LONERGAN IN THE WORLD

JAMES L. MARSH

Lonergan in the World

Self-Appropriation, Otherness, and Justice

UNIVERSITY OF TORONTO PRESS
Toronto Buffalo London

Toronto Buffalo London
www.utppublishing.com

ISBN 978-1-4426-4897-5 (cloth)

Lonergan Studies

Library and Archives Canada Cataloguing in Publication

Marsh, James L., author
Lonergan in the world : self-appropriation, otherness, and justice / James L. Marsh.

(Lonergan studies)
Includes bibliographical references and index.
ISBN 978-1-4426-4897-5 (bound)

1. Lonergan, Bernard J.F. (Bernard Joseph Francis), 1904–1984. I. Title. II. Series: Lonergan studies

B995.L654M37 2014 191 C2014-902500-9

University of Toronto Press acknowledges the financial assistance to its publishing program of the Canada Council for the Arts and the Ontario Arts Council, an agency of the Government of Ontario.

University of Toronto Press acknowledges the financial support of the Government of Canada through the Canada Book Fund for its publishing activities.

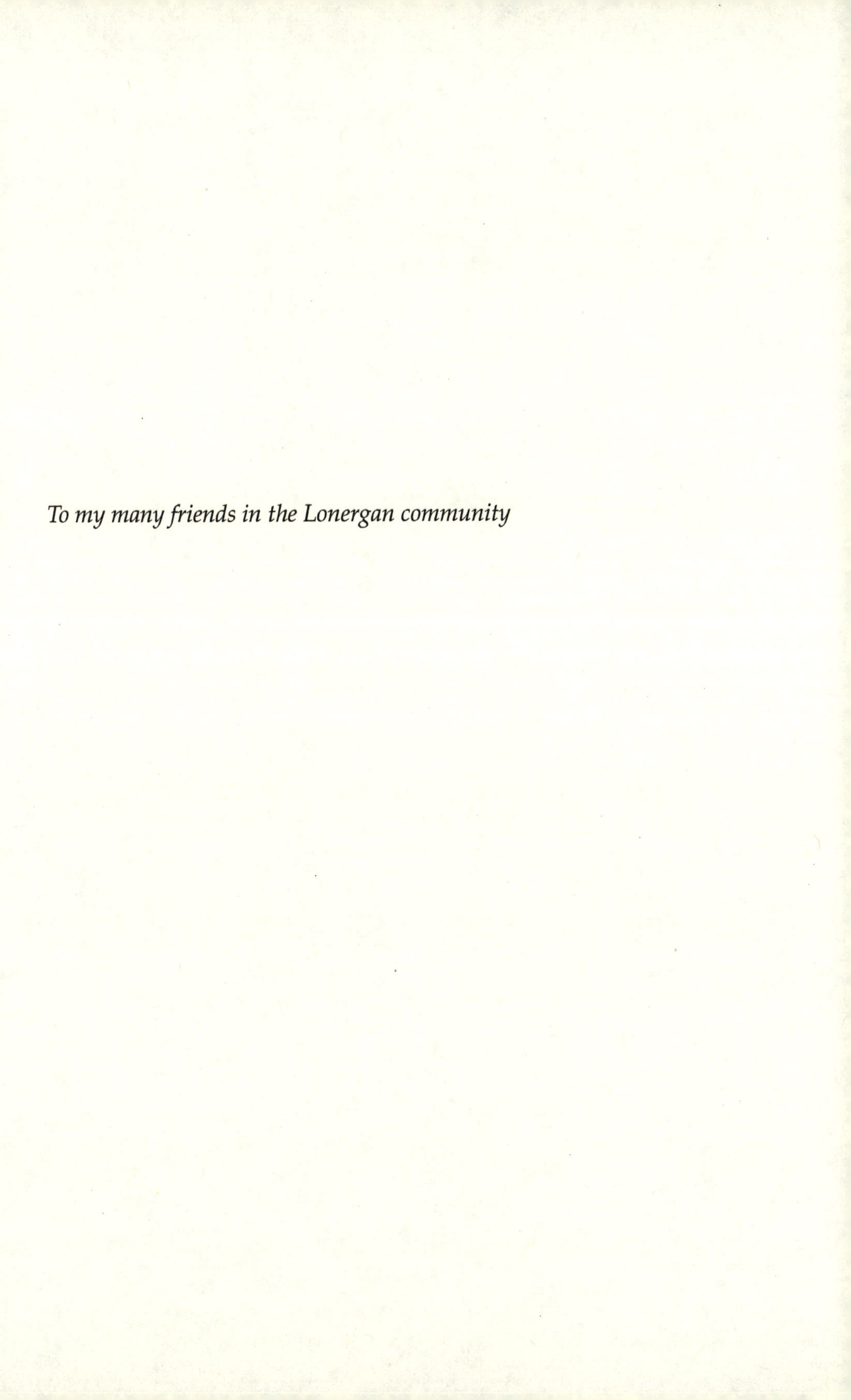

To my many friends in the Lonergan community

Contents

Preface

This book is an attempt to pay a long-held debt, owed to Lonergan as the thinker who has been the deepest influence on my approach to philosophy. He encouraged me through his work, especially *Insight* and *Method in Theology*, to become more than a plaster cast of a man, to stand on my own two feet in the doing of philosophy, and to become the best and first edition of myself.[1]

Then, after I had ceased to study Lonergan formally, I went to graduate school at Northwestern, wrote my dissertation on Hegel and Kierkegaard, and then embarked on a career of teaching twentieth-century Continental philosophy, first at St Louis University from 1970 to 1985 and then at Fordham University from 1985 to 2006, at which point I retired from the teaching of philosophy but not the doing of philosophy itself. As a colleague and friend William Desmond likes to say, "They pay you to be a professor, but you do philosophy for free," because that is part of who you are.

My first published book in philosophy, *Post-Cartesian Meditations* (PCM), was in my own voice, as were the two volumes that followed upon it, *Critique, Action, and Liberation* (CAL), and *Process, Praxis, and Transcendence* (PPT). I am sure it was Lonergan's influence that enabled me to have the self-confidence to do this kind of work, going counter to the usual academic trend of first publishing one or two or four or seven books on another thinker or thinkers and then, when I am in my dotage, trying to do something more original.[2]

The three volumes are a trilogy in which I develop my own cognitional-volitional theory in PCM, expand that horizontally into ethics and social theory in CAL, and vertically into a metaphysics, philosophy of religion, and liberation theology in PPT.

Reflecting some years later on this achievement, I realize that, especially in PCM, the influence of Lonergan is less explicitly present than was that of other thinkers such as Merleau-Ponty, Ricoeur, Marx, and Habermas. The reason is that the philosopher that I had become as a result of Lonergan's influence made it less necessary to mention him explicitly as I dealt with issues of epistemology, ethics, social theory, metaphysics, and theology. Thanks to Lonergan's enabling me to become my own man as a thinker and human being, I was able to take positions and make arguments that were, to some extent at least, independent of him.

Consequently I have been able to reflect in the group of essays presented here upon this paradoxical dependence and independence. As a result of the self-appropriation which Lonergan enabled me to undertake, the pearl of great price articulated in the first essay, I have realized the contradiction between such self-knowledge and self-authoring and being a "Lonerganian." I am not a "Lonerganian" any more than a "Habermasian," a "Ricoeurian," or a "Marxist," even though all these thinkers have influenced me profoundly – though none so much as Lonergan.

His influence is the deepest; it was at his feet that I learned to do philosophy. It is my conviction that he is not only the greatest Roman Catholic thinker, but also the greatest philosopher of the twentieth century. If we compare *Insight* with two other important works of the last two hundred years, Kant's *Critique of Pure Reason* and Hegel's *Phenomenology of Spirit*, we find that Lonergan learns from them, criticizes them, and goes beyond them to a higher synthesis. He learns about transcendental method from Kant and historical development from Hegel, criticizes Kant's doctrine of things in themselves and Hegel's objective idealism, and moves to a higher viewpoint. In such a viewpoint, he conceives a philosophical method that is both transcendental and dialectical, employs that method to generate an epistemology, ethics, and metaphysics, and retains elements from Aquinas in his synthesis.

One regular reminder of Lonergan's greatness as a thinker for me over the years was the way I was "forced" to return to him as I was doing my own work. Thus, in the second chapter in PCM, in order to make adequate sense out of the relationship among perception, expression, and reflection, I had recourse to Lonergan's distinction in *Insight* between cognitional structure and patterns of experience. In chapter 3, on objectivity, I found myself returning to Lonergan's discussion in *Insight* of the four kinds of objectivity – principal, absolute, normative, and experimental. And in chapter 4, on freedom and the self, I found myself having recourse to Lonergan's notion of transcendental method as the most fundamental kind of praxis, from which other kinds of ethical and political praxis emerge. At several places in this group of essays, I note that kind of experience, that Lonergan had already "preceded me" in asking the right questions and coming up with the requisite insights.[3]

The essays in this volume have their own kind of trajectory, moving from the initial essay through more detailed, particular discussions such as the link between thought and expression, self-appropriation and alterity, hermeneutics, post-modernism, and Marxism to the final two more synthetic essays, "On Really Living" and "Self-Appropriation as a Way of Life." Thus, in a way that is both Lonerganian and Hegelian, I inscribe a movement from identity through difference to a unity of identity and difference, from the relative immediacy of the beginning to the mediated immediacy of the concluding chapters. Thus, this group of essays, while they can be fruitfully read as individual essays on particular topics, can most fruitfully be read as a systematic argument from beginning to end.

Finally, I wish to express my gratitude to Mark Morelli, who over the last few decades has hosted conferences in the spring on Lonergan's thought at Loyola Marymount in Los Angeles. Most of the chapters in this book were initially presented there and received encouraging and critical commentary. I wish to thank also my assistant Jamie Aroosi, who has supplied indispensable help with such matters as email and has given invaluable advice and counsel as the manuscript has progressed through various stages to publication. I wish to thank John Maxwell for an excellent job of word processing the entire manuscript, and Joe Catalano for a fine job of proofreading. Finally, the University of Toronto Press has been welcoming, hospitable, and super-competent. Here I wish to mention especially Ron Schoeffel, Richard Ratzlaff, and John St James.

LONERGAN IN THE WORLD

1 Self-Appropriation: Lonergan's Pearl of Great Price

There are many philosophers who have proposed one of their ideas as a key to understanding the world. Examples that come to mind are Plato's theory of forms, Aristotle's account of the good, Kant's transcendental deduction, and Hegel's *Begriff*. But for my money, Lonergan's self-appropriation is the most valuable of all keys. One reason for Lonergan's superiority is that he draws on and incorporates into a new, higher synthesis aspects of all these thinkers. But his own contribution is significant and important too.

Yet one can easily miss the centrality of self-appropriation in Lonergan's work, especially in his work *Insight*, reading it as a treatise in epistemology or philosophy of science or metaphysics rather than seeing the book's main purpose as self-appropriation, the cognitive and existential taking possession of oneself as a knower, chooser, actor, and lover in relation to being. Such enterprises as philosophy of science or metaphysics only have relevance in *Insight* as instances, effects, and implications of self-appropriation.

I propose in this essay, therefore, to discuss self-appropriation, first by articulating and reflecting on some basic Lonerganian texts on the issue, then, in the context of contemporary philosophy, showing how such self-knowledge can illumine and resolve perplexities arising from inadequate self-knowledge, then reflecting on my own work as an instance of self-appropriation, and concluding with some reflections on the human subject. Who and what is the subject, and how is the subject related to self-appropriation?

One reason for reflecting on my work in this context is that in thinking about the issue, I have been led to discover or rediscover an autobiographical or individual element in the notion of self-appropriation.

Self-appropriation enables me as a knower and chooser and actor to discover and create myself as a unique and transcendentally universal self. By "transcendental" here I refer to a structure of selfhood that is a priori, present in the subject as the condition of possibility of engaging with the world in an a posteriori way. Consequently, my own work is an expression of my own unique self-appropriation, and so it might be of interest to reflect on my work in that light. Different people can do different things and become different people as a result of self-appropriation, and the effect on a community of self-appropriated selves can be complementary, mutually enriching and enabling fruitful mutual and individual self-criticism. Different self-appropriated knowers can mutually illumine and enrich and criticize one another in both a negative and positively constructive manner.

Lonergan on Self-Appropriation

Clues to the centrality of self-appropriation in Lonergan are given in the introduction to *Insight*. Here Lonergan says that this book "is not about mathematics, nor a book on science, nor a book on common sense, nor a book of metaphysics; indeed, in a sense, it is not even a book on knowledge."[1] On a first level, the book contains sentences about mathematicians or science or common sense. On a second level, their meaning and significance are to be grasped "only by going beyond the scraps of mathematics or science or common sense or metaphysics to the dynamic, cognitional structure that is exemplified in knowing them."[2] On a third level, "the dynamic cognitional structure to be reached is not the transcendental ego of Fichtean speculation, nor the abstract patterns of relationships in Tom or Dick or Harry, but the personally appropriated structure of one's own experiencing, one's own intelligent inquiry and insights, one's own critical reflection and judging and deciding."[3] Already we see Lonergan emphasizing the personal and unique in relation to the transcendental and universal.

Lonergan goes on. The crucial issue is an experimental one, and the experiments will be performed not publicly but privately: "It will consist in one's own rational self-consciousness clearly and distinctly taking possession of itself as rational self-consciousness. Up to that decisive achievement, all leads. From it, all follows."[4] Here we see further evidence for the private, individual aspect of self-appropriation, linked to universal aspects. No one else, no matter what his knowledge, eloquence, logical rigor, or persuasiveness, can do it for me. Nonetheless, the act has public antecedents and consequences. The private and individual are linked to the public and universal. And just in case we have not gotten the point, Lonergan drives it home: "In the third place, then, more than all else, the aim of the book is to issue an invitation to a personal, decisive act."[5]

Self-Appropriation and Contemporary Philosophy

One major aspect and consequence of self-appropriation is transcendental method, the experiencing, understanding, judging, and choosing of myself as an experiencing, understanding, judging, and choosing subject in relation to being. By "subject" I mean simply the human being as conscious or self-aware in intentionally relating to the world. In transcendental method, self-appropriation takes explicit, full possession of itself. As he articulates this concept in the first chapter of *Method in Theology*, in my opinion one of the most important chapters Lonergan ever wrote, we see a more explicit emphasis on, and articulation of, the so-called fourth level of freedom, decision, and love, already present in *Insight*, of course, in the insistence on rational self-consciousness, as distinct from the rational consciousness of reflection and judgment.

But this emphasis on freedom and choice as essential to method invites comparison with thinkers such as Heidegger in *Being and Time*, in which freedom and authenticity are also essential to Heidegger's version of the existential phenomenological version of the transcendental project.[6] And Lonergan is also implicitly critical of Heidegger insofar as the full story about intentionality in relation to being is not simply finitude but infinitude, and a dialectic between limitation and transcendence.[7] Moreover, this conception of transcendental method overcomes the dichotomy in Gadamer between truth and method. Method, Lonergan insists, is not the automatic grinding out of results like sausage from a sausage machine, but rather "a normative pattern of recurrent and related operations yielding cumulative and progressive results."[8] Method is not, as Gadamer seems to think, a set of rules that can be followed blindly by anyone as on an assembly line.[9]

Self-appropriation as a project of self-knowledge is a modern project which, for Lonergan, has its antecedents in Descartes, Kant, Hegel, and Kierkegaard, but which also has affinities with Ricoeur, Heidegger, Sartre, and Husserl. As such, it is a philosophical pearl of great price that one ignores and rejects at one's peril. Various postmodern interpretations of reason, for example, as identitarian, technocratic, logocentric, disciplinary, or one-sidedly conceptual reveal themselves to be one-sided, undifferentiated caricatures of reason. Lonergan emerges as the true or truer friend of difference.[10]

In Lonergan's account of knowing, there is a movement from preconceptual to conceptual, question to answer, insight to concept, particular experience to universal conceptual formulation. In the magnificent chapter 1 of *Insight*, for example, Lonergan traces the genesis of the definition of a circle from data to question to preconceptual guess to insight to definition. In chapter 10, on reflective judgments, there is a similar genesis of judgment from evidence to questions about its sufficiency to grasp of the virtually unconditioned to judgment. Again, there are active and passive aspects on each level of knowing. On the level of experience, I have to be attentive to data, allowing the appropriate images to emerge. On the level of understanding, I have to be intelligently receptive to the emergence of insights, going where the preconceptual hints and guesses seem to lead. On the level of judgment, I have to be open to all the evidence, and, if the evidence is not there or contradicts my hypothesis, to recognize that. Human knowing, as Lonergan conceives it, is not one-sidedly conceptual or judgmental or active, imposing itself on a recalcitrant field of experience. Such conceptions show themselves, in Lonergan's account, to be one-sided caricatures of reason.[11]

Because data can be of two kinds, data of sense and data of consciousness, there are two kinds of science and method, empirical science and generalized empirical method, or in the later language of *Method*, transcendental method. Because philosophical judgments can be verified in data of consciousness, philosophy can be regarded as scientific in a way different from, and yet similar to, empirical science. There is an affinity of Lonergan's approach to Husserl's in *The Crisis of European Sciences and Transcendental Phenomenology* and *Formal and Transcendental Logic*, in which Husserl argues that if the basic orientation of logic and science is judgments grounded in evidence, then transcendental phenomenology and transcendental logic fulfill that orientation more adequately and rigorously and with greater certitude than empirical science and formal logic. Indeed, these disciplines receive their adequate ground and basic premises from transcendental phenomenology and transcendental logic.[12]

Like Husserl, then, and against postmoderns, Lonergan can say, "Be logical" or "Be scientific." These are legitimate enterprises. If one does that, then formal logic requires a grounding in transcendental method, and empirical science in generalized empirical method. The premise underlying both enterprises – that being is intelligible – is grounded and justified in transcendental method and in the metaphysics flowing from it. Moreover, because philosophy is most fundamentally method and not logic, logic is relativized as merely a product of understanding. Because empirical science is distinguished from, and grounded in, generalized empirical method, knowing cannot be legitimately equated with empirical science or technology. I am not tempted, therefore, in a postmodern manner to look for a post-rational, post-conceptual, post-metaphysical alternative outside of reason or knowing or metaphysics.[13]

Because knowing is fueled by desire, it is not neutral or value-free as some modernists and postmodernists are inclined to say. Rather, knowing is passionately interested in the truth, guided intrinsically by the transcendental precepts, scientifically by the canons of empirical method, and hermeneutically by the canons of hermeneutics. Knowing is disinterested in the sense that it is, or should be, free from the influence of bias. Because such is the case, Lonergan can distinguish, in a way analogous to Habermas, between knowledge-constitutive interests and those that are extrinsic to, or nonessential to, knowledge. But in a way that is deeper than Habermas, enterprises like science or hermeneutics or ethical-political liberation, Habermas's three knowledge-constitutive interests, are more like Lonergan's patterns of experience, which require for their grounding and unity cognitional theory and transcendental method articulating the structure common to all patterns of experience.[14]

Because knowing, therefore, is essentially internally value-laden, and because objectivity is the fruit of authentic subjectivity, there is not the consequence of relativism that haunts thinkers like Nietzsche or Foucault who make claims about the value-laden character of knowledge. Lonergan rejects, as they do, the notion of purely neutral, value-free, objectivist reason, but unlike them this is not a reason for rejecting reason or modernist reason. Rather, their accounts are a postmodern caricature of reason. Because reason is essentially value-laden and not value-free, he avoids the pitfalls of a purely objectivist, disinterested concept of reason rooted in the idea of knowing as looking. Because he can distinguish between values, norms, and desires intrinsic to and those extrinsic to reason, postmodernist relativism can be avoided. Scientists, logicians, or philosophers will do good science, mathematics, or philosophy to the extent that they are authentic, guided by the transcendental precepts and canons of scientific and hermeneutical method.[15]

Moreover, because being is the known unknown towards which the desire to know heads, there is an awareness of, and orientation to, mystery on a psychic, emotional, intellectual, and spiritual level. I respond in felt wonder to a universe that is perceived as wonderful, worthy of questioning, worthy to be responded to in gratitude for the gift of being. Lonergan's conception of metaphysics and theology based on self-appropriation is not closed to mystery and devoted to mastering it, but open to it, accepting it and valuing it. For this reason, dicta of the late Heidegger, such as that questioning is the piety of thinking and such as thinking as thanking, have a place within philosophy, theology, and metaphysics, not outside them. Because Heidegger's concept of metaphysics is so narrow, conceived as closed to mystery and oriented to mastery, he thinks one has to go beyond metaphysics to incorporate and practice such dicta. Contemplative, wondering appreciation of the world is a foundation and consequence of self-appropriation. Self-appropriation begins with a question, "What and who am I?" or "Why is there something rather than nothing?" and ends in a kind of second immediacy, a wondering, appreciative response to mystery, in which my answers have inspired only further questions about the known unknown.[16]

The active receptivity of the four transcendental precepts finds its proper completion in a surrender to God as mystery, a "falling in love with God."[17] And because of the vertical movement downward of such surrender, occurring in such a way as to influence the activities of experiencing, understanding, judging, and deciding on more mundane levels, then that surrender to divine mystery on the fourth level intensifies the receptivity already functioning in these levels and expressed in the transcendental precepts. The religiously converted philosopher, as a result of religious conversion, is able in his own daily, mundane work of philosophy to engage in a kind of Lonerganian "thinking as thanking."

My Own Work as a Consequence of My Self-Appropriation

Now I come to the third part of this chapter, which is to reflect on my own work as an expression of self-appropriation. This expression is most clearly present in my three-volume trilogy, which begins with cognitional theory and phenomenology in *Post-Cartesian Mediations,* moves into an ethics and social theory in *Critique, Action, and Liberation,* and concludes in metaphysics, philosophy of religion, and theology of liberation in *Process, Praxis, and Transcendence.* Thus, the trajectory of the work follows, in its own way, Lonergan's description of cognitional theory as the basis and pronouncements on ethical, metaphysical, and religious issue as the expansion.[18] PCM is the basis of my philosophy and CAL and PPT are its horizontal and vertical expansions.

In addition, in each work there are specific ways in which Lonergan's influence is present: in chapter 3 on objectivity in PCM, in the grounding of critical theory in self-appropriation in CAL, and in the discussion of intellectual, moral, and religious conversation as radical conversion in PPT. This last point suggests what is perhaps my main, most original, and controversial expression of self-appropriation, namely, that its aim implies a radical critique and overcoming of capitalism. Even this move, I have become recently convinced, has its undeveloped roots and antecedents in Lonergan, such as the remark in *Insight* about going beyond the liberal thesis and Marxist antithesis and in works written after *Method* which claim that there is a necessity to go beyond the reign of the multinational corporation and that the basic principles of capitalism are flawed. Fidelity to both Lonergan's theory and to recognizing a contradictory, social reality demands that radical self-appropriation be completed by a radical, liberationist ethics, politics, and theology.[19]

Another way of putting this point is to say that I, along with Lonergan and such thinkers as Matthew Lamb and Robert Doran, argue for a plague on the houses of both late capitalism and state socialism. In the context of such agreement, there is still room for fruitful discussion, agreement, and disagreement among self-appropriated Lonerganian knowers, choosers, lovers, and doers on such issues as the status of Marxism. Is it all or mostly counter-positional, as Lonergan seems to say, or a contradictory unity of position and counter-position, as Lamb and Doran are inclined to say, or mostly or totally positional, as I am inclined to say and argue exhaustively in my three volumes? Here such issues come up for discussion as whether and how much Marx is to be distinguished from Marxism-Leninism as a reductionist aberration (and this I am inclined to say is counter-positional, both bad Marx and bad social theory) and from a non-reductionist Western Marxism, including such thinkers as Herbert Marcuse, the late Jean-Paul Sartre, and Antonio Gramsci as a fruitful development. I am inclined to make this move, as are Lamb and Doran, I sense, up to a certain point, but Lonergan is much less inclined to do so.

The discussion among us would be guided by the canons of hermeneutics. Among us we'll agree that self-appropriation leads to a radical, ethical, political, and theological critique and overcoming of the capitalist New World Order and agree also about the importance of a culture influenced by the scale of values – vital, social, cultural, personal, and religious – and three conversions radiating downward into the politics and economics of our current situation and transforming these. Even this point, I think, is somewhat present in Marx, but is underdeveloped and is more thoroughly developed by later Western Marxism, for which economy, polity, and culture interact in a reciprocal way, not in a one-way, deterministic manner.[20]

My own conviction, about which I confess to being pretty confident, is that while such a radical critique and overcoming will and should draw on sources that are non-Marxist, as I do myself, we deprive ourselves of a precious resource if we ignore Marx and Western Marxism. Such an attempt strikes me as similar to attempts to think about transcendental philosophy while ignoring Kant, physics while ignoring Einstein, or biology while ignoring Darwin. All of these represent forward moves in the learning of the human race that we ignore at our peril. And I am inclined to think that because the capitalism of which he was the first, deepest, and most comprehensive critic is now virtually worldwide, Marx is not dead, but is more relevant than ever. As Derrida put it in a recent book, there is no decent, humane future without Marx. His ghost hovers over our current, somewhat uneasy, quasi-manic celebration of the New World Order. Maybe he is right about the irrationality of the capitalist system.[21]

Self-Appropriation and the Subject

I turn now to my fourth main point, the status of the subject and its relationship to self-appropriation. First of all, the subject is the agent of self-appropriation. Self-appropriation is or leads up to the decisive personal act that no one can do for me. Second, the subject is the object of self-appropriation, in the sense of explicit objectification and in the sense of intended result or goal. Third, the subject is the conscious dynamism of self-appropriation as it moves from starting point to goal. Fourth, the subject is the dynamic, dialectical unity of opposites such as sensible and intellectual, cognitive and existential, psychic and spiritual, transcendental and historical. Fifth, the subject is a unity of "what" and "who," universal and individual. In self-appropriation, I become, philosophically and existentially, my own original, unique, authentic man or woman, but not in such a way as to sever individuality and uniqueness from the transcendental and universal.

Indeed, self-appropriation helps to overcome unenlightened attempts to sever these opposites, and other sets of opposites as well. Self-appropriation leads to an intellectual and existential overcoming of one-sidedness. Consequently, my self-appropriated presence is similar to, yet different even from, that of Lonergan himself or of other Lonerganians. As a result, there is a basis for affirmation and celebration of difference not present in postmodernism, which tends undialectically to split apart difference from sameness, individuality from universality. As self-appropriated persons, we can legitimately claim, against postmodernists, to be the true or truer friends of difference.

Conclusion

A final way to view self-appropriation is to see it as a pathway to, and achievement of, personal freedom. In a real sense, *Insight* and *Method in Theology* are the "introduction to the non-Fascist life," in a way different from and yet similar to and superior to Foucault's description of Deleuze and Guattari in an introduction to *Anti-Oedipus*. In being my own man or woman, I am joyfully and rhapsodically "anti-Oedipal," free from any external or internal fathers or masters. Indeed, in a certain sense, I become non-Lonerganian in the sense of being able and willing to move or try to move beyond his thought, reading and learning from thinkers he did not read or to whom he was unsympathetic, both avoiding excessive reliance on Lonergan's doctrine and refusing to rely excessively on his authority. The move to philosophical enlightenment demands, finally, kicking away the Lonerganian ladder and slaying all internalized fathers, even Lonergan himself.[22]

And here I am inclined to think about and affirm the way in which Bob Doran, in a move apparently endorsed by Lonergan himself, has explored psychic conversion as a necessary complement to intellectual, moral, and religious conversion. Full self-appropriation, then, is about the whole self, psychic as well as spiritual, feeling as well as thought, unconscious as well as conscious. Liberation is not only political but also personal, not only from external victimization of unjust social structures but also from the internal victimization of a violated psyche. Coming to accept and empathize with my violated psyche opens me up to identification with external victims – the poor, the exploited, and the oppressed – and, similarly, empathy with external victims opens me up to greater awareness of psychic victimization. Radical psychic conversion, mediated by intellectual, moral, and religious conversion, leads to radical political conversion.

The way up is the way down. Moving to the heights of intellectual, moral, and religious conversion implies moving down into the depths of solidarity with the oppressed. In opposition to the inauthentic upward mobility of a mind, heart, and spirit "capitalized" and colonized by the New World Order is the downward mobility of someone who has recognized his or her own solidarity with the victim both in the psyche and in the current oppressive social order. This downward mobility rooted in full psychic and spiritual freedom is the final manifestation and fruit of self-appropriation.[23]

2 Thought and Expression in Lonergan

We have begun by initially thinking about self-appropriation, its conditions, and its implications. Now we have to move more fully into more detailed, particular reflections on its conditions and implications. One question that can arise is that concerning thought and expression. Self-appropriation results from a second-level reflection on thought and its relationship to experience and freedom. To reflect on self-appropriation as we did is to engage in a thinking, a thematizing, a definition, and an expression of that definition. Our thinking about and expressing our ideas about self-appropriation is an instance of the relationship between thought and expression discussed in this chapter.

Here there are three main possibilities: expression as just an external instrument for a thought already complete in itself, thought as all or mostly reducible to expression in such a way that there is no thought that must precede expression logically or experientially, or thought and expression as two distinct interrelated aspects of a whole, a thought-expression unity, in which each aspect needs and requires the other. My position and Lonergan's is that the third possibility is the one that is truest and most comprehensive. Expression completes thought and makes it fully articulate, but thought precedes expression logically and temporally. Expression completes thought in the sense that I do not know what I have to say until I have said it, but thought precedes expression in guiding it to the most proper or best expression. I would not be able to come up with the best expression if I did not know in an inchoate way what I want to say.

The two aspects, thought and expression, have been emphasized and developed differently in the two main branches of contemporary philosophy, Continental and analytic. Continental philosophy, especially in its earlier phenomenological versions in thinkers like Husserl, tends to focus on thought and de-emphasize expression in such a way as at least to flirt with the idea of thought already complete in itself. Analytic philosophy, especially in its early versions in thinkers like Wittgenstein, tends to emphasize expression and to de-emphasize or ignore thought as distinct from expression. Lonergan's integration of thought and expression can give us a basis for integrating, criticizing, and sublating these two forms of contemporary philosophy.[1]

In this essay, I will first focus on Lonergan's initial discussion of the issue in *Insight* and then on his deepening, clarifying, and amplifying of his account in *Method in Theology*.

Insight

We begin with Lonergan's marvelous first chapter in *Insight*, "Elements," where he describes the emergence, development, and completion of insight. When one perceives a cartwheel, a question can arise about the meaning of the circularity of the cartwheel. What makes it circular? Why is it round? What if we were to allow the spokes and rim to thin out into lines and reduce the hub to a point? If there were an infinity of spokes and all were perfectly equal, the rim would have to be perfectly round. Conversely, if the spokes were unequal, the rim could not avoid having bumps or dents. Hence, we can say that the wheel is necessarily round inasmuch as the distance from the center of the hub to the outside of the rim is always the same. Consequently, we can formulate the definition of a circle as a locus of coplanar points equidistant from a center.[2]

A number of observations are in order. The first is that points and lines cannot be imagined. We can imagine an extremely small dot or extremely thin line, but no matter how small or how thin, they still have magnitude. But to reach a point or line, all magnitude must vanish, and, if magnitude vanishes, then so also do the point or line as imagined. Second, points and lines are concepts. Concepts are creations of the mind that can be thought but not imagined. Concepts thus have two properties: they are constituted by the mere activity of supposing, thinking, considering, formulating, defining; and they do not occur at random but in the act of supposing, thinking, considering, formulating, and defining. And such activity occurs in conjunction with an act of insight. Third, the image is necessary for the insight. Points and lines cannot be imagined, nor can necessity or impossibility. But these are conceived in relation to a concrete, particular circle. We do not have a necessity in general, but a necessity of roundness resulting from these equal radii in this imagined circle. Eliminate the image of the center, radii, and curve, and by that same stroke all necessity vanishes.[3]

Fourth, there is the question expressed in words: "Why is the wheel round?" Underlying the question expressed in words is the pure question, a spirit of inquiry or desire. Although this question is prior to the insight, concepts, and words, nonetheless it presupposes experience and images. Just as insight is into the concretely real or imagined, so also the pure question is about the concrete given or imagined. We do not just wonder; we wonder about something.[4]

A final point is to distinguish moments in the genesis of a definition. The first moment is the awakening of wonder. The second moment is the clue: what would happen if we reduced the hub to a point, the spokes to lines, and the rim to a circle? The third moment is a process of moving from image to wonder expressed in a question to insight getting hold of a clue to full-blown definition. There is a movement from image to insight, preconceptual to conceptual, particular to universal, question to answer. Language is present in the definition of the circle, as well as in the concepts of points and lines. The concept expressed in the words of the definition perfects and completes an already inchoate, vague insight. Language is also present in the initial perceptual context, in which I perceive a "circular cartwheel." And underlying and guiding the process is the desire to know that could have kept the process going indefinitely if its requirements had not been met. And one of these requirements is to find the right definition expressed in the right words; not just any definition or any words will do.[5]

Just as there is movement from pre-conceptual to conceptual, prelinguistic to linguistic in the emergence of a definition, so also is there in the emergence of a judgment, "it is so." In chapter 10, "Reflective Understanding," Lonergan considers an instance of a concrete judgment of fact. A man returns to his home in the evening and finds that its windows are smashed, smoke is in the air, and water on the floor. Let us suppose him to make the extremely restrained judgment, "Something happened."[6]

This is a virtually unconditioned judgment, a judgment that has conditions for its being made, and has three elements: a conditioned, a link between the conditioned and its conditions, and the fulfillment of the conditions. When a question for reflection is raised, the prospective judgment is a conditioned standing in need of evidence sufficient for reasonable judgment. The aim of reflective understanding is to transform a prospective judgment from the status of a conditioned to the status of a virtually unconditioned; and this occurs when reflective understanding grasps the conditions and their fulfillment.[7]

In the above example, the conditioned is the judgment that something happened. The fulfilling conditions are two sets of data: the remembered data of the home he left in the morning and the present data of the home he returns to in the evening. The fulfilling conditions are found on the level of presentations. The fulfilling conditions are not insights or judgments, but simply lie on the level of present and past experience. The link between the conditioned and the fulfilling conditions is a structure immanent and operative in cognitional process. It is not a judgment or a concept or a set of concepts. It is simply a way of doing things, a procedure within the cognitional field.[8]

When he returns home, the weary worker experiences present data and recalls past data, but refers both sets to the same set of things, which he calls his home. This insight has a double function: it refers two sets of data to one identical set of things, and a second level of cognitional process is added to a first. The two contain a specific structure of this process, which we may name "knowing change." He combines in his reflection three elements: on the level of presentations there are two sets of data. On the level of intelligence there is an insight referring both sets to the same things. When both levels are taken together, there is involved the notion of knowing change. Reflective understanding grasps all three to ground the judgment, "Something happened."[9]

That judgment here is a statement. But prior to judgment and statement, a structure or procedure is preconceptually and pre-linguistically operative in cognitional process itself. Just as there is a presentation of the cartwheel giving rise to direct insight, so also there is presentation of data that act as fulfilling conditions. Just as there is the question, "What is a circle," giving rise to direct insight, so also there is a question about the sufficiency of the evidence giving rise to reflective insight. Just as there is a definition that emerges as a fruit of the process of coming to an insight, so also there is a judgment that emerges as a result of the process of arriving at reflective understanding. Just as the definition expressed in a verbal definition completes the insight, so also the judgment expressed completes reflective insight. Insight and definition, reflective understanding and judgment are internally related, essential for one another.

In a further chapter, "Metaphysics as Dialectic," Lonergan affirms an isomorphism or correlation between knowledge and expression. To the utterance as linguistic affirmation or negation corresponds reflection and judgment. To the expression as a significant combination of words corresponds insight and conception. To the expression as instrumental multiplicity corresponds the material multiplicity of experience and imagination.[10]

The isomorphism of knowledge is not to be taken for an identity. It is one thing to assert and another to judge, for men can lie. It is one thing to understand experience and another to hit upon the happy and effective combination of words and sentences. It is one thing to be rich in experience and another to be fluent in words. To the insight of knowledge, expression adds a further practical insight governing the verbal flow towards its end of communication. Finally, the manifold of presentations of sense and representations of imagination is succeeded by the manifold of conventional signs.[11]

If knowledge is distinct from expression, they also interpenetrate. Because coming to know is a process, it advances in stages in which inquiry leads to insights only to give rise to further questions and further insights. At each stage of the process, it is helpful to fix what has been learned and to formulate in some way what remains to be sought. Consequently, expression enters into the very process of learning, and the attainment of knowledge tends to coincide with attaining the ability to express it. Also, as our accounts of understanding and judgment show, the inner words of definition and judgment are themselves already linguistic before we express them externally. Because of the interpenetration of knowledge and expression, there is a solidarity, almost a fusion, between the development of knowledge and the development of expression. The more sophisticated the knowledge, the more sophisticated the expression, and vice versa.[12]

As we conclude our discussion of *Insight*, one lingering doubt remains. Does not the use of "instrumental" to describe expression indicate a merely external relationship such that we run the risk of affirming a non-linguistic thought complete in itself, for which expression remains optional. Our distinction between internal and external word should reassure us on this issue. The definition of a circle and the judgment that something happened are already conceptually-linguistically mediated and their external expression is a further linguistic addition, such that I may choose between different possibilities. But a further point is to realize that the ability to express internally what something is or that something is is the result of a process of learning and development in which I first learned as a child in a community how to use words and at a certain stage of maturity learned to think within myself at times without necessarily expressing externally what I am thinking. The process of learning reaches great heights of sophistication, but all the way along there is not only an interplay between preconceptual/pre-linguistic and conceptual-linguistic, but also between internal and external, private and public. Subjectivity is intersubjectivity, and intersubjectivity is subjectivity.[13]

Method in Theology

In this part of the chapter, I undertake two tasks: first, to reflect on Lonergan's answer to an objection to his position by Edward Mackinnon, a disciple of Wittgenstein. Then, I propose to consider one long quotation that updates, deepens, and synthesizes his teaching on the relationship of thought to expression.

The discussion of Mackinnon occurs in the chapter "Dialectic," in which Lonergan confronts positions that have become more prominent since the publication of *Insight* in 1957. Mackinnon defends the notion that the meaningfulness of language is essentially public and only derivatively private. If this were not so, language could not be a vehicle of intersubjective communication. The meaning of a term accordingly is to be explained by its use or the family of usages associated with it, which are learned in public interaction between and among human beings. Once such learning occurs, one can think privately about such meaning, but it has been learned publicly. The meaning of a word is not explicable by reference to private mental acts.[14]

Lonergan responds as follows. First, he does not believe that mental acts occur without a sustaining flow of expression. Such expression may or may not be linguistic, but it is essential. Indeed, Ernst Cassirer has reported that students of aphasia, agnosia, and apraxia have found these disorders of speech, knowledge, and action to be interrelated.[15]

Second, he has no doubt that the ordinary meaningfulness of ordinary language is essentially public and only derivatively private. For language is ordinary if it is in common use. It is in common use, not because some isolated individual has decided what it is to mean, but because all individuals of the relevant group know what it means. Similarly, it is by performing expressed mental acts that children and foreigners come to learn a language. But they learn that language by learning how it is ordinarily used, so that their private knowledge of ordinary usage is derived from the common usage that is essentially public.[16]

Third, what is true of the ordinary meaningfulness of ordinary language is not true of the original meaningfulness of any language, ordinary, literary, or technical. For all language develops and, at any time, any language consists in the sedimentation of the developments that have occurred and have not become obsolete. Developments consist in discovering new uses for existing words, inventing new words, and diffusing the discoveries and inventions. All three are a matter of expressed mental acts. The discovery of a new usage is a mental act expressed by the new usage. The discovery of a new word is a mental act expressed by the new word. The communication of the discoveries and inventions can be done through a process of trial and error in which a new usage takes shape. Unlike ordinary meaningfulness, then, unqualified meaningfulness originates in expressed mental acts, is communicated and perfected through mental acts, and attains ordinariness when the perfected communication is extended to a large enough number of individuals.[17]

Fourth, another confusion lurks behind this confusion of ordinary and original meaningfulness. Two quite different meanings can be given to the statement that all philosophical problems are linguistic problems. If one conceives language as the expression of mental acts, one will conclude that philosophical problems have their source not only in linguistic expression but also in mental acts, and it could happen that one would devote much more attention to the mental acts than to their linguistic expression. But one may feel that mental acts are just occult entities or, if they really exist, the philosophers are just going to keep floundering around if they pay any attention to them. On a reductionist view, then, or on a weaker or stronger methodological option, one may decide to limit philosophical inquiry to the usage of ordinary language, illumined, perhaps, by the metalanguage of syntax, semantics, and pragmatics.[18]

If one adopts this approach, however, he cannot account for the meaningfulness of language by appealing to its originating mental acts. Ordinary language can only capture part of a whole that includes interaction between public and private, ordinary meaningfulness and originary meaningfulness, expression and thought.[19]

The final discussion of Lonergan that clinches the point for me occurs in the chapter on meaning, in his account of the origin of early language. I will quote the passage in full.

> In the first stage there occurs the development of language. But if we have referred to language as an instrumental act of meaning and contrasted

> it with potential, formal, full, and active acts, still this must not be taken to imply that language is some optional adjunct that may or may not accompany the other acts. On the contrary, some sensible expression is intrinsic to the pattern of our conscious and intentional aspirations. Just as inquiry presupposes sensible data, just as insight occurs with respect to some schematic image, just as the reflective act occurs with respect to a summation of the relevant evidence, so inversely the interior acts of conceiving, judging, and of deciding demand the sensible and proportionate substrate we call expression. Indeed, so rigorous is this demand that Ernst Cassirer has been able to put together a pathology of symbolic consciousness: motor disturbances that result in aphasia are accompanied with disturbances in perception, in thought, and in action.[20]

Some aspects of this passage stand out as significant. First, our doubts about the word "instrumental" are laid to rest. It is not an optional adjunct but an essential aspect of meaning. Some sensible expression is "intrinsic" to our conscious operations of experiencing, understanding, judging, and deciding. Second, Lonergan develops a correlation. Just as inquiry presupposes sensible data, insight occurs with respect to some schematic image, and reflective understanding requires evidence, so also do conceiving, judging, and deciding require expression, a point that Lonergan has already made in *Insight*. Third, when I wrote *Post-Cartesian Meditations*, I developed a similar correlation in chapter 2, "Perception, Expression, and Reflection." What I was not aware of sufficiently when I wrote this chapter was that Lonergan not only agreed with this account, but had articulated it before I wrote the above account.[21]

In summary, then, we see Lonergan developing a phenomenology of thought and expression in *Insight* and *Method*. In *Method*, we see him developing, deepening, and expanding his account in encounter with developments in Continental philosophy and analytic philosophy that he did not consider in *Insight*. Perhaps the major challenge to his position, Mackinnon's, is confronted by showing that language as originating presupposes mental acts of insight, judgment, and decision that are expressed sensibly. Finally, we see him in the last passage explicitly rejecting a false interpretation of "instrumental" as merely external and optional. Moreover, we see Lonergan in other parts of *Method* showing the dependence of thought not only on ordinary language, but on history. He goes further than Mackinnon does in de-absolutizing "interiority," so as to satisfy our postmodern friends, freeing interiority from any lingering sense of false presence.

Conclusion

If I am right about Lonergan and we are both right about the relationship between thought and expression, then two possible implications occur to me. The first is that we have a firm transcendental basis for overcoming the split between Continental and analytic philosophy. If the first, especially in its early phases, emphasized in a one-sided way interiority, and the second, especially in its early phases, emphasized expression, Lonergan shows himself to be more comprehensive than either in integrating them.

Both of these traditions, of course, in their developments go through mutations. Phenomenology, especially the thought of Merleau-Ponty, and hermeneutics, in the thought of Gadamer and Ricoeur, develop an account of language that comes closer to Lonergan's; postmodernism in its recent incarnations tends to shade too much over into the side of language; and Habermas goes too much in the direction of analytic philosophy in his rejection of a "philosophy of consciousness" in *The Theory of Communicative Action*. But Lonergan's comprehensiveness, nuance, and depth stand superior to both of these traditions in their recent or not so recent versions. This is not to say, of course, that at times these do not supplement, enrich, and fill out Lonergan's account. I think here, for examples, of Merleau-Ponty's discussion of embodiment, perception, and expression; and Ricoeur's of decision, which I have incorporated into my own accounts in *Post-Cartesian Meditations*.[22]

Second, perhaps most interestingly and controversially, if all of the foregoing is true, we have the basis for dealing with the issue of alterity as discussed by Derrida and Levinas; we will pursue this issue in a further chapter. If Lonergan is correct, then all other beings, non-human and human others, are present to us in our experience, understanding, and judgment. Others are not hidden behind some set of appearances in some noumenal realm beyond knowledge. The other is present to me as thematizable and objectifiable in a way that does not violate her or alienate her or reduce her to an illegitimate sameness. In such knowing of the other, I come to express myself and to know the meaning and reality of the other as similarly disclosed in her actions in the world that express her own interiority. More of this anon.

3 Continental Hermeneutics: A Lonerganian Response

I am entitling this chapter "Continental Hermeneutics: A Lonerganian Response" rather than "Continental Hermeneutics: Lonergan's Response" for several different reasons. First of all and perhaps dominantly, I can use Lonergan's account to go into issues that he did not go into in his writings. In so doing, I will be drawing on various pieces I have written "under the Lonerganian influence," for example, chapter 6 in *Post-Cartesian Mediations,* "The Hermeneutical Turn: From Retrieval to Suspicion," and chapter 2 in *Critique, Action, and Liberation,* "Understanding and Explanation," in which there is an operative interplay between my Lonergan-influenced philosophical self, speaking in my own voice, and certain Continental voices, especially Gadamer and Ricoeur. Thus, the result seems to be, or promises to be, richer than just confining myself to what Lonergan said. Which is not to deny, of course, that I will use explicit Lonerganian claims whenever desirable or necessary, or that a study confining itself to what Lonergan said is also desirable and necessary.

A second qualifier to note is that I will be focusing on the universal viewpoint and "upper blade" as articulated in *Insight,* chapter 17, "Metaphysics as Dialectic," and not so much on the chapters on history, interpretation, dialectic, and foundations in *Method in Theology,* valuable as they are. The reason is that the discussion in *Insight* has a philosophical rigor and clarity and salience that is especially germane to what is basically a philosophical discussion of hermeneutics, and that chapter seems to be presupposed by the chapters in *Method,* while they in turn expand, particularize, and make concrete what hermeneutics means in the domain of theology. The discussion in *Insight* thus stands to the discussion in *Method* as universal to particular application, unity to multiplicity (the multiple chapters in *Method*), potential to fulfillment. It has seemed to me that the discussion in *Insight* has been underutilized and underappreciated compared to other parts of Lonergan's work. And this point continues to be true in spite of the marvelous book by Coelho on the topic, typical of much very recent, illuminating scholarship on Lonergan.[1]

My strategy in this chapter will be the following. After laying out brief descriptions of Lonergan, Gadamer, and Ricoeur on hermeneutics, I will argue that Lonergan corrects Continental hermeneutics in a major way in his insistence on the meaning and expression components on the upper blade interacting with the lower blade; Gadamer and Ricoeur, to some extent at least, are confined too much to a hermeneutics of finitude. Gadamer and Ricoeur, on the other hand, complement Lonergan in what they say about the lower blade of interpretive procedure and practice. But Lonergan's remains the more comprehensive and more critically grounded hermeneutics, because it rests on self-appropriation, epistemology, and metaphysics. On this issue, as on so many others, self-appropriation is the pearl of great price in philosophy. One way in which Gadamer and Ricoeur complement Lonergan and confirm or verify what he says is in their strong rejection of a hermeneutics of immediate looking or hearing in favor of a hermeneutics of mediation. In fact, one striking aspect of this discussion is the way *Insight* anticipates a discussion in Continental hermeneutics that does not really get off the ground until the 1960s and 1970s. This should not, of course, surprise those of us who for many years have been influenced by Lonergan's undoubted genius.

Lonergan, Gadamer, and Ricoeur on Hermeneutics

In *Insight* Lonergan's account of interpretation rests on self-appropriation and the epistemology and metaphysics that flow from it. The necessity for it emerges from the need for an account of interpretation as scientific that would enable Lonergan to give an account not only of his position but of how it relates to and is superior to other positions. If his account is to be scientific, then it has to show how there cannot be a range of different, conflicting, equally valid interpretations rooted in individual, group, and general biases or the historical context of the different experts. If hermeneutics is to be scientific, then it has to discover some method of conceiving and determining the habitual development of all audiences, and it has to invent the technique with which its expression escapes relativity to particular and incidental audiences.[2]

Enter the universal viewpoint. It meets the issue head on; the universal viewpoint "is a potential totality of genetically and dialectically ordered viewpoints."[3] It is potential in that it is not universal history like Hegel's dialectic, complete apart from matters of fact. The totality is of viewpoints and is thus concerned with principal acts of meaning that lie in insights and judgments, and it reaches these principal acts by directing attention to the experience, understanding, and judgment of the interpreter. The universal viewpoint is an ordered totality of viewpoints, which has as its base adequate self-knowledge and the consequent metaphysics. It has a retrospective expansion in the various genetic series of discourses through which human beings could advance to present knowledge, and a dialectical expansion in the many formulations of discoveries due to the polymorphic consciousness of human beings, in the possibility of positions, true claims based on mediated understanding, leading to further development, and in the necessity of counter-positions, false claims based on one-sided immediacy, reversing themselves. The universal viewpoint can reach a concrete presentation of any formulation of any discovery by identifying in personal experience the elements that, as confused or related under this or that orientation of polymorphic consciousness, could be combined to make the position or counter-position humanly convincing.

As the totality is potential, so also is the ordering of viewpoints. Because the totality is a heuristic structure, its contents are sequences of unknowns. There are genetic sequences, but the same discoveries can be made in different manners. There are dialectically opposed formulations with their contrasting invitations to development and reversal, but these are not clear-cut and merge in the ambivalence of the aesthetic, dramatic, and practical patterns of experience, give rise to unsolved and inadequately conceived questions, and make their clearest appearance not in the field of knowledge but in the volitional tension between moral aspiration and practical living.[4]

Not only is the ordering potential, but what is ordered in itself in its linguistic expression advances from the generic to the specific, undifferentiated to differentiated, from the awkward, the global, and spontaneous to the expert, the precise, and the methodical. One example of this tendency is the description in *Method* of stages of meaning, such that a movement occurs from fundamentally undifferentiated consciousness to the classical differentiation between theory and common sense, sense and understanding, to the modern differentiation among science, common sense, interiority, and religious transcendence. All people in all epochs experience, understand, judge, and decide, but the differentiated consciousness understands the undifferentiated consciousness in a way that the undifferentiated consciousness can understand neither itself nor differentiated consciousness.[5]

The universal viewpoint is universal not by abstractness but by potential completeness, which is attained not by stripping subjects of their particularities, but by envisaging subjects in their concreteness. Because there are no interpretations without interpreters, there are no interpreters without polymorphic unities of empirical, intelligent, and rational consciousness. If the interpreter assigns any meaning to what he interprets, then its experiential components have to lie in his experience, its intellectual component in his intelligence, and its rational component in his critical reflection on the critical reflection of another.

To put the matter differently, if the core of meaning is the protean notion of being, then being is or is thought to be whatever is grasped intelligently and affirmed reasonably. There is, then, a universe of meaning, and its four dimensions are the full range of possible combinations of experiences and lack of experience, of insight and lack of insight, of judgments and failures to judge, and the various orientations of polymorphic consciousness. In the measure that I have explored these dimensions, then I become capable, when provided with the appropriate data, of interpreting any expression whatever.[6]

Is this just a matter, Lonergan asks, of his arbitrarily naming his own philosophy as the basis for the universal viewpoint? In one sense, of course, it is; it is Lonergan's discovery in a certain place and time of a certain point of view which is admittedly his. But if one distinguishes between personal expression and what that refers to, then this is a particular philosophy that takes its stand on the dynamic structure of human cognitional activity, distinguishes the various elements involved in that structure, and affirms a basis for constructing any possible philosophical position or counter-position in the history of philosophy. Such a genuine philosophical basis, though particular, becomes a philosophy of philosophies able to account not only for its own position but for its own difference and superiority to counter-positions. The Hegelian influence on Lonergan here is very strong, at least as strong, I have concluded from a recent rereading of *Insight*, as Kant's.[7]

Lonergan moves on to discuss an upper blade and a lower blade in interpretation. The upper blade is one of generalities, and the lower blade is the techniques and practices of scholars enabling the generalities to be determined with greater accuracy. The upper blade has two components of meaning and expression. For the totalities of meanings, the upper blade is the assertion that the protean notion of being is differentiated by a series of genetically and dialectically related unknowns. For the totality of modes of expression, the upper blade is the assertion that there is a genetic process in which modes of expression move towards their specialization and differentiation on sharply distinguishable levels. Because it meets the problem of knowing how an interpretation can be true or approximately true and how it can be based on evidence, the upper blade meets the problem of relativism squarely.[8]

Helping to specify the universal viewpoint are the canons of hermeneutics. As the canons of empirical method spell out the criteria of operative, concrete intelligence and reasonableness, so the canons for a methodical hermeneutics simply spell out explicitly the criteria involved in any concrete process of intelligent and reasonable interpretation. There is a canon of relevance, demanding that the interpreter begin from the protean notion of being, and that the interpreter come up with some differentiation of this notion. Second is the canon of complete explanation. Not only must the interpretation be explanatory rather than descriptive, but, all other things being equal, an interpretation will be more preferable the more comprehensive and nuanced and differentiated it is in relation to the surface of the text. Third is the canon of successive approximations. Because self-knowledge can increase or decrease, because that self-knowledge can increase or decrease the adequacy of the interpretation of the text, because the universal viewpoint can be more or less present in the interpretation of a text, and because modes of expression move from general to specific, undifferentiated to differentiated, there can be a progressive approximation to what is actually being said in a text by the same interpreter or series of interpreters.

Fourth is the canon of parsimony. Negatively, it excludes the unverified and unverifiable, for example, what private feelings or thoughts the writer was having at the time he wrote. Positively, the canon relates to what can be verified in the surface of the text, initially just a series of marks on paper. Finally, there is the canon of residues. Just as physical science contains a non-systematic component, so also does the field of meaning. Because any text can contain both the genetic and dialectical, positions and counter-positions, more advanced and differentiated positions in tension with less advanced and differentiated positions, we have to have a principled openness to such possibilities, and the canon of residues is such a principle. In my own work I have argued that such a principle captures what Derrida is getting at in his practice of deconstruction, but neither Lonergan nor I make it the whole story about interpretation as Derrida does. There are positive insights as well as inverse, systematic as well as non-systematic aspects in the text, positions as well as counter-positions.[9]

The canons for a methodical hermeneutics enable one to distinguish between positions and counter-positions not only in texts but in interpretations of texts. If positions call for development in the light of the protean notion of being, the counter-positions call for the opposite. Here the ideal of interpretation is a form of immediate intuition, to let the real Plato or Aristotle or Kant speak for himself in as immediate a way as possible. Yet the fact is that the real Plato, Aristotle, and Kant speak for themselves in remarkably different tongues, depending on the stance of the interpreter. As we shall see, Lonergan's stance on this issue anticipates Gadamer and Ricoeur and is confirmed by them. They, also, give up the ideal of any immediate hermeneutics.[10]

Moving to Gadamer, we see that the basic kind of such an invalid hermeneutics is romantic hermeneutics, one instance of which is Schleiermacher. For Schleiermacher the object of interpretation is to understand an author better than he understands himself by gaining an immediate, intuitive contact with the subjectivity of the author. The aim here is primarily to understand the subjectivity of the author, not his published work. This individuality can be grasped "by, as it were, transforming oneself into the author." What we are aiming at here is inner divination of the subjectivity of the author.[11]

Gadamer questions whether this account captures the intent of an adequate hermeneutics. Is the intent to understand the work or the author? Is the method one of immediate divination or a more mediated process where indeed a fusion of horizons occurs, but one that is not total or infallible, because both author and interpreter are in a mediated world of meaning, in which they "are" language and project a world linguistically. Their daseins are situated in place and time, and such a presence makes immediate divination neither possible nor desirable.[12]

Schleiermacher correctly sees that in some sense a "thou" is involved when I interpret a text. But this "thou" is highly mediated and ultimately known through my encounter with the text. Thus, Gadamer suggests that the process of interpreting a text is one of give and take in which I question the text and it questions me. In such interpretive play between myself and the text, I discover that I am in over my head. I am in an intersubjective and historical process over which I have no control. The game of interpretation plays me as much as I play it. Such serious, playful encounter with the text is possible because the text and I share a common bond of language and tradition. Because I have learned a tradition and language that have become sedimented in me, part of my habitual lived past expressing itself in my present, I can encounter the text. Because the text is part of the same language and same tradition, I can be related to it and it to me.

As in the intentional relation between two subjects in the present, two historical monads encounter one another; intentionality becomes historical. The text as historical encounters me as historical, temporal, social, and in the world. Because I am essentially historical, I can have a past and encounter the past. Because I am essentially historical, the text is other but not alien. I encounter it as part of my temporal and spatial world, illumining and enriching that world. There is a legitimate sense to be given to the notion that the tradition speaks through us. Nonetheless, such a recognition entails not relinquishing the subject, as postmodernists advise, but only qualifying its claim to autonomy and independence from society and history. Such a recognition entails not transcending phenomenology into thought, but transcending transcendental, Cartesian-Husserlian phenomenology into existential and hermeneutical phenomenology.[13]

Because I am in this interpretive game of play, in over my head in a process of question and answer, I am subject to historical and interpretive experience. I can encounter something new that can disappoint and frustrate as well as fulfill and confirm. And such expectations are what Gadamer calls prejudice: presuppositions, values, premises, anticipations that enable interpretation rather than frustrating it. Because of the exploitation and domination abroad, for example, wrought by a national and international capital intent on globalization, the war on terror, and wars in Iraq and Afghanistan, more people are discovering the relevance of prejudice in a new way. One block that modern thought throws up to understanding interpretation correctly is the "prejudice against prejudice." Think of Descartes's search for presuppositionlessness in the first meditation of his *Meditations* or Husserl's in his opening meditation of the *Cartesian Meditations*. Prejudice is not an obstacle to understanding, but a condition of understanding.[14]

One consequence of Gadamer's approach to interpretation is that it is anti-scientific and anti-positivistic. Because interpretation is a process of give-and-take, question and answer, it is not amenable to prediction and control; rather, the opposite. Hermeneutical understanding is an ongoing invitation to loss of control and loss of self, which results in enrichment of self and regaining of self. Gadamer critically articulates and verifies a domain of knowing that is extra-scientific, and this is salutary, a real gain. What is problematic here for Lonergan is that he severs such a gaining of truth from that of method. More of that anon.[15]

Paul Ricoeur picks up on this account of Gadamer's, including his critique of romantic hermeneutics, and departs from, and expands it in at least a couple of different ways. For my discussion of Ricoeur here I am drawing primarily on his *Interpretation Theory: Discourse and the Surplus of Meaning*. One of Ricoeur's departures is in his notion of discourse as a unity of speaking and writing, structural form and semantic content, event and meaning. Gadamer tends to emphasize the former of these sets of opposites; Ricoeur insists on their dialectical unity. In one and the same speech act there is an objective, propositional content and a subjective, event character. The propositional content encompasses both sense and reference, which correspond noematically to understanding and judgment respectively. When I understand what the sentence "Sartre was the conscience of a generation in France" means, then I grasp its sense. When I judge that the sentence is true, I grasp its reference. In addition to its objective semantic content, there is the semiological form on phonological and syntactical levels. Ricoeur thus blends Gadamer's dominantly first-person, relatively immediate dialogical aspect with an explanatory, third-person aspect.

Within the objective prepositional content, there is also a dialectic between singular identification and universal predication. When I say that Sartre was the conscience of a generation in France, the subject of the sentence identifies Sartre as a singular individual and the predicate posits certain universals as instantiated in him. This unity of singular and universal in the sentence is its basic, most important structure. The semiological dimension relates to the semantic dimension as form to content. The full reality of the objective dimension of the sentence, therefore, is a unity of singular and universal, form and content. Although we are conscious of the semantic content, we are usually not conscious of the form. We must try to reach such form through a movement from understanding to explanation.

On the subjective, event side of discourse are the self-reference of the sentence – the implicit or explicit reference through such grammatical devices as pronouns and such non-linguistic devices as physical expression and gestures in the speaker, the illocutionary dimension in which the same locutionary content, that "Sartre was the conscience of a generation in France," is asserted, questioned, or exclaimed over – and the perlocutionary reference to the hearer, its attempt to influence the hearer. As subjective, the act of speaking is noetic; as objective, it is noematic and public. Event and meaning imply one another. "If all discourse is actualized as event, all discourse is understood as meaning."[16]

Because discourse even as speech already has a public, universal, objective content, it can take the form of writing. When writing occurs, there is a distinction of the meaning from the subjectivity and immediate situation of the author. A distanciation and an objectification of meaning occurs that is not negative and obfuscating, but positive and enlightening. For what writing does is to free the meaning disclosed in the initial author's situation from the limited confines of that situation for the comprehension of a wider public. Writing, rather than being confined to the here and now of one author and one group, becomes accessible to millions in many different historical epochs. An objectification occurs in such expression that is not alienating but liberating.

We note here a dialectic between immediate Gadamerian belonging and distanciation that I find very fruitful. We also note here fruitful dialogue between immediate speech and "writing" in the structuralist and post-structuralist sense that represents Ricoeur's critique and sublation of an immediate phenomenology of speech in Husserl, Merleau-Ponty, and Gadamer with a structuralist or post-structuralist emphasis on writing. At the same time, he retains Gadamer's sense of the way a reader is informed by and educated by a text, but now in a proper dialectic of appropriation and distanciation. I make the text my own, but I do it by a kind of dispossession of self or losing of myself in relation to the text. The process is one of dispossessing the possessive ego in favour of the non-possessive self. This process of dispossession is the work of a kind of universality and atemporality emphasized in explanatory procedures, which are in turn linked to the disclosing power of the text that can never be mastered and in this sense is always "other" to me. I lose myself in order to find myself enriched by the disclosive powers of the text.[17]

A second advance that Ricoeur makes over Gadamer is in his contrast between receptive retrieval of a tradition and critique or suspicion of it. Here Ricoeur picks up on Habermas's critique of Gadamer as not allowing for the possibility of a different kind of bias in a tradition and, therefore, being too uncritical of it. There is, however, in Habermas's critique and alternative to Gadamer a danger of not recognizing our embeddedness in tradition and dependence on it in a positive way. Ricoeur, in perhaps the best discussion of the debate between Gadamer and Habermas, argues that both aspects, listening to the tradition and critiquing it, are necessary and necessarily dialectical. I can only criticize tradition, for example, if I already belong to it. Habermas's having recourse to ideology critique is beholden to a tradition that goes back at least to Hegel and Marx. On the other hand, tradition nourishes critique insofar as it is the source of different values by which to criticize and make possible and encourage a limited distanciation from tradition.

What I find myself pointing to in this brief discussion is a gradually expanding and progressive trajectory from Heidegger, on whom both Gadamer and Ricoeur depend, through Gadamer to Ricoeur. In this sense, Ricoeur's approach seems to be the one that is most adequate and most approximates Lonergan's position. On the other hand, Lonergan's method allow us to move back down in a descending trajectory that criticizes, reclaims, and sublates Ricoeur, Gadamer, and Heidegger. It is to this issue of the relationship, the dialogue and dialectic between their approaches, that I now turn.

The Dialogue and Dialectic between Lonergan and Continental Hermeneutics

Although the difficulties and limits are more serious in Gadamer than in Ricoeur, Lonergan's upper blade corrects Continental hermeneutics in a major way. Gadamer with his emphasis on truth clearly intends a non-relativist viewpoint, but the question is whether he is able to achieve that adequately. Because all interpretation is mediated by prejudice, the question becomes one of distinguishing between legitimate and illegitimate prejudice. Lonergan's distinction between bias, on the one hand, and transcendental precepts and canons of methodical hermeneutics, on the other hand, is a great help here. But because Gadamer separates truth from method, one does not enter interpretation with the a priori guidelines supplied by method and is totally on his own on the lower blade of interpreting questions and answers. Because the horizon within which interpretation goes on is a limited one deriving from a particular tradition, we do not have the resources in Gadamer's approach for knowing whether we are excluding certain possibilities illegitimately or focusing on them legitimately.[18] Because Gadamerian interpretation implies a moral knowledge that emerges on the spot in the process of interpretation, there are again no criteria that can be employed for verifying one interpretation as true and another as false.[19]

I think that there is a basis in Gadamer for developing or moving towards a universal viewpoint in his discussion of the logic of question and answer and the horizon of being and life-world in the last part of *Truth and Method*, but he does not do this. Thus, we are left too much on the lower blade of hermeneutical dialogue, of give and take, of being oriented towards positive and negative judgments, but Gadamer gives us insufficient guidance on how to reach these.[20]

Ricoeur does somewhat better, indeed a lot better, but still is insufficient. In his account, the process of coming to a correct interpretation is one of moving from guess to validation, roughly correlated with understanding and judgment. Validation gives us not total certainty about a text, but one that is more or less probable and guided by what he calls a "logic of probability." But what the content of this logic is he leaves unspecified. Nor is there discussion of the metaphysical horizon within which interpretation takes place. Perhaps this lack is due to Ricoeur's rejection of metaphysics, which, following Kant, he denies that we can have. But he does agree with Lonergan that not all interpretations are equal; we must move between the limits of dogmatism and skepticism.[21]

As an aspect or corollary of his correcting Continental hermeneutics, Lonergan links truth and method. With regards to Gadamer's disjunction, several things can be said. First, one reason for Gadamer's position may be that he conceives method as thoughtlessly automatic, like a sausage machine, rather than operating intelligently and reasonably according to explicit criteria of intelligent and reasonable discourse. Second, method is not to be identified with science; rather, science is an instance of the mind operating intelligently and reasonably in inquiry into data of sense in the intellectual pattern of experience. Another instance of method is philosophy reflecting on data of consciousness as "generalized empirical method" or, as later named in *Method*, transcendental method. Third, it may be that Gadamer does not distinguish adequately between a legitimate science and technology, on the one hand, and an illegitimate scientism and technocracy, on the other hand, such that science and technology equal rationality.[22]

Fourth, related to this distinction is that between the legitimate prediction and control exercised by science, an orientation compatible with and proceeding from scientific wonder, and the illegitimate control and domination exercised by scientism and technocracy. Gadamer's term "domination" does not adequately capture this distinction. Fifth, we note positive use of science and mathematics in *Insight* in which they are legitimate instances of knowing and give striking instances of the distinction between sensible and intellectual knowing, knowing as looking and knowing as mediated experience, understanding, and judgment. Lonergan's positive evaluation of science and technology corrects a tendency in Continental philosophy, present somewhat in Gadamer and much less so in Ricoeur, to stress the dark side of these activities. Finally, this negativity and darkness is less attributable to science and technology as such than to their misuse in the service of systematic injustice rooted in class and group domination, manifest most fully and obviously in state socialism and late capitalism. Making this distinction allows one to avoid the postmodern temptation to identify domination with reason as such or with science and technology as such or modern reason as such, *Gestell* as Heidegger puts it in his *The Question of Technology*.[23]

Continental hermeneutics also complements Lonergan fruitfully in different ways. One of these is the way Lonergan's critique of hermeneutics as looking is verified by Gadamer's and Ricoeur's critique of romantic hermeneutics. It is clear that interpretation is not a matter of getting at the private subjectivity of the author, but rather at the meaning of a publicly available text. Correspondingly, hermeneutical meaning and truth is not in the intention of the private author outside of and behind his text nor in the immediate historical situation of the author and his readers nor in the expectations and feelings of the original author and his readers. Gadamer and Ricoeur show the fruitfulness of Lonergan's account here and develop it with more detail and historical, philosophical nuance.[24]

Another way in which Continental hermeneutics complements a Lonerganian approach is in the logic of question and answer, developed most fully by Gadamer in a very persuasive, insightful way. This account expands Lonergan's emphasis on the primacy of the question, asserted among other places in the first chapter of *Insight*, where understanding begins with the question about the meaning of the cartwheel, moves to pre-conceptual insight, and ends with definition. In the dialogal situation between myself and the text, I learn the art of putting questions to the text and letting it challenge me, of letting the questioning of the desire to know be guided by the text, letting it educate me in developing a path for fruitful questioning and allowing myself to be educated by historical, hermeneutical experience, by its negativity, by its newness. In this way, analogously to a fruitful conversation between two people, I become more of a self as a result of encountering the text, and I give up any lingering ideals of total domination or mastery. I learn in hermeneutical experience the art of losing myself and finding myself in relation to the text, in being in over my head and being comfortable with that, in learning the way of questioning and answering appropriate to the text.[25]

On the basis of this complementarity, I think an apparent one-sidedness in Lonergan's discussion of the universal viewpoint and the lower blade can be overcome. The mistaken impression can be given that the fully self-appropriated Lonerganian interpreter approaches texts already fully knowledgeable, already self-sufficient, and thus we can miss the way such an achievement is already formed by hermeneutical experience, as Lonergan himself admits later in *Insight*, in which he talks about the way he has reached up to the mind of Aquinas in a way that has changed him profoundly. But as *Insight* manifests, it is not just St Thomas who has formed and educated Lonergan, but the history of modern philosophy, especially Kant and Hegel. The universal viewpoint and upper blade is not just a norm to be applied to the lower blade of hermeneutical practice, but is itself a product of that practice. The interaction between upper blade and lower blade goes both ways. The upper blade without the lower blade is empty and excessively naive and innocent; the lower blade without the upper is relativistic and arbitrary.[26]

It may be, therefore, that what I am getting at in this dialectic between upper and lower blade, between self-appropriation and appropriation by and with the textual other is just an instance of a more general phenomenon. Self-appropriation always takes place in a social context in which I am involved in dialogue and dialectic with the other. As a result, I never achieve full mastery of either the other or myself. Self-appropriation is always processive, incomplete. As Kierkegaard says somewhere about being a Christian, I am never fully self-appropriated, but always on the way.

A final kind of complementarity between Lonergan and Continental hermeneutics occurs in Ricoeur's account of the dialectic between receptivity to tradition and suspicion of it. Lonergan mentions this distinction in one of his post-*Method* writings, but does not develop it systematically. But there is a basis in Lonergan's text for such a development in his distinction between bias, about which one should be suspicious both in ourselves and in the text, and the canons for a methodical hermeneutics, and in the distinction between understanding and judgment, which can be negative as well as positive, suspicious as well as affirming. In my own work, I have developed this distinction by my conception of dialectical phenomenology as a receptive listening to the past, descriptive, eidetic elucidation of the lived present, and suspicious questioning leading to a radically transformed personal and social future. But since I will discuss such matters in future chapters, I will not go into them here.[27]

Conclusion

Is there a universal viewpoint? Is there an upper blade? At times, in the way Continental philosophy has asked this question, these stances seem like an unreachable, hubristic ideal to which it seems unreasonable to aspire. "Embrace your finitude" seems to be the motto. For Lonergan, however, the universal viewpoint is a matter of verifiable, concrete fact. If I have a desire to know oriented to a notion of being leading to a metaphysics of proportionate being, then I have a universal viewpoint and upper blade. If I do not have a universal viewpoint, then, by *modus tollens*, I do not have a metaphysics of proportionate being, notion of being, and self-affirmation. I cannot deny having a universal viewpoint and upper blade without contradicting myself performatively and logically.

Like metaphysics, the universal viewpoint is in the mind. Like metaphysics, the universal viewpoint can move from latent to problematic to explicit. Anyone who affirms a proposition as true implies latently that such a claim could be defended against all comers. All articulation of the universal viewpoint does is to make that point explicit.

Insight, as the rich book it is, can be read forwards and backwards such that earlier viewpoints anticipate later viewpoints and can be included in a higher viewpoint, and later stances can be taken as instances of earlier ones. As I understand the matter, the universal viewpoint and upper blade functioning in a methodical hermeneutics is an instance of genuineness, which admits and maintains the fruitful tension between finitude and infinitude, limitation and transcendence. Genuineness or authenticity in hermeneutics is maintaining that tension and allowing both poles to play their appropriate role, the lower blade of hermeneutical practice and the upper, infinite blade of meaning and expression. There is a failure in genuineness, therefore, when I exclude or minimize or maximize either pole one-sidedly, moving into a one-sided emphasis on infinitude or becoming dogmatically sunk in finitude. It is this latter tendency that is present at least as a temptation and danger and possibility in Continental hermeneutics and then rushes, like a massive flood, into postmodernism and post-structuralism. By Lonergan's criteria, Continental hermeneutics falls prey, more or less, in whole or in part, completely or incompletely, in its modernist or postmodern variants to an inauthentic hermeneutics of finitude.

I end with Lonergan's moving testimony to genuineness in *Insight*:

> Genuineness is the admission of that tension into consciousness, and so it is the necessary condition of the harmonious cooperation of the conscious and unconscious components of development. It does not brush questions aside, smother doubts, push problems down, escape to activity, to chatter, to passive entertainment, to sleep, to narcotics. It confronts issues, inspects them, studies their many aspects, works out their various implications, contemplates their concrete consequences in one's own life and in the lives of others. If it respects inertial tendencies as necessary conservative forces, it does not conclude that a defective routine is to be maintained because one has grown accustomed to it. Though it fears the cold plunge into becoming other than one is, it does not dodge the issue, nor pretend bravery, nor act out of bravado. It is capable of assurance and confidence, not only in what has been tried before and found successful, but also in what is yet to be tried. It grows weary with the perpetual renewal of further questions to be faced, it longs for rest, it falters and it fails, but it knows its weakness and its failures, and it does not try to rationalize them.[28]

4 Self-Appropriation and Alterity

At first, it seems that there must be an incompatibility between self-appropriation, with its focus on the self, and alterity, with its focus on the other outside of the self. A minute's reflection, however, indicates that this is not the case. For the self that is appropriated is intentionally oriented to the other, and alterity, even or especially the human alterity that is the concern of this chapter, is included in the being to which, according to Lonergan, we are intentionally oriented.[1] Two of Lonergan's famous formulations from *Method* indicate this point: "Man achieves authenticity in self-transcendence" and "objectivity is ... the consequence of authentic subjectivity."[2] The first formula indicates that we become authentic the more we relate to the other as intellectually, morally, and religiously real. And the second formula suggests that objectivity and alterity are reached to the extent that we are authentic. Objectivity does not just drop from the skies, but is the result of the work of self-transcendence.

Just mentioning a couple of Lonergan's formulations, as insightful as they are, is not sufficient. For alterity, the alterity of the human other, has recently emerged as an issue in the work of certain postmodern thinkers such as Derrida and Levinas. While the issue as they raise it has certain common ground with earlier thinkers such as Husserl, Sartre, and Marcel, there are also strong differences. And one of these differences is a much more thoroughgoing questioning or rejection of the relationship between self-appropriation and alterity stated above.

My procedure in this chapter, therefore, will be to lay out a Lonerganian response to the contemporary debate over alterity. That response will be phenomenological-transcendental, in the sense of laying out a descriptively grounded, positive account of alterity, and dialectical, in the sense of developing a criticism of the current postmodern account of alterity. Why should I prefer a Lonerganian account to that of Derrida and Levinas? Here I am operating in the spirit of Lonergan's method in presenting not only a positive but a dialectical reflection on why my position is superior to that of others.[3]

A Phenomenology of the Other

Let us imagine ourselves on a subway in one of our major cities. I am sitting minding my own business peaceably, and all of a sudden I see a beggar walking down the length of the car inviting the inhabitants to contribute whatever they can. It is an experience that I have had hundreds of times in the last twenty-nine years of my life in New York City.

What a relatively presuppositionless description reveals in a prima facie manner is at least the following. First, the other is present to me perceptually, morally, and politically. I perceive the other as black or white, rich or poor, male or female, well or poorly dressed, and I respond or do not respond to her appeal. Second, there is an asymmetry involved in the situation of the other contrasted to mine. I am relatively well-off whereas she is poor, clean whereas she, perhaps, is dirty, happy whereas she is unhappy. The appeal of the other is the appeal to a set of moral or political or religious beliefs which she presumably shares with us, in the light of which she is deprived or marginalized. "I am poor and needy and require help to live a fully human life and even to get through the day." There is asymmetry here, but it is related to symmetrically shared, communal beliefs as more fundamental.

A third aspect is that the appeal of the beggar to me is mediated, not immediate. Our prior discussion of the shared moral and communal context supports this point. If I am sympathetic to the plight of the other, for example, as having a right to my aid on liberal, secular grounds or as being the poor person who is Christ or, perhaps, as a victim of class injustice, I will give to her. If, however, I am a neoliberal individual who does not think that such an appeal has any merit and that the plight of the person is her fault, due to her own laziness and dissolute living, then I will keep reading my newspaper and give her nothing. The point is that the call of the other, whether heeded or not, is mediate, not immediate.

A final aspect is the primacy of perception, even when I respond to the other morally and compassionately. I have to perceive the other sensuously before I respond to her morally. One indication of this point is that I can be aware of the other perceptually when she appears on the train, before she reveals herself as a beggar. When she starts her appeal, then a moral dimension arises, but that presumes cognition on the perceptual level.

This description may seem straightforward and plausible, but it is questioned or denied by postmodern accounts. First, in relation to the first aspect, the other is regarded as totally other, "tout autre" as it goes in the French. Second, asymmetry is not derivative, presuming a more fundamental symmetry of belief, but fundamental. The asymmetrical call of the other from the margins constitutes the obligation to give to the other. Symmetry is later constituted through a mediating third. Further, the other's call has an immediacy about it that seems to deny or downplay mediating factors. It puts me in question in a way that I cannot question. Questions about the legitimacy of the call seem not to arise or to be illegitimate. The other is "nude," totally proximate, and non-metaphorically present. Finally, the stress on the moral appeal, as opposed to the cognitive, brings into question whether there is any necessary logical priority of perception to moral appeal and response.[4] Thinkers like Levinas, therefore, force us to go deeper, both to ground more profoundly our account of the other and to account for our disagreement with him.

Self-Appropriation and Alterity: A Lonerganian Account

I refer to my account as "Lonerganian" to give myself room not only to make use of his very valuable insights but to avail myself of insights and arguments that I have developed in my own work. Those further considerations, while my own, are inspired by and compatible with Lonergan's spirit and method.

We start with a review of what Lonergan means by self-appropriation. This is, as he tells us in the introduction to *Insight*, the coming to terms with, knowing, and choosing my own cognitive and existential self in intentional relation to being. As fully constituted in the transcendental method described by Lonergan in the first chapter of *Method*, self-appropriation is the experiencing, understanding, judging, and choosing of myself as an experiencing, understanding, judging, and choosing subject in relation to being. And this cognition and choice are not just the cognition and choice of any Tom, Dick, or Harry, but my own personal individual, knowing, choosing, and loving. This individual aspect, of course, is always linked to universal aspects, most fundamentally the transcendental structure of human intentionality itself.[5]

This unity of individual and universal aspects of the human self has significant implications, we will see, for our account of relating to other persons, for others will be definitely *other* to us, not just in their similar transcendental structure, but *different* from us in their individuality. A Lonerganian account of alterity gives full recognition to a legitimate play of difference or *différance*.

Human intentionally has as its object being, the object of the pure desire to know. "Being," therefore, includes everything in its purview, all the legitimate answered and unanswered questions; outside of being there is nothing. Consequently, the distinction between self and other is included within the notion of being. Already we can see why, in a Lonerganian sense, there can be only a relative, not an absolute, alterity. Even God, though absolute in other senses, is the object of our own understanding and love and, therefore, only relatively other. Absolute alterity in the postmodern sense, or in any other senses, makes no sense, and we can know that in an a priori way based on the notion of being.[6]

Lonergan's notion of objectivity follows from this discussion of the notion of being. In addition to the principal notion of objectivity occurring in a patterned context of judgments – "I exist," "you exist," and "I am not you" – there are three other aspects of objectivity corresponding to experience, understanding, and judgment: experiential objectivity presenting us with the given into which we inquire, normative objectivity governing the desire to understand, and the absolute objectivity of fact. Otherness or alterity emerges most fully for Lonergan in this discussion of objectivity. The alterity of the human other is simply a particular instance of a more general objectivity or alterity.[7]

Two further comments are in order here: for Lonergan an analysis of alterity based on intentionality does not do in or deny or destroy alterity, but rather gives us the other. I can thematize you, for example, in saying that "you are a good philosopher" or "you are a generous person" without denying your otherness, degrading it, or reducing it to sameness. This is a point denied by Levinas's account of alterity, and by others as well. Rather, receiving such compliments, you feel or should feel your subjectivity enhanced or enabled or lifted up. Objectification and thematization do not in themselves lead to alienation, although one particular kind does. When I exploit Joan or insult her or whistle at her in a sexist way, that certainly is unacceptable alienation and objectification. The danger here is to confuse that form of objectification with objectification as such.[8]

A second point is that in *Post-Cartesian Meditations*, I laid out phenomenologically five different aspects of experiential objectivity, going more deeply into Lonergan's notion. These are briefly the contrasts between my own lived body "here" and the body of the other "there," at a distance: between the massive, implicit certainty of my own conscious lived body given to me in an originary way and the merely presumptive certainty about the other (the apparently bent stick in the water turns out to be straight); between the multiplicity of conscious acts moving around the perceived object, seeing it, touching it, and the unified object perceived through a multiplicity of profiles; between the non-perspectival presence of my own lived body and the perspectival presence of the object perceived from a point of view; and between my awareness of my perceptual acts as dependent on me and the independent content of the perceived object. Whether I like it or not, the table is brown, not red; rectangular, not triangular; and large, not small. This list of aspects, I argue, enriches Lonergan's notion of experiential objectivity while being compatible with it, and these aspects are among the conditions I know in making the virtually unconditioned judgments that I exist, you exist, and I am not you.[9]

In a Lonerganian framework, then, the knowledge of human otherness is just a specific instance of a more general orientation to being and objectivity. Just as I can say that Joan exists, I exist, and I am not Joan, so I am aware of Joan experientially in the different above aspects. I am aware normatively in my conversation with Joan of the necessity to be consistent, clear, and open, and I am aware of the brute factuality of Joan. If she is truly here now, then she cannot not be here, and the truth of that judgment will reverberate down through the centuries.

In *Post-Cartesian Meditations*, I have summed up and rendered systematic the argument in the following manner. If I know other experiencing, understanding, judging, and choosing subjects through their own embodied behavior, then I know other persons. Here we have a conditioned, a condition, and the link between the two. The conditioned is simply the conclusion that I know other persons, and the link between the conditioned and condition is a materially analytic claim, defining what other persons are, as they are or may be known in concrete judgments of fact. To know other persons is to experience, understand, and judge them. The other person will not be a noumenal spirit in some noetic heaven, but one essentially embodied and manifesting herself in her own embodied behavior, in a body known as distinct from mine.[10]

The fulfillment of the conditions is given in phenomenological reflection upon conscious experience. Here, as in the discussion of perceptual objectivity, it is not a matter of inference from private states of consciousness, but of explicating evidence that is already there implicitly. Such an explication has four steps: the evidence for otherness in general, the evidence for specific kinds of otherness, the evidence for other persons, and a stronger, richer sense of objectivity.[11]

Let us describe these briefly. The evidence for otherness in general lies in the five notes of perceptual objectivity listed above, leading to virtually unconditioned judgments that other things exist that are distinct from me. Second, we become aware of and know specific kinds of otherness. Rocks, trees, and dogs are objects of my consciousness and, therefore, independent of me, but rocks, trees, and dogs are specifically, qualitatively different from one another – they have a different kind of presence. I can make a tree grow, but not a rock; I can train Fido to hunt ducks, but not a tree.[12]

In this context of multiple kinds of otherness, I know other persons. For what becomes clear is that there is another kind of embodied life with a different kind of presence. It not only grows, senses, and moves, but talks, gestures, and paints pictures. I can talk *at* Fido, but I can talk *with* this other kind of life, which can also talk back and disagree with me. I can put my plants anywhere I want in my apartment with no protest from them, but these other beings can resist me, disobey me, refuse to do what I want or be where I wish. I can train and indoctrinate Fido, but these other strange beings can resist being trained and indoctrinated and express their indignation in being so treated.[13]

With the presence of the other, we have objectivity in the full sense of the word. Objectivity in the full sense means not simply what I experience, understand, and judge for myself but what is or can be intersubjectively true. The perceived thing is present to me as something that not only I perceive but the other perceives from her point of view there, and her perceptions can correct, complement, or deepen mine. An objective claim in science, mathematics, or philosophy is one that is or can be universally true for all persons. Absolute objectivity – that Columbus traveled to America in 1492 – is knowable not just by me but by everybody.[14]

Such is my brief account of what it means to know other persons. Already, however, on a cognitive level, certain claims in our initial phenomenological description are confirmed as true. First, the other is relatively, not absolutely, other, known through my own conscious experience. Second, the other is not immediately other, known in "a good look" or "a good hear," but known mediately through experience, understanding, and judgment.

Existential Encounter with the Other

After this first stage of the cognitive relationship with the other, in which I have been basically dealing with issues raised by Merleau-Ponty and Husserl, there is another, founded stage in which existential, free encounter with the other takes place. Here the turf occupied is that of Marcel and Sartre, the Sartre of *Being and Nothingness*. Is the relationship between two or more people basically conflictual, as Sartre argues, or is there the possibility and actuality of a beneficial, mutually respectful relationship? In the spirit of Lonergan, I opt for the latter alternative, all the while admitting that some conflict does occur in some kinds of situations.[15]

One problem with denying beneficially mutual relationships is that the claim is self-refuting. If I defend such a proposition to another person with reasons and arguments, I am implicitly presupposing mutuality. I am implicitly presupposing the non-violent, non-coercive value of a discussion between equals and that only the "force" of the better argument should prevail. If I wish to claim such validity for my claim, then I am implicitly excepting my own argument from the general claim that all discourse is conflictual and coercive. If, in order to avoid performative inconsistency, I wish my argument to be included, then it loses its validity; it's just a form of arbitrary self-assertion and attempt to dominate the other.[16]

A second problem with Sartre's claim is that it does violence to differences present in our experience. Contrary to his claim that all encounters can be subsumed under the hostile, dominating look, we experience the encouraging look, the loving look, and the respectful look. In addition to the manipulative discourse that tries to subdue the freedom of the other in a non-reciprocal way, there is also a non-manipulative discourse animated by a genuine desire for truth in which the transcendental precepts and the desire to know prevail over the intrusion of bias.[17]

One assumption in early Sartre, as I have concluded in past work, that makes his position tempting is a one-sided conception of freedom, such that it is totally active and non-receptive to the world. If this is so, the choice of human beings in encounter is either to dominate or submit, conquer or be conquered, manipulate or be manipulated. But one influenced by Lonergan is aware of an active receptivity or receptive activity in her approach to the world. There are receptive as well as active aspects, for example, in each one of the transcendental precepts: "be attentive," "be intelligent," in the sense of allowing insights into phantasms to occur, "be reasonable," in the sense of being open to evidence, even evidence that invalidates my claims, and "be responsible," in the sense of being open to the other in her individual difference, otherness, and freedom.[18]

The Ethical Presence of the Other

Let us briefly recapitulate. We have argued for the possible and actual presence of the other in a relative, not absolute manner, and in a mediated way. Such cognitive presence is a pre-condition for existential encounter with the other; I have to perceive the other before I can be hostile or friendly to him. We have also become aware of a possible and actual symmetrical cognitive and existential community, in which each of us becomes aware of sharing a common human humanity, motivated by the desire to know and by transcendental percepts, and able to be mutually receptive and open. The ethical level, as I am going to unfold it, presumes these two levels and is founded on them.

Let us imagine a community of inquirers in a philosophical discussion at a conference. A particular topic is introduced, discussed, agreement or disagreement ensues, and perhaps some general consensus is arrived at, perhaps not. But the discussion has generally been animated by fidelity to the desire to know and by mutual respect and openness. Let us also assume that part of the shared ethical background of such a discussion is Lonergan's form of the categorical imperative: doing should conform to knowing. And let us imagine that such an imperative has been adhered to in the discussion, even though the pattern of experience is intellectual. Everyone has been treated with respect and openness and everyone has been animated by the desire to know and by transcendental precepts.[19]

So far, so good! So far no unacceptable, asymmetrical marginalization or exploitation has occurred. But let us imagine a situation in which somebody is not allowed to speak or is put down or is disagreed with for motives of racial or sexual or class bias, forms of group bias. Let us imagine that such a person has been materially deprived of services before or during the conference, such as inadequate notification or inadequate lodging or food. Let us imagine further that such a person explicitly complains about such marginalization and material deprivation. "I have been subject to racial, sexual, or class bias in ways that violate the desire to know, transcendental percepts, and the categorical imperative. Because of material deprivation, I have not been able to participate fully and equally in the conference."

We have here an instance of what I, drawing on Dussel, in *Critique, Action, and Liberation,* called an "interpellative speech act."[20] The marginalized and deprived other appeals to the community gathered at the conference that is violating its own symmetrically generated and shared criteria and norms and, because of material deprivation, has not been able to participate adequately, fully. But note here that asymmetrical exclusion and deprivation are derivative, less fundamental than the shared criteria and norms. It is to these that the marginalized other appeals in trying to right an injustice done to her.

She is marginalized and deprived, nonetheless, and is other to us asymmetrically, but is not absolutely other to us. She is still present to us cognitively and existentially, but normative symmetry is presupposed, both as what is appealed to in order to right the wrong and what should be restored in a fuller way once the wrong is righted. Moreover, such a moral process is mediated, not only by prior cognitive and moral meaning, but also as morally interpreted in the interpellative speech act: "I have been unjustly marginalized and deprived by you." Finally, as the existential level presupposes the cognitive level, so also the moral level presupposes and is founded on the cognitive and existential levels. I have to be present to the other as a knower and chooser in order to be present to her morally.

Conclusion

Our Lonerganian account thus confirms our initial phenomenological description of the marginalized other on the subway. Alterity is relative, not absolute, derivative as asymmetrical from symmetrical community, mediated, and, as moral, undergirded by a cognitive and existential presence to the other. Levinasian postmodernism, while it has some insights into alterity and the importance of responding to the marginalized other, goes wrong in many different ways.

Why and how does it go wrong? First, there does seem to be a problem of a model of knowing as immediate looking or hearing, especially with regard to the third issue of mediation. Second, Levinas's affirmation of absolute alterity seems to be a reincarnation of the Kantian noumenon on the level of interpersonal relations, and is, perhaps, either the result of inadequately answering Kant on that question or of not taking advantage of answers that have already emerged in Hegel, phenomenology, and critical theory. To the extent that Lonergan most adequately and most deeply answers Kant, as I believe he does, then we have a basis for dealing with this most recent outbreak of "noumenality." Third, other problems emerge in Levinas's account that flow from a bad or inadequate phenomenology. His account of intentionality, for example, as I have already suggested, seems to be that intentionality does not give us access to the other as such, but rather does violence to the other, reduces her to sameness. Thus, the real other is beyond intentionality, totally other.

Fourth, there seems to be a problem of logical inconsistency between, for example, the claim that the other is totally other and the demand that I should hear the other, implying that she is at least somewhat present to me. Fifth, there is an issue of performative consistency between assertion and the content of what is asserted. The question arises, "Why should I listen to the other, speaking to me from on high?" If I simply take her word for what she demands of me, accepting it on her authority, what is arbitrarily asserted can be rationally questioned or denied. If I question her demand, asking her for reasons, then I am on a level of implicit equality with her in that we are both oriented to giving reasons in a context of argument and dialogue. In any event, a dangerous implication of simply accepting her authority dogmatically is that we seem very close to Jonestown.

What are some of the implications of my account? One of them, as I see it, is that the meaning of alterity has at least two other levels or stages, the political either within or between states, and the metaphysical-religious in relating to being, God, and Christ. These levels sublate and presuppose the cognitive, existential, and moral levels. To the extent that there is racial, sexual, class exploitation and marginalization on national or international levels, then issues arise similar to those already discussed. What is the normative basis on which such evils can be criticized and overcome? At this point in my own work, as that has developed in *Critique, Action, and Liberation* and *Process, Praxis, and Transcendence*, I bring up and critically discuss issues of capitalism, imperialism, and militarism.[21]

One way in which the Christian religious level, taking the form in my work of a theology of liberation from the imperial center, sublates prior levels is that for the Christian, the poor, exploited other is responded to as Christ in a preferential option for the poor. If I am correct, there is such an option that can be argued for even on a philosophical level. As I have argued the point elsewhere, and will argue it later here, radical political conversion, the movement to a post-capitalist, post-imperialist standpoint in feeling, thought, and commitment, flows from intellectual and moral conversion, and solidarity with the marginalized, exploited other flows from radical political conversion. In radical political conversion I hear and respond to the call of the oppressed other as illuminated by the demands of intellectual and moral conversion.[22]

I conclude with a quotation from *Process, Praxis, and Transcendence* that may help put the discussion in context.

> The desire to know, our questioning orientation to being, expresses itself in an ever increasing identification with otherness as it is in its otherness. Being as other to me and as including me is the object of the pure desire to know. To experience, understand, judge, choose, and love, in line with the transcendental precepts, is progressively to say "yes" to the other, to be converted to the other. We have here a deepening receptivity to the other. "Receptivity" and "otherness" are correlative.[23]

5 The Unity of the Right and the Good in Lonergan's Ethics

Let me supply some context for this chapter. About fifteen to twenty years ago, when I was writing *Critique, Action, and Liberation,* it seemed to me that there was an ethical Humpty Dumpty operative in the United States: right versus good, deontology vs. teleology, duty vs. happiness, universal, normative justification vs. concrete prudential application. Some of the major players on the scene were Habermas, Taylor, McIntyre, Gadamer, Sandal, and Apel. What seemed to me to be the case was that these dichotomies needed to be overcome dialectically: different, contrasting perspectives needed to be reconciled in a higher viewpoint, which I proceeded to work out in three chapters.[1]

Years later, to my delight and surprise, when I was rereading chapter 18 of *Insight* on the possibility of ethics, I discovered, lo and behold, that Lonergan was already there before me, in his attempt to reconcile the right and the good, the perspectives of Kant and Aristotle-Aquinas. This experience is not the first and only one I have had with Lonergan in this regard, and represents one kind of evidence for me of his greatness as a thinker. In my opinion, in the twentieth century there is Lonergan and there is everyone else, trailing far behind. Nor do these experiences invalidate my own effort, which was worked out in far greater detail than Lonergan's and has its own kind of validity and originality. Nonetheless it seems to be profitable to reflect on Lonergan's account, worked out fifty years ago in *Insight*. Consequently, I will first consider Lonergan's treatment of the issues in *Insight* and briefly reflect in my conclusion on some possible implications.

The Right and the Good in *Insight*

Lonergan begins his discussion by asking whether there is a method for ethics similar to that of metaphysics, the implementation of the integral, heuristic structure of proportionate being. His "yes" answer is worked out in chapter 18 in three steps: first, to define such notions as the good, will, virtue, and obligation, from which will follow an account of the method of ethics and a cosmic, ontological account of the good. Second, he envisages the account of ethics from the point of view of freedom and responsibility, the relevance of the canon of statistical residues is considered, the nature of practical insight, practical reflection, and the act of decision is outlined, and the fact of the human being's freedom and responsibility is concluded. Third, he considers the possibility of effective, moral liberation. In this chapter I will be focusing on the first two of these sections.[2]

In reflecting on the good, Lonergan affirms that, as being is one and intelligible, so also it is good. But while the unity and intelligibility of being follow from the fact that being is grasped intelligently and affirmed reasonably, the goodness of being comes to light when we consider the extension of intelligent activity into the domain of deliberation and decision, choice and will. There are three levels of the good: the good as the object of desire, to be experienced as pleasurable, enjoyable, satisfying; the good of order arising from the desire to know's tendency to move beyond the immediate domain of pain and pleasure to the mediated domain of institutions such as the polity, economy, and family, ways of organizing and supplying immediate, particular goods; and the good of value emerging on the level of reflection and judgment, deliberation and choice.

Possible goods of order such as individualism, capitalism, and socialism can be affirmed or denied, chosen or rejected, valued or disvalued. When human beings reflect on possible goods of order and choose some and reject others, they do so with all the ardor of their being, because human intelligence here is not only speculative but practical, not only disinterested but interested, not only detached but attached. Thus, perhaps, if belief in God is on the decline in some communities and religion a matter of indifference, to question our economic system, neoliberalism, and foreign policy in Iraq are fighting words. "Put up or shut up."[3]

Will is intellectual or spiritual appetite. As the capacity for sensitive hunger stands to sensible food, so will stands to objects presented by intellect. Besides the bare capacity to will, there is the habitual willingness, specialized in particular directions, to carry out what intelligence and reasonableness demand, and there is the act of willing. It is an event, and so it alone is revealed directly. Further, willing is rational and, therefore, moral. The detached, disinterested desire grasps intelligently and reasonably not only the facts of the universe of being but practical possibilities. These include not just transformation of the environment but human beings themselves. The empirical, intelligent, critical subject becomes a morally self-conscious subject. Because human beings are not only knowers but doers, there occurs an exigency for self-consistency between knowing and doing.[4]

It is difficult enough for cognitional activities to be dominated by the pure, disinterested desire to know, but even more difficult is the area of moral living, and not a little of evidence for the exigency lies in human beings' efforts to dodge it. The three main forms of avoidance are the flight from self-consciousness – the unexamined life is definitely not worth living; rationalization, in which knowing is brought forcibly into harmony with doing; and moral renunciation.[5]

In our own way, Lonergan says, we have already been dealing with the meaning of the word "ought." Our answer differs from the Kantian doctrine, for if we agree in offering a categorical imperative, we disagree insofar as we derive it wholly from speculative intelligence.[6] Lonergan's answer differs from Freud's insofar as his "ought" is not neurotic, but is distinct from any basis in psychoneural events and from concomitant moral emotions and moral sentiments. Thus, we have already seen in Lonergan's first few pages a relating and distinguishing between the good and the right, speculative and practical reason, "is" and "ought." These themes will continue to be developed in the following pages.[7]

In rational, moral self-consciousness, the good as value comes to light; value here means the good as a possible object of rational choice. From this claim, a triple cross-division of values results. They are true insofar as they are chosen rationally, but false insofar as they result from a flight from self-consciousness, rationalization, and moral renunciation. They are terminal insofar as they are objects of rational choices, but originating insofar as directly or indirectly, explicitly or implicitly, they modify our habitual willingness to do good. Finally, they are actual or in process or in prospect, insofar as they have been realized already, or are in the course of being realized, or are merely under consideration.[8]

Values, moreover, are hierarchic. Objects of desire are values only as they fall under some intelligible order, and the goods of order are values only insofar as they are actually chosen and realized. Terminal values are subordinate to originating values, because the originating value grounds good will, and good will grounds the realization of terminal values. Within terminal values themselves there is a hierarchy, for each is an intelligible order, but some of these orders include others, some are conditioning and others conditioned, some conditions are more general and others less. From this cognitive, moral dynamism unfolds a body of moral precepts that extends fully to the concrete domain of human living and realizes in the concrete the full consistency between knowing and doing.[9]

From these reflections comes to light the method of ethics as parallel to and interpenetrating metaphysics. Just as the structure of knowing grounds a metaphysics, so also the prolongation of that structure into human doing grounds an ethics. Just as the universe of proportionate being is a compound of potency, form, and act, because it is to be known through experience, understanding, and judgment, so the universe of proportionate good is a compound of objects of desire, intelligible orders, and values, because the good is initially known as an object of desire, then subsumed under a good of order, and finally rationally chosen. Just as metaphysics is a set of positions and counter-positions, so also values are true or false, ordered or disordered, intelligently and rationally chosen, or unintelligently and irrationally chosen.

Just as the counter-positions invite their own reversal, so also the basically similar counter-positions of the ethical order through the longer cycle of decline either invite their own reversal or destroy their carriers. Just as the heuristic structure of proportionate being, being as intended through a totality of possible questions, reveals an upwardly directed dynamism of finality towards ever fuller being, so the obligatory structure of our own rational self-consciousness finds its materials and its basis in the products of universal finality, is itself finality on the level of intelligent and rational consciousness, and is itself finally confronted with the alternative of choosing either development and progress or decline and extinction.[10]

The ontology of the good flows from this account. Instead of speaking merely of objects of desire, intelligible orders, and terminal and original values, we can speak of parallel intelligibilities of potential, formal, and actual goods, where the potential good is identical with potential intelligibility and so includes but goes beyond objects of desire, where the formal good includes but goes beyond goods of order, where the actual good is identical with actual intelligibilities and so includes but goes beyond human values. The goods intended by human desire, the good of order, and humanly chosen values are, in other words, parts and aspects of a larger universe that precedes, envelops, and transcends what human beings create. Because this broad generalization may seem too sweeping and easy, Lonergan says, we take our stand on an identification of being and the good that surpasses human feeling and sentiments and resides exclusively upon intelligible order and rational value. To the hedonist who equates the good with what is experienced as pleasurable, we insist that, though one begins with objects of desire, the full good resides not in them alone but in the total manifold of the universe that needs to be understood, judged, and chosen.[11]

As the identification of being with the good in no way denies or minimizes pain and suffering, so it has not the slightest implication of a denial of unordered manifolds, disorder, or false values. The middle term of the identification of the good with being is intelligibility, and intelligibility is to be grasped not only by direct but by inverse insight, not by a single method but by a fourfold totality of classical and genetic, statistical and dialectical methods. Thus, the identification of the good with being is not the affirmation of an ideal intelligibility of some postulated utopia, but the ascertainable intelligibility of the universe that exists in all of its order and disorder, perfection and imperfection, value and disvalue.[12]

Now that we have finished our first task of discussing the good, will, value, and obligation, we will explore freedom and responsibility. Beginning with a discussion of statistical residues, Lonergan argues that their significance lies not in implying freedom but in suggesting the possibility of higher viewpoints. There can be autonomous sciences of physics, chemistry, biology, and psychology because at each lower level of systematization there are statistical residues consisting of a merely coincidental manifold to be systematized at a higher level. Consequently, higher laws and schemes of recurrence cannot be deduced from lower levels, nor can events at any given level be deduced systematically from all laws and schemes of recurrence on that level or on all prior levels. In excluding determinism, such reflection makes possible a positive account of freedom, which remains to be given.[13]

In such a positive account, there are four main elements: the underlying sensitive flow, the practical insight, the process of practical reflection, and decision.[14] A set of corollaries follows. First, practical reflection is an actuation of rational self-consciousness, building on but going beyond empirical, intelligent, and rational consciousness. Second, though such reflection heads beyond knowing to doing, still it is merely knowing. Third, such reflection has not an internal but an external term, "for the reflection is just knowing, but the term is an ulterior deciding and doing."[15]

Fourth, because the reflection has no internal term, it can, like Hamlet deciding whether or not to kill Claudius, expand indefinitely. Fifth, one can reflect reasonably on the possibility of reflection expanding indefinitely, on the incompatibility between such expansion and the business of living, and on the unreasonableness of the expansion. One can decide to act more like a Fortinbras. Sixth, while there is normal duration for the reflection, it is not reflection but decision that enforces the norm.[16]

Decision, the fourth element in our analysis, needs to be distinguished from its manifestation in execution, in knowledge, or expression of that knowledge. The nature of decision can be revealed by comparing and contrasting it to judgment. It resembles judgment in that it selects from a set of contradictories; as judgment affirms or denies, decision consents or refuses. Like judgment, decision is concerned with actuality, but judgment is concerned with what already is, whereas decision is concerned with bringing actuality into being. Finally, both decision and judgment are rational, because both deal with objects apprehended by insight and both occur because of a reflective grasp of reasons.[17]

Nonetheless, there is a radical difference between the rationality of judgment and that of decision. Judgment is an act of rational consciousness, but decision is an act of rational self-consciousness. The rationality of judgment emerges as an unfolding of the detached, disinterested desire to know being, but the rationality of decision emerges as the demand of the rationally self-conscious subject for consistency between knowing and doing. The rationality of judgment occurs if in fact a reasonable judgment occurs, but the rationality of decision emerges if in fact a reasonable decision occurs. Finally, the effective rationality of rational consciousness is radically negative in not allowing other desires to interfere with the unfolding of the pure desire to know, but the effective rationality of the rationally self-conscious subject is radically positive insofar as the demand for the consistency between knowing and doing leads to new deciding and doing consistent with the knowing.[18]

What we notice is a succession of enlargements of consciousness as it moves from dreaming to awakening to empirical to intelligent to rational to rational self-consciousness. The final enlargement, in which I become most fully a self, consists in the empirically, intelligently, and rationally conscious self demanding consistency between his knowing and his doing and acceding to that demand by acting reasonably.

Here also a set of corollaries follows. First, we see why practical reflection lacks an internal term, because what brings it to an end is not knowing but decision. Second, the transformation of consciousness illumines both the meaning and frequent inefficacy of obligation. For it is possible for practical reflection to reach with certitude that the emergence of an obligation is the emergence of a rational necessity, but because I can fail to decide to meet the obligation and act on it, the iron law of necessity can seem like a wisp of straw. For in addition to the contingency of being and being known, there is also the contingency of the decision and of acting on it. What is rationally necessary in knowing an obligation becomes contingent in an enlarged context of knowing leading to doing. In paraphrasing St Paul, that which I would do, that I find myself not doing, and that which I would not do, that I find myself doing.[19]

Coming to a discussion of freedom, the main topic of this section, Lonergan argues that it can only be understood as a higher viewpoint of integration on the level of intellect and will, a spiritual intelligibility that is both intelligible and intelligent. Practical insight, reflection, and decision have a legislative function. Instead of being subject to law, as are psychical, chemical, and psychological events, freedom lays down laws for human beings. There are laws of matter and laws of spirit. The laws of matter are discovered by empirical scientists, but the laws of spirit are the principles and norms that govern spirit in the exercise of its legislative functions. Thus, we see spirit as an emerging demand for consistency between knowing and doing and a body of ethical precepts resulting from living up to this demand. As metaphysics is a corollary to the structure of knowing, so ethics is a corollary to the structure of knowing and doing. As ethics resides in the structure, so the concrete applications of ethics are worked out by spirit inasmuch as it operates within the structure to reflect and decide upon the courses of action that it adopts.[20]

Notice the Kantian tenor of this language. The contingency of freedom is not that of a coincidental manifold on the physical level, but the contingency of a freely chosen consistency between knowing and doing, principles that follow from it, and concrete courses of action that follow from acting on the principles. Freedom, in a sense, gives itself its own law. As such, it has not only the negative aspect of excluding necessity, but the positive aspect of responsibility, because "the measure of the freedom with which the act occurs also is the measure of [the subject's] responsibility for it."[21]

Conclusion

Some interesting possible implications flow from this interpretation of Lonergan. I stress "possible," because I have not had the time or space to verify them here, although I have done some of that work elsewhere. First, if Kant is important negatively and positively for the emergence of Lonergan's cognitional theory, epistemology, and metaphysics, then he may be important in a similar way for Lonergan's ethics. As Kant is important negatively for Lonergan's rejecting such doctrines as the unknown and unknowable thing in itself and important positively for influencing Lonergan's notion of transcendental method, so Kant may be important negatively for Lonergan's overcoming of Kant's dichotomy of the right and good and important positively for influencing Lonergan's account of the categorical imperative, freedom, obligation, and responsibility. As there is a *Prolegomena to Any Future Metaphysics*, behind which self-appropriated knowers cannot fall in their practice of cognitional theory, epistemology, and metaphysics, so also do Kant's ethical writings constitute a prolegomena to any future ethics, behind which we cannot fall ethically.

Second, as Lonergan's turn to the subject in metaphysics represents a step forward and a turn away from exclusively object-based metaphysics, so his Kant-inspired ethical revolution represents a step forward from precept-dominated versions of natural law to transcendental self-legislation. Just as the cognitive, metaphysical revolution represents a turn away from knowing as taking a good look at an already out there now real, so the ethical revolution represents a turn away from obligation seen as looking at an "already out there valuable," perhaps rooted in a so-called natural tendency. Ethical value, similar to metaphysical truth, results from experiencing, understanding, judging, and deciding. Like metaphysical truth, ethical value is rooted in mediated, not an immediate, realism.

Third, as a later essay, "Natural Right and Historical-Mindedness," shows, the basis of natural law or natural right shifts to the transcendental dynamism of experiencing, understanding, judging, and deciding.[22] Consequently, ethical precepts themselves as products of this dynamism are subject to change, modification, and development, as Lonergan himself saw in dealing with contraception in the context of marriage.[23] Consequently, Lonergan's ethics, like his cognitional theory, epistemology, and metaphysics, is an integration of the opposites of transcendentality and historicality, unchangeableness and changeableness, invariance and variability.

Fourth, illegitimate regression to some safe point in the past, "the thirteenth, the greatest of the centuries," is not the same as legitimate historical retrieval. Lonergan's retrieval of an Aristotelian-Thomistic notion of the good and his sublating this into a higher viewpoint, using Kant's insights into the categorical imperative, freedom, and responsibility, is a beautiful example of such historical retrieval.

Fifth, with the emphasis on freedom, responsibility, self-legislation, and legislation for the world as an aspect of emergent probability, we can see how in a very real sense Lonergan lays the foundation for a philosophy and theology of liberation. As ethics becomes part of an emerging politics and philosophy of history, it becomes merely not self-legislation but legislation for the universe of proportionate being promoting progress rather than decline. In this expanded context of politics and philosophy of history, we move from the terrain of Kant to that of Hegel and Marx.[24]

Sixth, as both Bob Doran and I have shown elsewhere,[25] trying to develop Lonergan's genuine insights and spirit, including what is implicit in his work, promoting progress rather than decline in history – liberation, negatively – would mean liberation from two imperialisms, capitalist and state socialist, that limit, exploit, and destroy not only human beings but also the natural environment. Here there is room to develop in a Lonerganian vein the two other formulations of the categorical imperative, treating human beings as ends in themselves and working for a community of ends. Capitalism and state socialism violate not only the imperative for consistency between knowing and doing, but these other imperatives as well. Both systems treat the human being as a mere means to profit and power, and both violate the community of ends by subordinating the good of the whole community to the good of a particular class, group, or party. The emergence of a world-wide community of ends receptive to the environment in a non-exploitative way would be the positive content of a philosophy, theology, and praxis of liberation.

6 Rationality and Mystery in Lonergan

The topic of this chapter gives me a chance to do something I have wished to do for a long time, namely, to reflect on the relationship between rationality and mystery in Lonergan. Are they mutually inclusive or exclusive? If they are mutually inclusive, then authentic rationality leads to an openness to and affirmation of mystery. Such openness and affirmation, in a sense, complete rationality. If they are mutually exclusive, then the more rational I am, the more I will tend to exclude mystery, to see it as the enemy of rationality, to overcome it in the name of being more completely rational. The more rationality, the less mystery. The contrast ends up being, as we will see more fully, between surrendering to mystery or even serving it, and mastering or dominating mystery.[1]

The exclusivist view has been promoted by what has come to be known as postmodernism, a style of philosophizing or anti-philosophizing that is rooted in Nietzsche in the nineteenth century and flowers in the work of such thinkers as the late Heidegger, Derrida, Foucault, and Rorty in the twentieth century. One of the common complaints of these thinkers is that philosophy in its traditional, modern, and contemporary practice tends to eliminate its "other," whether that be defined as difference, alterity (the human other), or mystery. The late Heidegger, for example, in works such as *The Question of Technology and Other Essays*, argues that Western philosophy leads to a domination of technological reason that minimizes or eliminates mystery. Thus, we must question or reject that kind of approach and move to a post-metaphysical thinking or *Denken*. Such thinking leads us to a reverential, wondering stance before being, questioning as the piety of thinking, or thinking as thanking. In a very real sense, the postmodern thinkers accept the same tension as traditional philosophy (as they see it) between rationality and mystery. They simply opt for mystery in an either-or manner.[2]

In this essay I propose to interrogate Lonergan on this issue. Where does he stand on the relationship of rationality and mystery? Interestingly and paradoxically enough, even in *Insight*, Lonergan's most "rationalistic" book, he finds rationality and mystery to be mutually implicatory. The more I appropriate rationality, my own desire to know, the more I become open to and affirm an openness to the known unknown. The more, by contrast, I give into false, one-sided notions of rationality, the more they, rationality and mystery, will seem to be opposed. But Lonergan's approach gives us a method of criticizing those notions of rationality and, therefore, of overcoming the postmodernism which responds to them, making the mistake of identifying those one-sided versions with rationality itself and philosophy itself.

Lonergan on Rationality and Mystery

I propose to move directly to Lonergan's chapter on the notion of being in *Insight* in order to get to the heart of the matter quickly and easily. In this chapter, being is identified as the object of the pure desire to know, as a totality of possibly correct answers to a totality of possibly correct questions. But because we are finite knowers, we will never completely eliminate the unanswered questions. Only God's unrestricted act of understanding does that. There is, then, a crucial distinction that Lonergan makes between being as the heuristically intended known unknown towards which we are heading in our intellectual striving, and any particular finite account or set of answers, even very impressive accounts such as Hegel's, which tend to stress the known. Philosophers tend to get off the track more and more to the extent that they collapse those levels, thus leaving themselves open to the postmodern critique. More of this anon.[3]

In any event, in our first foray into Lonergan's thought, we can see a principled connection between rationality and mystery. To affirm ourselves as knowers, we need to affirm the desire to know as oriented to being, the known unknown, the questions we have answered and those we have not. Being is a heuristic notion that we can never fully exhaust or fill or fulfill. Consequently, we are in principle already oriented to mystery, to the known as known in a context of mystery. Not to affirm this point or deny it or to insist on the known as the whole story is fundamentally to fail in the task of self-appropriation and working out its implications. The word "mystery," at this point, is mine, not Lonergan's, but my usage, as we will see, is faithful to his thought.

Lonergan becomes more explicit about these matters in a later chapter, "Metaphysics as Dialectic." There he affirms, first of all, the paradoxical category of the "known unknown." Because being is the objective of the pure desire to know, it is the totality of what is to be known through intelligent and reasonable answers. But in fact, our questions outnumber our answers, so that we know of an unknown through unanswered questions. Second, domains of concrete being involve a succession of levels of higher integration and a principle of correspondence between otherwise coincidental manifolds on each lower level and systematizing forms on the next higher level. These higher integrations on organic, physic, and intellectual levels are not static but dynamic systems on the move, not only integrator but also operator. Third, on the intellectual level, the operator is the pure desire to know, ever heading towards further knowledge, "oriented to the known unknown." The principle of dynamic correspondence calls for a harmonious orientation on the psychic level, and "from the nature of the case such an orientation would have to consist in some cosmic dimension, some intimation of unplumbed depths, that accrued to man's feelings, emotions, sentiments."[4]

Fourth, such feelings, emotions, and sentiments become integrated into the flow of psychic events inasmuch as they are preceded by distinctive presentations and inasmuch as they issue forth in exclamations and bodily movements, in rites and ceremonies, in song and speech. Feelings of awe and wonder demand to be expressed; we are incarnate beings. A pragmatic distinction emerges between a sphere of the profane, domesticated, familiar, common; and the sphere of the ulterior unknown, of the unexplored and strange, of the undefined surplus of significance and momentousness. "The two spheres are variable and change with any knowledge of proportionate being. They may be as separate as Sundays and weekdays, or they may interpenetrate so that, as for Wordsworth in his youth, 'the earth and every sight take on the glory and freshness of a dream.'"[5]

Finally, the primary field of mystery consists in the affect-laden images and names that have to do with the second sphere. However, because the primary field is not the only field, it is well to distinguish between the image as image, the image as symbol, and the image as sign. The image as image is the sensible content as operative on the sensitive level. The image as symbol is the image as standing in correspondence with activities and elements on the intellectual level indicating the known unknown. The image as sign is linked with some interpretation that offers to indicate the import of the image.[6]

Lonergan has thus expanded his account to show a principle of correspondence that can and does operate between the psychic and intellectual levels in human consciousness. I take it that such correspondence is an instance of the genuineness Lonergan affirms in an earlier chapter, in which a lived unity-in-tension between finite and infinite operates. To achieve such genuineness is to advance further in the task of achieving an authentic, integrated self. To fail in such a task, to overemphasize the intellectual operator at the expense of the psychic finite, is to fail in genuineness. There is a Lonerganian "between" that is exemplary and that can serve us well, a stance, by the way, that he shares with Voegelin and Desmond.[7]

With a few quick strokes, then, we have sketched a Lonerganian account of mystery that responds to the postmodern challenge. Because mystery is rooted in the desire to know's orientation to the known unknown and in its correspondence with its sensible awareness and feeling, there is no need to go outside of human rationality or metaphysics in order to recover mystery, as late Heidegger thought he had to do. Indeed, the origin of metaphysics in wonder is an old story in philosophy, going back as far as Plato and Aristotle. William Desmond, responding to Heidegger, argues that he is putting old metaphysical wine into new post-metaphysical wineskins.[8]

Postmoderns like Heidegger do have a point, however, in indicating a tendency in modern philosophy to move away from wonder and towards the mastery of mystery. Hegel's claim in *Phenomenology of Spirit* that philosophy is a science of the whole, not a Socratic quest, is an indication of this tendency. And we can note here the criticism that Lonergan makes of Hegel. For Hegel, dialectic is conceptualist, closed, necessitarian, and immanental, whereas for Lonergan dialectic is intellectualist, open, factual, and normative. The appeal to heuristic structures, to accumulating insights, to verdicts awaited from nature and history goes outside the conceptual field to acts of understanding that begin with questions, arise upon appearances, and are controlled by critical reflection. The differences have a common source in that Hegel pours everything into the concept, into what is known, whereas Lonergan sees concepts as products of acts of understanding that are rooted in questions and head towards a known unknown.[9]

Lonergan, then, gives a critical basis for avoiding both the Heideggerian Scylla of saying too little and the Hegelian Charybdis of saying too much, and goes to the roots of postmodern criticism and concerns by arguing that a conception such as Hegel's of philosophy as totalizing knowledge is not to be identified with philosophy as such, but to a deficient version of it. And the solution to that problem is not to give up philosophy and metaphysics, but to come up with a better version of them such that Hegel's positive insights, and they are many, can be retained in a higher viewpoint.

Nor is this all that can be said. Heidegger in *The Question concerning Technology* and other works does indicate a problematic identification of reason with science and science with technocracy, scientism, and technocracy. But Lonergan shows that, in thought and unfortunate historical tendencies, both identifications are wrong. First of all, in addition to scientific reflection on data of sense, there is generalized empirical method oriented to data of consciousness, what Lonergan later calls transcendental method. Second, whereas the scientist depends on the investigations and results of other scientists, the philosopher has to understand and verify every philosophical claim for himself. "Philosophy is the flowering of the individual's rational consciousness in its coming to know and take possession of itself. To that event its traditional schools, its treatises, and its history are but contributions; and without that event they are stripped of real significance."[10]

Third, if reason is not identical with science, if philosophy is also an affair of reason, then reason is not identified with technocracy, with applied science, nor is science to be identified with technology. Fourth, the alternative to globetrotting, arrogant entrepreneurs like Kissinger, Brzezinski, and Kerry traveling around the world and bringing it into line with America's imperial designs is a public sphere, which Lonergan calls "cosmopolis," in which many different kinds of intellectuals, social and physical scientists, philosophers, artists, and theologians, reflect in a public, deliberative way on the level of culture about what policies should obtain on the lower levels of polity, technology, and economy.[11]

Fifth, there is a striking parallel between Heidegger's rather gloomy account given above of the darkening of the modern age due to the emergence of technocracy and the eclipse of being, and Lonergan's account of the longer cycle, in which over centuries there is a devolving series of lower viewpoints leading to various kinds of total control, technocracy, and totalitarianism. Whereas for Lonergan this longer cycle is a result of flight from understanding leading to a minimizing or elimination of philosophy and metaphysics, for Heidegger such a state of affairs is a result of a forgetfulness of being rooted in philosophy and metaphysics. If I am correct in my above conclusions, there is much to recommend in adopting Lonergan's account and rejecting Heidegger's. The point to note here is that "overcoming metaphysics" for Heidegger is not just a speculative matter but is deeply practical and is fraught with implications for the world and for struggling humanity. But the same is true for Lonergan.[12]

Lonergan's account of rationality and its relationship expands and deepens in *Method in Theology*. Here, as is well known, he develops the fourth level of freedom, commitment, and love, discusses the role of feeling in human life, and reflects on the role of conversion – intellectual, moral, and religious. The most important theme for us is religious conversion, falling in love with God. This is rooted in our capacity for self-transcendence, through which we achieve authenticity. The transcendental notions rooted in our questions for intelligence, reflection, and deliberation constitute our capacity for self-transcendence. This capacity becomes actualized when we fall in love. Falling in love can take the form of the intimacy of husband and wife, parents and children. It can take the form of a love for humankind manifesting itself in work for welfare and justice. Finally, it can take the form of a love for God with one's whole heart and whole soul, with all one's mind and all one's strength.[13]

As the question of God is implicit in all our questioning, so being in love with God is the basic fulfillment of our conscious intentionality. It is being in love without reservation. It is a deep-set joy, radical peace, and love for human beings that strives to bring about the kingdom of God on earth. To say that this dynamic state is conscious is not to say that it is known. "Because the dynamic state is conscious without being known, it is an experience of mystery. Because it is being in love, the mystery is not merely attractive but fascinating; to it one belongs; by it one is possessed. Because it is an unmeasured love, the mystery evokes awe."[14]

We can see here that Lonergan's account of mystery completes and deepens his account of mystery in *Insight*. Whereas the emphasis in *Insight* is on the relationship of rationality to mystery, here the emphasis is on the relationship of love to mystery. If there is a basic openness to mystery on the three levels of cognition, here in *Method* the falling in love is the proper fulfillment of that orientation. Religious mystery is not rooted in any mediated cognitional or volitional striving, but is a gift, and we are invited to be in wonder and awe over that gift.

Because, as Lonergan says later on in *Method*, the fourth level sublates the cognitional level, here the religious love of mystery sublates cognitional openness to mystery. If, as he says also, religious conversion generally precedes and leads to moral and intellectual conversion, then a religious sense of mystery can inform and permeate our moral and intellectual striving. The world and being are no longer simply the object of the pure desire to know and love, but are enveloped in and flowing from divine mystery and informed by the faith which is the "knowledge born of religious love." Feelings as the mass and momentum and power of conscious living complement our cognition and love, and find their expression in religious awe, wonder, reverence, and love. The world becomes not just something I question, but something I reverence.[15]

Conclusion

In summing up and reflecting on implications of my account, I must say, first, that the postmodern challenge that is the occasion for my reflection is not merely to be rejected and dismissed. Even though as a whole it, postmodernism, is mostly or dominantly counter-positional, even in that counter-positionality it can serve to deepen and broaden our thought as Lonerganian philosophers.

I find also, second, that postmodernism is or can be positively insightful in a way that can be incorporated into my account. Elsewhere, for example, I have shown how Heidegger's notions of "thinking as thanking" or "questioning as the piety of thinking" can be incorporated into a transcendental account of knowing. Because rationality is not the narrow caricature that Heidegger makes it to be, there is a way of incorporating such notions into our account of questioning, thinking, and loving in a way that enriches our account of those activities. There are reasons why, as Lonerganians, we must be pious, reverential questioners grateful for the gift that motivates us to question.[16]

Consequently, third, there is no reason why I cannot on good Lonerganian grounds approach the world in my daily and professional activities with a sense of reverential awe and wonder and gratitude and emphasize these more than he did. Lonergan says that while "Rahner emphasizes mystery a lot, I have a few clear things to say."[17] But I do not have to be beholden to Lonergan's emphasis here; I can on good transcendental grounds choose to emphasize mystery, wonder, and awe more than he did, and move into domains beyond the intellectual pattern more than he did. Here I find another thinker, William Desmond, very suggestive.[18]

Fourth, it is only fair to say that Bob Doran's notion of psychic conversion is another fruitful addition to Lonergan's thought, which Lonergan himself endorsed.[19] To understand psychic conversion as a way of being open to and affirming the psychic flow and mass of feeling, image, and affect is to see such conversion as another essential complement not only to religious conversion but to the other conversions as well. I wish to note especially here Doran's claim that psychic conversion enables us to be open to the finite poles – psychic, intersubjective, and cosmological – of the three dialectics of the subject, society, and culture. Thus, psychic conversion becomes an important addition to the theme of genuineness as living in the tension between finite and infinite, Lonergan's version of the "between."[20]

Finally, one interesting implication of the interplay between conscious intentionality and mystery is Lonergan's doctrine of dogmatic and systematic theology. Dogmas are not rationalistic accounts given by dominating intelligence, nor is the systematic understanding of dogmas. Rather, dogmas are a response to mystery, and systematic understanding is an imperfect, fallible, limited attempt to make sense of these dogmas.[21]

I conclude with a quotation from William Desmond that expresses nicely the spirit and sense of my reflections.

> The advent of metaphysical thinking is a primal astonishment. Astonishment is itself primal. It is elemental and irreducible. Plato speaks of *thaumazein* as the stance of the philosopher. This is sometimes translated as *wonder* and this is not inappropriate. Astonishment, however, captures the sense of being rocked back on one's heels, as it were, by the otherness of being in its givenness ... There is a suffering, an undergoing; there is patience of being; there is a receiving that is not the production of the metaphysician or mind ... We might call astonishment the innocence of the mind as agapaic. That is, it articulates a spontaneous transcendence of mind towards the otherness of being as other ... This is what agapaic astonishment is primarily: a love of other-being as other, which is not first chosen by self-conscious will but given, a gift of self-being ... We discover something *childlike* about such beginnings. I do not say childish, though this has been said. The childlike opening is our finding ourselves

> astonished already in the openness of being ... Metaphysics is initiated, carried, renewed by singular thinkers, not just by anonymous systems ... The more mature a singular metaphysician becomes, the more there is a refinement of childlike astonishment.[22]

I cannot resist commenting on this quotation by Desmond. First, his insistence on the singularity of metaphysical thinking recalls us to Lonergan's sense of self-appropriation as a fundamentally personal project, not that carried out by any Tom, Dick, or Harry. In insisting on the singularity of metaphysical thinking, Desmond reminds us that the personal orientation of self-appropriation extends into metaphysics. Second, note the fundamentality of wonder, which we ground in the desire to know. Third, his noting of the child-likeness of metaphysical questioning, inviting us Lonerganian seekers to a new or second innocence, a second naiveté. Fourth, his insistence on wonder as manifesting a kind of love for other-being as other. Here I can only articulate Lonergan's sense of transcendental method as an experiencing, understanding, judging, and choosing of ourselves as experiencing, understanding, judging, and choosing subjects in relation to being. To be self-appropriated, then, is to choose and love the being to which we are ordered, and, therefore, to be loving and receptive and reverential to the being and beings that disclose themselves to our wondering and questioning. Fifth, transcendental method alerts us not only to what happens inside the intellectual pattern of experience, but to what happens outside it in our daily life as we inhabit it more and more as awe-filled lovers of being. In this way transcendental method enables us to recover and be conscious of a spontaneous wonder that arises in such daily life, going all the way back to childhood. Sixth, religious conversion only intensifies an orientation present already in daily life and in philosophical reflection on it, and philosophy can lead us to the threshold of religious conversion.

7 Postmodernism: A Lonerganian Retrieval and Critique

A Lonerganian critique of postmodernism might seem appropriate now, since Lonergan certainly is an example of a kind of enthusiastic modernist who draws the critical fire of postmodernism. The methodical, systematic character of his work, its grounding in the knowing, choosing self, its orientation to universality and to metaphysics, and its unabashed commitment to modern, Western rationality make Lonergan an apt target of postmodern critique. Indeed, such critiques have already begun.[1]

A natural question that arises in this context, therefore, is whether Lonergan has any kind of response. It is my conviction that he does and, moreover, that on a Lonerganian basis one can construct a critique of postmodernism that is compelling, and that, while incorporating valid aspects of its project, brings it into question.

My stance in this chapter, therefore, is sympathetic towards and critical of postmodernism. I believe Lonergan is basically correct on the fundamental issues that divide him from postmodernism and in relation to which there is a judgmental and volitional "either/or." But I think that postmodernism raises questions that deserve consideration, comes to insights that Lonergan and other modernists can employ and incorporate, and interprets the pathology of the modern in a way that has to be taken seriously. The Lonergan, then, that emerges from the encounter with postmodernism is different, chastened, broader, deeper, more conscious of the limits of rationality, more fallibilistic, more aware of the ways in which human reason and history can go wrong, more committed to a progressive social agenda.

The Postmodernist Critique of Rationality

Modernism is committed to the project of self-reflective, critical rationality and freedom. From Kant's concept of the Enlightenment as the emergence from self-incurred tutelage to Husserl's return to the things themselves, modernism at its best is characterized by this orientation to reflexive, self-conscious understanding and critique. Postmodernism is a challenging, insightful, profound attempt to undermine that project. In the grip of such a *Ratio*, being tends to be covered over and difference and individuality tend to be submerged. Western *Ratio*, in the eyes of postmodernists such as the late Heidegger, Derrida, Adorno, and Foucault, is oriented towards an identity that excludes difference and an active, conceptualizing stance that inhibits receptivity to being.[2]

The motivation for such a critique of reason is, second, that modern reason itself, as defined and described by the postmoderns, is oriented to totalizing, alienating objectification. The description of rationality as such a closed, objectifying system rests upon three models or descriptions that interact and complement one another. First, rationality is equated with science and technology, either in the sense of explicit identification, generalizing the traits of dominance, prediction, objectification, and control to the whole domain of rationality, or emphasizing and thematizing scientific rationality as the dominant form of rationality and leaving other forms unthematized. Second is the model of the logical system, which Derrida criticizes in structuralism. Third is the metaphysical or ontological system or systematic approaches, which Adorno and Derrida criticize in their treatments of Husserl and Hegel.[3]

These three models interact within and between each postmodernist thinker in various ways. For example, if metaphysics for Heidegger has a long history of the forgetfulness of being, science and technology are the final, most recent flowering of such a forgetfulness. If for Adorno an illegitimate identitarian thinking is present in such thinkers as Hegel and Husserl, science and technology linked to and in the service of late capitalism become the most important contemporary versions of such thinking, reducing all persons and things to versions of such thinking, reducing all persons and things to versions of the same quantified, commodified logic. We could say in general that operating in all these thinkers is a disillusioned scientism, a cynical logicism, and a metaphysics ill at ease with itself. These different models come together in each thinker to form a concept of rationality as repressively totalizing: "instrumental reason" in Adorno, "logocentrism" in Derrida, "calculative thinking" in Heidegger, "discipline" in Foucault.[4]

Because of such an equation of rationality with totalizing objectification and because such an equation, according to the postmodernists, necessarily covers up or obscures reality, the only alternative is an overcoming of metaphysics, a transcendence of evidential reality, a movement beyond conceptual objectification. This alternative is not irrationalism, but rather a form of reflection claiming to go beyond traditional Western concerns with method, evidence, argument, and definition.[5]

We note here a similarity to and difference from positivism, scientism, logicism, and technocracy, in general, with those who equate rationality with describing or affirming an actual or possible state of affairs. If we recall the positivists' triumphalistic equation of reason with science, technology, and formal logic, and come to a negative rather than a positive evaluation of the equation, then we have an essential element of the postmodern stance. In many respects the postmodernist reflects a disillusionment with positivism and technocracy; "reason" in these senses has not worked and needs to be transcended. For this reason we have the strong emphasis on negativity in most of these thinkers, strongest in Adorno and Derrida, but present in Foucault and Heidegger as well. Negative is to positive, in their eyes, as postmodern is to modern.

On another more concrete, hermeneutical level, there is a similar disenchantment. If we recall Comte's triumphalistic account of the progress from religion to metaphysics to science as defining the modern and add a sign of negation, we have essentially the postmodernist hermeneutics of modernity. Modernity is essentially a development and consolidation of scientific and technological control. Development is essentially progress in domination, whether that is defined as increase in the reign of "instrumental reason," "logocentrism," "calculative thinking," or "discipline." Such movement, postmodernists powerfully argue, covers up, dominates, and alienates nature, human beings and being. The final form of modernity is an iron cage, from which there is little or no exit.[6]

Finally, at the most concrete level, the political implications that flow from such a stance are dire and pessimistic. If reason equals science and if modernity is essentially growth in the dominance of instrumental reason, then, even though in postmodernism an ethical-political will to transcendence of modernity exists, there would seem to be little possibility of transcendence, few counter-tendencies contesting the reign of one-dimensionality. The historical dominance of instrumental reason leads to a one-dimensional society in which all or most traces of transcendence are rubbed out. Again, we can contrast the negative reading of this situation in such works as *Dialectic of Enlightenment* with the positive reading present in such works as Luhmann's *The Differentiation of Society* or Skinner's *Beyond Freedom and Dignity*. Depending on whether one is a technocrat or postmodernist, being a mere object for political, economic, and social technique can be either good or bad.[7]

I need to qualify this characterization in the following way. Any attempt to catch a group of thinkers under a conceptual rubric, here that of postmodernism, runs risks and has inevitable limits. First of all, there are real differences among these thinkers; Foucault, for example, is politically leftist in a way that Heidegger is not. Second, I do not think that all of them are consistently postmodernist. In Adorno, for example, there are strong modernist elements coexisting with postmodernism. Third, I do not mean to suggest or imply that the pessimistic political implications of postmodernist thought necessarily are manifest in the lives of those thinkers. Foucault and Derrida, for example, have been politically active in a way that may not square with their own thought. These, then, are the traits of postmodernism as I am characterizing it here: a questioning of modern, Western evidential rationality, a definition of such rationality as a closed, totalizing, objectivizing system, a negative hermeneutics of history, and a generalizing of the thesis of one-dimensionality as it applies to politics and economics. Because this definition of postmodernism moves from abstract to concrete, from rationality to ethics and politics, my critique will similarly move from abstract to concrete in four different interrelated stages: logical (in a self-referential sense), descriptive, hermeneutical, and ethical-political.

A Lonerganian Critique: The Issue of Self-Referentiality

Lonergan, along with Habermas, is perhaps the most adept contemporary practitioner of the self-referential argument, that is, the argument that anyone in attempting to deny or reject rationality inevitably ends up contradicting herself or being arbitrary. Either the critique of rationality is made rationally with evidence or it is not. If it is made rationally, then the critique of rationality is self-contradictory. If it is made without evidence, what is arbitrarily asserted can be rationally questioned or denied.[8]

One important place where such an argument occurs in Lonergan is in the chapter in *Insight* on the self-affirmation of the knower. Let us recall that argument briefly as Lonergan sets it up in syllogistic form. If I am an experiencing, understanding, judging subject characterized as a unity-identity whole and characterized by acts of seeing, perceiving, imagining, inquiring, understanding, formulating, reflecting, and grasping the unconditioned, then I am a knower.

The unconditioned is a combination of a conditioned, a link between the conditions and the conditioned, and the fulfillment of the conditions. The conditioned is the claim "I am a knower." The link between the conditions and the conditioned is given in the major premise. The fulfillment is given in consciousness.

The conditioned is clear and offers no difficulty. The link between conditioned and conditions offers no difficulty because it is just a statement of meaning, a definition of what it means to be a knower. The problematic aspect is the fulfillment of the conditions in consciousness as stated in the minor premise. Consciousness for Lonergan is not an immanent look at oneself but an awareness accompanying cognitional acts. Whether I am seeing a colour, hearing a symphony, understanding a proposition, or judging a truth claim, I am aware not only of the contents of these acts, but of these acts themselves and of myself as a unified subject performing these acts. One indication of this point is that I can recall later what I was thinking about or doing at a certain time when I was not explicitly adverting to my acts at the time I was performing them: "What were you thinking about when you were driving home?" Recall of what I was thinking would be impossible if I were not implicitly aware of my acts and of myself performing the acts at the time I was performing them. Explicit remembering is founded on implicit awareness of myself as a knower.[9]

Consciousness is, then, an awareness immanent in cognitional acts. Since such acts differ in kind, the awareness differs in kind. An empirical awareness is present in seeing and hearing, an intelligent awareness in understanding, in activities of inquiry, insight, and conceptualization, asking and answering the questions "What is it?," "Why is it?," and "How is it?"; and reflective or rational consciousness in acts of reflection and judgment, asking and answering the questions "Is it so?" and "is it true?"[10]

Consciousness not only is diverse, it is also unified. Contents culminate in unities; what is perceived is what is inquired about; what is inquired about is what is understood; what is understood is what is formulated; what is formulated is what is reflected upon as possibly true or false; what is reflected upon is grasped as unconditioned, as having the conditions for its truth fulfilled; what is grasped as unconditioned is affirmed. Similarly, we note a unity on the side of the subject who moves from experiencing to understanding to judging. I see the body fall, I formulate the law of falling bodies, and I judge that as true after I have performed certain verifying experiments. Lonergan argues that were the unity of consciousness not given, it would have to be deduced in a Kantian sense; otherwise the diverse contents could not coalesce into one known. Since such a unity is given, however, we have the basic evidence for affirming the subject as a unity-identity-whole.[11]

Now that we have indicated what we mean and do not mean by consciousness and the fulfillment of conditions in consciousness, we can turn to the question "Am I a knower?" Here each one has to ask the question for himself or herself, and there are two possibilities. Either I affirm that I am a knower, or I do not. If I affirm that I am, the answer is coherent, for, if I am a knower, I can know that fact by having recourse to conditions present in consciousness. Do I see or not? Do I understand or not? Do I judge or not? But the answer "no" is either arbitrary or incoherent, inconsistent, self-contradictory. If it is arbitrary, what is arbitrarily asserted can be rationally questioned or denied. If the claim is made with evidence, then I have experienced the evidence, understood the proposition "I am not a knower," and have made the judgment. "I truly know that I do not know" is a self-contradiction.[12]

How does this line of argument apply to postmodernism? The Lonerganian move here is to treat postmodernism as a self-referentially inconsistent kind of skepticism that is incoherent because of its total negation of modern, Western reason. Postmodernism falls into a contradiction between the present transcendental condition for knowing and the negative content that denies such knowing. If I criticize rationality, either I do that rationally or not. If I do it rationally, then I experience, understand, define, reflect, and judge. I am in fact affirming *in actu* what I explicitly deny. If I do not make the critique rationally, what is arbitrarily asserted can be rationally questioned or denied.

The dilemma works itself out differently in each postmodernist. If rationality is described in Adornian terms as instrumental rationality, science and technology oriented to class or group domination, then a rational critique of instrumental rationality becomes impossible. Adorno and Horkheimer posit a *mimesis*, a dialogical, reciprocal relationship with nature, as a way out of the iron cage of modernity, but they can argue this point only with a *theory of mimesis*, which they are incapable of providing because such a theory would presuppose the possibility of a non-instrumental conception of rationality. They are caught in the trap of setting instrumental reason on the path of truth and yet contesting the idea of truth itself. In Habermas's words, the "critique of instrumental reason conceptualized as negative dialectics renounces the theoretical claim while operating with the means of theory."[13]

If with Heidegger we say that the kind of reason to be transcended is calculative, science-technology that eclipses being, the question arises about why we are to do that. Either such transcendence is arbitrarily asserted or it is not. If it is arbitrarily asserted, it can be rationally questioned or denied. If the claim is argued, then from Heidegger's perspective I am using a form of metaphysics, calculative thinking, to transcend calculative thinking.

One further aspect or implication of this argument for the self-affirmation of the knower is the reality and necessity of the self as subject. If Lonergan is correct, the judgment that I am a knower implies the subject: "I am a self" or "I am a subject." Such an implication renders problematic postmodern minimizing or denying of selfhood, the "end of man" as Foucault put it. One cannot, without self-referential inconsistency, deny knowing, the value of rationality, and the reality of the self.[14]

Descriptive Adequacy

From a Lonerganian perspective, the descriptive question that arises about postmodernism is whether it is too one-dimensional. Are there not different forms of the experience of reason, some pathological, some not. Lonergan, I argue, has in *Insight* and *Method in Theology* a phenomenology of the different forms of rational activity that allow him to claim against postmodernism that he is the true or truer friend of difference.

Let us briefly recall some of these different forms. (a) First of all, already noted, is the distinction among experience, understanding, and judgment. When we add to these the fourth level of freedom, of choosing, committing myself, loving, then we have a four-level transcendental structure of the self as experiencing, understanding, judging, and choosing. Such transcendental structure functions as a genuine Lonerganian a priori which the human subject brings to different forms of activity.[15]

(b) Lonergan distinguishes between science as a form of empirical method oriented to external data of sense, quantitative formulation of hypotheses, and experimental verification; and philosophy as a form of generalized empirical method reflecting on data of consciousness, qualitative definition, and self-affirmation. Both are expressions of cognitive structure, but each is different in having a different kind of data to reflect upon, different goals, different criteria of certainty.[16]

(c) Lonergan affirms different patterns of experience of which each is an expression of cognitional-volitional structure, but each of which is essentially different from the others in aim, criteria, and object reflected upon. Common sense is pragmatically oriented towards short-range results, whereas the intellectual pattern of experience is oriented to rigorous knowledge for its own sake. The aesthetic pattern of experience is oriented to perceptible patterns of experience in a way that the religious pattern is not. The religious pattern of experience, falling in love with God, has a transcendent object in a way that common sense or science or art do not.[17]

(d) Lonergan distinguishes among different aspects or stages on different levels of cognition; for example, the movement from question to insight to definition on the level of understanding or the movement from evidence to reflective grasp of the unconditioned to assertion on the level of judgment. (e) Lonergan distinguishes among different kinds of bias – egoistic, group, dramatic, and general oriented to the short range and empirical and indifferent to the long range and speculative solution, on the one hand; and the immanent, norm-guided dynamism of inquiring intelligence and reasonableness, on the other hand.[18]

(f) There is a distinction between authentic subjectivity, in which the self's thought and behavior correspond to the transcendental structure of experience, understanding, judgment, and decision; and inauthentic subjectivity, in which there is contradiction between one's behavior and the structure. (g) Finally, we note the difference between a just society that institutionalizes the imperatives of inquiring intelligence and reasonableness and one that does not, that engages in domination and exploitation. I will develop this distinction further in the last section, in which I show how instrumental rationality illegitimately dominates practical, lived moral intersubjectivity.[19]

The relevance of these distinctions to the postmodernist problematic is salient. In general, the tendency to identify reason with science, technology, or domination is simplistic, in that it misses the experienced, lived difference in forms of rationality. More specifically, we can say, first, that science-technology is just one form of rationality, legitimate when in its own sphere, but not equal to reason as such. Second, one reason that such an equation is invalid is that philosophy as a form of generalized empirical method is distinct from science. Third, because of the interplay between conceptual and preconceptual on the levels of understanding and judgment, any rejection of reason as simply logical or conceptual is invalid. Logicism and conceptualism are one-sided accounts of rationality that ignore its preconceptual aspects. Fourth, because of Lonergan's broad conception of reason and of rational method, he can incorporate valid postmodern insights. Heidegger's claim, for example, that questioning is the piety of thinking can enrich and be enriched by Lonergan's account, which already gives a high priority to questioning.

Derrida's critique of immediate presence and his emphasis on the structural dimensions of language can enrich Lonergan's critique of immediate realism by adding insights into language not developed by Lonergan. The insistence that the meaning of a thing is not simply itself but is mediated by a play of difference is a further basis for rejecting the claim that knowing is merely immediate looking. Lonergan already has a critique of presence that can enrich and be enriched by Derrida's critique of presence. If one conceives rationality and philosophy in a sufficiently broad and deep way, the question oriented to being and the linguistic play of difference are within rationality and philosophy, not outside of them. All that the postmodern prodigal thinks he has to leave home to find is already present in modernist rationality as he is welcomed home, penitent and forgiven by his modernist father.[20]

Fifth, because of the distinctions between authentic and inauthentic subjectivity, just and unjust societies, reason does not equal domination, injustice, exploitation. Rather these can be criticized in the light of rationality as irrational, as at best incomplete, truncated manifestations of a deformed rationality. Finally, Lonergan recognizes a legitimacy in the desire present in postmodernism to transcend rationality, but he locates this transcendence in a movement to the fourth level of freedom, of commitment, of falling in love with persons or with God. Such transcendence does not reject rationality, but rather builds on and presupposes it. Transcendence of rationality is not rejection of it but completion. As he puts it, the fourth level necessarily sublates the first three cognitional levels. The desire to know naturally completes itself in the desire to love. All that glitters, therefore, in postmodern transcendence is not gold. Such legitimate transcendence also allows Lonergan to make a critique of presence: mystery is rooted in the desire to know's anticipation of a totality of correct answers contrasting with the finite set that we do have and the mystical experience proper to falling in love with God.[21]

Hermeneutical Adequacy

Lonergan's challenge to postmodernism on the level of a hermeneutics of history is similar to his challenge on the level of phenomenological description. Has the postmodernist given an account of history, modernity, and the development and/or devolution of modernist rationality that is too undifferentiated or de-differentiated and thus does violence to these realities? Has the postmodernist, contrary to his stated intentions to respect difference, obliterated or minimized it? Is the postmodern account of modernity, rather than being that of a dialectical interplay between positive and negative, progress and decline, forward moves and regressive moves, one-sidedly bleak and negative? The Lonerganian answer to all these questions is a resounding "yes."

As is well known, Lonergan's account of human cultural history presents it as moving through three stages of meaning. These stages progressively differentiate the patterns of experience, common sense, science, philosophy, and religious interiority, discussed in the previous section. The first stage is, in the language of *Insight*, mythic and, therefore, relatively undifferentiated. Common sense, science, philosophy, and religious interiority intermingle in a confused fashion. The second stage is the discovery of mind by the Greeks, in which theory is rigorously distinguished from common sense. To adequately define something, Socrates tells Meno, is not just to give particular examples of that reality in the manner of common sense, but to understand and formulate the essence of something as universal, the essence of justice or piety or courage. Philosophical enlightenment for Plato is moving out of the undifferentiated mythic reality of the Cave and into the sunlight of the Forms illumined by the Good.

The third stage of meaning characterizing modernity involves and implies a further distinguishing among science, philosophy as reflection on cognitive and volitional interiority, and religious interiority. Philosophy's proper function is to promote the self-appropriation that cuts to the root of and can resolve philosophical difference, and has the further function of distinguishing among the patterns of experience, grounding methods of science, and promoting their unification.[22]

To the extent that differentiation and integration have occurred in history, progress has occurred. But in addition to progress, there is also decline. In addition to genetic method allowing us to account for forward moves in history, there is also dialectical method that allows one to account for decline and to criticize it. Criteria for progress and decline are in the normative exigencies of the subject giving rise to four transcendental precepts – "Be attentive," "Be intelligent," "Be reasonable," and "Be responsible" – corresponding to the levels of experience, understanding, judgment, and decision respectively.[23]

Next, criteria for interpretation lie in the exigencies of the intelligent, rational, free subject, giving rise to the canons of the hermeneutics: relevance, complete explanation, successive approximations, parsimony, and residues. Relevance is oriented to the universal viewpoint of a totality of possible interpretations potentially and/or actually manifest in a series of genetically and dialectically related texts. Complete explanation demands that we achieve as complete and nuanced an interpretation of the text as possible. Successive approximations is an ideal of ever more closely approaching an adequate account of the text. Parsimony negatively excludes the unverified and unverifiable and positively invokes critical reflection verifying or invalidating claims by having recourse to passages in the text. Residues alerts us to the possibility and actuality of contradictions and anomalies in the text. Here Derrida's practice of "deconstruction" can be taken as a version of the canon of residues; in Lonergan, however, the canon of residues is linked to the other four canons in a way that it is not in Derrida.[24]

Finally, Lonergan can sharply distinguish between positions and counter-positions as they manifest themselves in the history of culture and philosophy. A philosophical claim will be a position if the real is being and not the immediate "already out there now," if the subject is known through intelligent and reasonable affirmation and not through some prior existential state or inward look, and if objectivity is the fruit of authentic subjectivity expressed in intelligent inquiry and reasonable reflection and not a property of vital anticipation, extroversion, and satisfaction. On the other hand, a claim will be a counter-position if it contradicts one or more of the above positions.[25]

All of the preceding relates to the postmodern critique of modernity in the following ways. (a) Lonergan has the advantage over postmodernism in that he can articulate precise criteria for progress and decline, whereas postmodernism's rejection of modernist normativity is so thoroughgoing that it has trouble specifying such criteria. It does often validly indicate and criticize decline, but, because postmodernism lacks criteria, its critique at a certain point becomes arbitrary. (b) If Lonergan is correct, differentiation is preferable to lack of differentiation and mediation to immediacy. To wish to move back in a Heideggerian manner to a Presocratic stage of unity and immediacy is to be fundamentally mistaken. Such a move confuses legitimate objectification with alienation, and the real with the immediate. Such orientation to a pre-critical immediacy has to be rejected in whole or in part as a counter-position.[26]

(c) Lonergan disagrees with the postmodernists over the interpretation of modern philosophy. Is it mostly or all a negative story, a gradual and progressive forgetfulness of being in favor of the calculable, a mostly triumphalistic story, or a dialectical story, a unity of truth and error, position and counter-position, light and darkness? Lonergan's argument with postmodernism is that the third alternative is the best and that his account of method can spell out why his method is preferable, whereas the postmodern critique of modern philosophy is negatively one-sided and cannot spell out criteria for its critique.

According to Lonergan's criterion of complete explanation, an account must be as comprehensive and as nuanced as possible. Thus, Descartes's turn to the subject is valid, but he sinks into dualism and overemphasizes apodicticity. Kant's discovery of the transcendental was valid, but in his doctrine of things in themselves he unwittingly falls prey to a pre-critical realism, claiming that knowing of the real world should be immediate. Hegel's notion of dialectic contains some acceptable insights but is overly conceptual, too much on the level of understanding and not enough on the level of judgment and of freedom.[27]

(d) Like Heidegger in his account of the gradual eclipse of being in modern history and philosophy, Lonergan discusses a longer cycle of decline rooted in the general bias of common sense towards practical, short-range solutions linked to group domination, manifested in ever more restricted viewpoints, and culminating in totalitarianism. Unlike Heidegger, however, Lonergan does not see such decline as testifying to the bankruptcy of metaphysics, but to its necessity. One feature of the longer cycle is its rejecting of detached, disinterested intelligence and subordinating it to solutions that are ever more short-sighted. If the pathology of the longer cycle is the gradual subordination of theory to common sense, then such pathology can be overcome only by a restoration of such detached, disinterested intelligence.[28]

To put the point in Heidegger's terms, metaphysics does not need to be overcome but to be restored, chastened and fallibilistic through its encounter with postmodernism. To put the point in Lonergan's terms, Heidegger's overcoming of metaphysics is part of the problem, not part of the solution: it is a cultural product of the longer cycle and mistakes rationality with one of its pathological, positivistic forms.

If rationality, however, is critical and dialectical, then the longer cycle that is the product of a contradictory relationship between narrow, commonsensical intersubjectivity and inquiring, disinterested intelligence can be reversed. The genuine modern discoveries about the subject, critique, and dialogue can be brought to bear on the concrete social order, which itself has progressed, in spite of the longer cycle, towards greater insight into human dignity, individual rights, democracy, and welfare. Modernity and human history show themselves to be genuinely dialectical, an interplay between truth and falsity, light and darkness, progress and decline, not simply or primarily negative as postmodernists are wont to say.[29]

Nonetheless, from a postmodern perspective, one can question whether Lonergan has done full justice to the pathology of the modern; his own politics may seem to lead to a liberalism too comfortable with and uncritical of the capitalist status quo currently taking the form of the New World Order. I make this point in spite of Lonergan's very critical understanding of modernity in his account of the long cycle of decline, to be discussed in the next section. One of the genuine contributions of postmodernism is found here, whether one talks about Heidegger's account of *Gestell* or "enframing," Adorno's instrumental reason functioning as a lackey of late capitalist domination, Derrida's critique of logocentrism, or Foucault's critique of capitalism as a disciplinary society oriented to domination, exploitation, and normalization. My own sympathies lie with the proponents of a left-wing Lonerganianism, such as Lamb and Doran, who argue for full democracy transcending the injustice of both late capitalism and state socialism. Only such a radical political solution does justice to both the exigencies of intellectual, moral, and religious conversion and the depths of modernist pathology. I will develop the implications of such conversion in the next section.[30]

Ethical-Political Cogency

When one reads *Insight* and *Method in Theology* together, it becomes apparent that Lonergan is more than just a cognitional theorist and metaphysician. What emerges more fully in *Method in Theology* is the importance of the fourth level of freedom, commitment, and love sublating the three cognitional levels, ethical value as a product of experience-feeling, understanding, judging, and choosing, the importance of intellectual, moral, and religious conversion, and objectivity as a fruit of authentic subjectivity. Objectivity, whether on the level of knowing or of ethical choice, is not a matter of taking a value-free look at something, but is itself a result of subjectivity functioning authentically in conformity with the four transcendental precepts and as a product of the three conversions.[31]

Lonergan up to this point can admit to some of the claims made by Foucault about the necessary link between truth and power: all truth claims are made as a result of my own will to power and are imbedded in discursive power-knowledge regimes such as science and technology serving late capitalism. Foucault thus denies that knowledge is a value-free look at data divorced from relations of power: interest, influence, domination, and submission between groups and individuals. Truth and power, he argues, are intrinsically related. Individuals and groups tend to interpret the world from the perspective of their own will to power: their will to dominate, to control, to direct the wills of other men. Women will thus have a different "take" on the world from men, labor from capital, black from white.[32]

One issue that arises here is that of relativism. If the world is interpreted according to my own particular will to power, then how are objective truth claims possible? How can Foucault's own claims, putatively true and universal, about modern disciplinary societies and the reign of bio-power, his preference for the oppressed, or his claim about truth and power be justified?[33]

Lonergan can respond to this *aporia* in the following ways. (a) He makes the distinction between authentic and inauthentic subjectivity. Thus, the rejection of a naive notion of objectivity and value, which rejection he shares with Foucault, does not entail relativism: "Objectivity is the fruit of authentic subjectivity." (b) Lonergan makes the distinction between cognitional structure and patterns of experience. Cognitional structure operates in each pattern of experience, but it operates according to different interests. The interest of the scientist in prediction and control is not the same as the aesthete's interest in beautiful works of art; the interest of common sense in a rough, pragmatic truth is not the same as the religious interest expressed in "falling in love with God." Yet these interests internal to the domains in question do not compromise their truth, objectivity, or normative rightness; they help constitute it. In a way analogous to Habermas, Lonergan can affirm knowledge-constitutive interests.[34]

(c) Such knowledge-constitutive interests are different from externally imposed claims rooted in power or domination. Thus, a scientific claim asserted because it is a more comprehensive account of the data is internal to the domain of scientific knowledge and legitimate; a claim made or rejected because it satisfies or fails to satisfy a certain group funding the project is external and illegitimate.

Lonergan, then, can make the distinction between legitimate and illegitimate forms of power in a way that Foucault cannot. He can also make the distinction between just and unjust forms of social interaction. Foucault here remains curiously decisionistic or self-contradictory. Either the decision to resist modern forms of power is morally justified or it is not. If it is morally justified, then there seems to be tacit appeal to a moral humanism and sense of right that Foucault has already rejected. If such a decision is not justified, what is arbitrarily asserted can be rationally questioned or denied. It is hard not to agree with Habermas when he asks, quoting Nancy Fraser, "Why is struggle preferable to submission? Why ought domination to be resisted? Only with the introduction of normative notions could he begin to tell us what is wrong with the modern power/knowledge regimes and why he ought to oppose it."[35] A possible way out for Foucault is his preference for the marginalized and subjugated forms of knowledge and groups. Indeed, there is something analogous to a "preferential option for the poor" or oppressed in his work that is exemplary and deserves attention. But here again the question arises, "Why should one prefer the oppressed?" and "Which groups of marginalized should one prefer?" An account of justice is lacking here that would allow Foucault to justify such preferences. Such an account is present in Lonergan; justice emerges when the dictates of authentic subjectivity and intersubjectivity take precedence over bias, the transcendental precepts are respected, the ethical demand for consistency between knowing and doing is fulfilled, and a society emerges that satisfies the legitimate demands of its citizens for human rights, participation, and human welfare; arbitrary exclusion for reasons of racial, sexual, or class bias, different kinds of group bias, is to be rejected. A just economy will be one that interacts fruitfully in a non-reductionist way with culture and the polity and that satisfies the material needs of all citizens, not simply or primarily the few at the top. It will ensure a fruitful dialectic between instrumental practicality and moral intersubjectivity. Foucault, however, has no way of distinguishing between the legitimately marginalized – racists, sexists, and classists whose values no longer obtain in a just society – and the illegitimately marginalized who are victims of racism, sexism, and classism. Why could not Donald Trump, Hugh Hefner, and George Wallace use *Discipline and Punish* or *The Order of Things* to make a comeback? In the hell of the marginalized, there are many shacks or mansions, not all of which deserve our compassion or sympathy.[36]

All of which is not to deny that on a concrete sociological and historical level there is much that is true and insightful in Foucault. His account of the disciplinary society as the growth of modern power/knowledge regimes that oppress and tame and normalize subjects in such a way that they become "good students," "good academics," or "good workers" in thrall to an unjust New World Order needs to be incorporated into Lonergan's account of the long cycle. In this way not only is Lonergan's thought enriched, but it becomes one that is more explicitly aligned with the oppressed. A marriage between Foucault and Lonergan on this level leads to a more radical Lonergan. The following seems plausible, although not fully proven in this chapter: if one is genuinely and fully intellectually, morally, and religiously converted, then a radical political conversion emerges that is on the side of the oppressed. Elsewhere and later in this book I develop this line of thought more fully. If I am committed to justice and to the critique of institutions that cause injustice, then I must side with the oppressed. The proposition is analytic, an analytic principle in Lonergan's terms.[37]

Conclusion

On the basic questions dividing Lonergan and postmodernism – self-referential consistency, descriptive adequacy, hermeneutical comprehensiveness, and normative cogency – I have given the nod to Lonergan. Postmodernism, however, raises certain questions, comes to certain insights, questions forms of modernist, capitalist, and state socialist pathology, and takes certain political stances that can be incorporated into a Lonerganian perspective. Heideggerian questioning as the piety of thinking, for example, can be incorporated into a philosophy of the subject that is metaphysically oriented. One does not need to go beyond metaphysics to do justice to such questioning, provided that one's conception of knowing is broad enough and nuanced enough. Again I have argued that Derrida's practice of deconstruction can enrich a Lonerganian use of the canon of residues, but now such practice is given a broader hermeneutical context and is linked to the other canons of interpretation.

Here I think that it is important to do full justice to the critique of presence offered by Derrida and others. Western metaphysics has certainly been guilty at times of trying to achieve illegitimate closure, excessive certainty, and repression of difference. Postmodernist insights can enrich and enhance a critique of presence already going on in Lonergan: his distinction between immediate knowing as looking and knowing as mediate experiencing, understanding, and judging, the distinction between the finite set of judgments that we have made and the totality of correct judgments anticipated by the desire to know, and the distinction between an inauthentic mythic consciousness and an authentic orientation to mystery rooted in the desire to know, anticipation of a totality of correct answers that it does not have, and the mystical experience of falling in love with God. Here postmodernism helps philosophy realize its own deepest *telos*; illegitimate presence is a betrayal of philosophy. Philosophy can, but does not necessarily have to, fall into such presence.

I have also argued that postmodern accounts of the pathology of modernity can enrich Lonergan's account of the longer cycle of modern history while being incorporated into a broader, deeper, more differentiated interpretation of modernity stressing its positive as well as its negative aspects. At the same time, it seems to me that the political radicalism of the French – Foucault, Derrida, Deleuze-Guattari, Lyotard, and Baudrillard – brings into question a bourgeois liberal or conservative Lonerganian reading of ethics and politics, in Lonergan himself and in some of his disciples. The question of the French to Lonergan himself is this: to the extent that rationality becomes merely bourgeois mirroring and justifying of an oppressive capitalist status quo, does not rationality compromise itself and mutilate itself? Does not rationality in its full cognitive, ethical, and religious range point towards liberation from all injustice: racist, sexist, classist? The question of Lonergan to the postmodernists is this: do you not cut the links between evidential reflective rationality and critique at your peril? Does not such critique negate itself as critique, becoming arbitrary, inconsistent, violent?

Continuing this mutual questioning, Lonergan could ask whether there is not at the root of some postmodern questioning of modern reason a hankering after an immediacy that a rigorous account of objectivity and knowledge shows that we cannot have. One thinks here of Heidegger's return to Presocratic immediacy and lack of differentiation as well as Adorno's and Horkheimer's positing of *mimesis*, an immediate oneness with a reconciled nature. Similarly, does not Derrida's post-structuralism betray one-sided idealistic tendencies present in a post-structural play of difference on the level of understanding and ignoring too much the complementary levels of experience and judgment? To what extent is Foucault's impatience with modern normativity and his problematizing of all mediated truth claims the result of one-sided hankering, coming to full expression in his late work, after an aesthetic immediacy and a one-sided voluntarism not doing justice to the three cognitive levels and turning reason into an instrument of the will to power? To such tendencies, Lonerganians would reply with the following dictum: positions tend to develop, counter-positions to reverse themselves.[38]

8 Self-Appropriation, Polymorphism, and Différance

I have, for some time now, been involved in writing a book on postmodernism, *French Ideology*, meant to complement my book on Habermas, *Unjust Legality: A Critique of Habermas's Philosophy of Law*, which was a critique, among other things, of the way his philosophy of law functions as an ideology for capitalism expressing, legitimating, and covering up its irrationality, exploitation, and oppression. Habermas's, I argue, while ultimately more insightful than postmodernism and on whose thought I draw in many positive ways, is a modernist ideology, whereas postmodernism is a form of postmodern ideology, aiming to criticize, transcend, and transform modernist forms of rationality and social life, but in attempting to do so, ending up, like Habermas, expressing, legitimating, and covering up capitalism.[1]

These two books are intended to complement, build on, extend, and test my earlier, three-volume, systematic trilogy: *Post-Cartesian Meditations*, *Critique, Action, and Liberation*, and *Process, Praxis, and Transcendence*. A phenomenology of self and self-appropriation leading horizontally to an ethics and social theory and vertically to a metaphysics and philosophy/theology of liberation. In these three books the main idea animating my thought is the link between rationality and radicalism, self-appropriation and liberation. No fully adequate rationality without radicalism, no adequate radicalism without a fully developed defense and account of rationality.[2]

In the light of this claim, both Habermas and postmodernism fall short, one by a deficit of radicalism, the other by a defect of rationality. In *French Ideology*, I also criticize postmodernism as counter-positional, inconsistent, experientially and hermeneutically oversimplified, and totalizing. In contrast to its proclamation of différance, postmodernism flattens out human experience and history in a way that minimizes or denies différance. Another task, however, is to give an account of positive, redeeming, fruitful questions and insights and claims that can be incorporated into a more adequate philosophy, social theory, and philosophy of religion. It is this task that I take on here.[3]

Unlike Mark Antony, therefore, I have come today not to bury postmodernism, but to praise it.[4] I was helped in conceiving this task by a very fine book on Lonergan by Gerard Walmsley, *Lonergan on Philosophic Pluralism: The Polymorphism of Consciousness as the Key to Philosophy*, one of the many fine books on Lonergan coming out of the University of Toronto Press. In this book, Walmsley links polymorphism and pluralism in philosophy, including the kind of pluralism represented by postmodernism. He contrasts an earlier more negative, less sympathetic critique influenced by *Insight* with a later, more nuanced version based on *Method*, able to do justice to both positive and negative aspects of postmodernism.[5]

I propose in this chapter to develop and emphasize the positive by discussing the link between self-appropriation, polymorphism, and *différance*, this latter term and concept referring not just to Derrida in a specific way, but also to a more general sense and emphasis running through many postmodern thinkers. Polymorphism becomes the middle term between self-appropriation and différance, used not only to criticize, but also to integrate postmodernism into a more adequate philosophical account, shorn of difficulties, counter-positions, and ideology, but also expanded to include the legitimate light postmodernism can throw on our shared human situation.

Polymorphism and Différance

"Polymorphism" is less well developed and emphasized by Lonergan than some of his other notions, but does turn out to be key. Indeed at one point, in *Insight*, he says that "the polymorphism of consciousness is the one and only key to philosophy."[6]

> Against the objectivity based on intelligent inquiry and reasonable reflection, there is the unquestioning orientation of an extroverted biological consciousness and its survival not only in dramatic and practical living but in much philosophical thought – knowing as taking a good look. Against the concrete universe of being, of all that can be intelligently conceived and reasonable affirmed, there stands an apparent prior completeness of

> the world of sense, in which the "real" and "apparent" are subdivisions within a vitally anticipated "already out here now real." Against the self-affirmation of a consciousness that is at once empirical, intelligent, and rational, there is the native bewilderment of the existential subject, revolted by mere animality, unsure of his way through the maze of philosophies, trying to live without a known purpose, suffering despite an unmotivated will, threatened with inevitable, and eventual death, and, before death, with disease and even insanity."[7]

This is a Beckettian, modern, and postmodern world.

There are not only logical but lived antitheses rooted in the concrete unity-in-tension that is the human being.

> For human consciousness is polymorphic. The pattern in which it flows may be biological, aesthetic, artistic, dramatic, practical, intellectual, or mystical. These patterns alternate; they blend or mix; they can interfere, conflict, lose their way, break down. The intellectual pattern of experience is supposed and expressed by our account of self-affirmation, of being, and of objectivity. But no man is born in that pattern; no one reaches it easily; no one remains in it permanently; and when some other pattern is dominant, the self of self-affirmation seems quite different from one's actual self, the universe of being seems as unreal as Plato's noetic heaven, and objectivity becomes a matter of meeting persons and dealing with things that are "really out there."[8]

These quotations of Lonergan are his initial formulation of polymorphism in *Insight*, and in reading it, we are struck by a negative emphasis: polymorphism is contrasted to self-affirmation, the universe of being, and true objectivity, and can lead us to human and philosophical stands that are false, counter-positional, and confused, but patterns of experience, though they may be confused, are not necessarily so, and they remain universal and necessary components of the human being. Common sense can become distorted, absolutized, and biased, but nonetheless it is necessary to deal practically with the world as we negotiate it and make a living and survive and flourish. Consequently, the task is not, as with the counter-positions, to eliminate patterns of experience, but to distinguish them and order them and to figure out their role and importance in our lives. Moreover, while cognition is important and essential, it is not everything; there are embodied, emotional, sexual, interpersonal, and aesthetic aspects to our lives on which postmodernism can shed light. Postmodernism as expressing a polymorphism can give us a salutary warning and caution against an overemphasis on cognition. "There are more things in heaven and earth, Horatio ..."[9]

I wish, therefore, to distinguish several different senses of polymorphism. The first is operational polymorphism, the fourfold level of consciousness, experience, understanding, judgment, and decision. The second is orientational polymorphism, the different patterns of experience and their interrelationships. Third is developmental polymorphism, the gradual differentiation and integration of human consciousness in society and history, the way in which, for example, science has become distinguished from philosophy, common sense, and religious experience. The fourth is foundational polymorphism, the distinction and relationship among different kinds of conversion, intellectual, moral, and religious. A fifth is deviant polymorphism, the reality and role of bias in human life and thought, general, dramatic, egoistic, and group. A final form, my own addition to Walmsley's list, is lived and philosophical counter-positionality. All these kinds of polymorphism can be seen as differentiation in a more general sense, a point I will develop later. Differentiation is related to polymorphism as a positive, making sense and articulation of it in a way that is essential to self-appropriation.[10]

In addition to these, Walmsley discusses other patterns mentioned but not developed by Lonergan, or mentioned and developed by commentators. There is an artistic pattern distinguished, in chapter 14 of *Insight*, from the aesthetic pattern. There is also a practical pattern rooted in our commonsensical orientation to getting things done, already mentioned in chapter 8 of *Insight*, and a mystical pattern. Commentators add symbolic patterns rooted in the expressive tendencies of the psyche and a moral pattern.[11]

I am content here just to mention further patterns of experience in Lonergan's account as sufficient for my purposes. What is more pertinent here is to quote Lonergan from *Understanding and Being*, as he discusses the issue of the number and kinds of patterns:

> Perhaps the most relevant thing with regard to those patterns of experience is this: the ones I give are simply indications of the fact that people differ from one another, that they live in different ways, that this or that is a possibility ... What I am trying to indicate is the possibility of different components that can enter into human living.[12]

Postmodernism expresses, gives rise to, and is rooted in both positive and negative versions of polymorphism. In articulating this point, one can make two mistakes. One is to so emphasize the negative that the positive insightfulness of postmodernism is missed; such has been the tendency the last fifteen to twenty years of some or many of the critics of postmodernism. The opposite mistake is to so emphasize the positive that deleterious, philosophically problematic, and ideologically pernicious aspects are missed.

The task of self-appropriation is to integrate polymorphic postmodernism in its different aspects and kinds into a properly differentiated consciousness and one coherent interpretation or story. For, as Lonergan says,

> [the] philosophers have been men of exceptional acumen and profundity. On the other hand, the many, contradictory disparate philosophies can all be contributions to the clarification of some basic but polymorphic fact; because the fact is basic, its implications range over the universe; but because it is polymorphic, its alternative forms ground diverse sets for implications.[13]

Self-appropriation and polymorphism go together. No adequate account of the difference of polymorphism without the unity of self-appropriation. No adequate unity without difference. Postmodernism in its negative and positive aspects can contribute to philosophical knowledge. Negatively, by raising questions and making claims, even erroneous claims, that deepen and clarify such knowledge; positively, by its insightfulness into the human condition.

But how does all of this relate to postmodern accounts of différance, such as Derrida's. I want to argue that, while the primary and dominant meaning of différance is linguistic, there are broader and deeper implications of that account. "Différance" is a concept of linguistic meaning that is differential and structural, meaning dispersed between and among linguistic units. A letter, syllable, word, or phrase does not mean simply itself, but refers in its meaning to other letters, syllables, words, or phrases. Meaning, in other words, is both differential and deferred; it links up with other linguistic units, and is deferred in its relationship to those units as they occur and recur in past, present, and future contexts. Because meaning is not simply present in one of its units, we see the basis here for Derrida's critique of presence.[14]

Perhaps a few examples will make the point clearer. When I utter a sentence in conversation, any words are apprehended in the immediate present as spontaneously linked to what came before in the utterance and what will come after. The letters of the alphabet, "a," "b," "c," and so on, need to be seen in relation to one another; "a" by itself or "b" by itself is more or less meaningless. This particular claim by Derrida should not be unwelcome to Lonerganians; he is simply making, in different words, a critique of one-sided immediacy.[15]

Linguistic meaning for Derrida is structured by "quasi-transcendentals"; "différance," "supplementarity," and the "trace" are examples. As commentators such as Caputo and Gasché describe them, quasi-transcendentals are "almost" transcendental, functioning up to a point in an a priori manner, but too intermingled with the body, world, and history to be purely or strictly transcendental. There are many such quasi-transcendentals, or "infrastructures," another word for the same reality. One distinction from traditional accounts such as Husserl's or Kant's is that there is no overarching unity, such as a transcendental ego.[16]

There is no "being," "subjectivity," or "objectivity" outside of différance or preceding différance. In this sense, there is nothing outside of language. Reality, then, whether subjective or objective, comes to us mediated by language. Because such is the case, I can talk about the "ontological" import of Derrida's thought. I take it, therefore, that when he describes "justice" as "undeconstructible" in *Specters of Marx*, he is referring to justice as another quasi-transcendental or infrastructure.[17]

Différance, therefore, even in the strict Derridean sense, opens onto reality. It becomes in a very real sense ontological, without being metaphysical. But it is sufficient, both linguistically and ontologically, to allow us to talk about différance within and related to the world. But do we have enough basis here for arguing that polymorphism as linked to self-appropriation is related to différance, albeit in a critically transformed sense?

Part of that critical transformation is to see Derrida's structural account of différance as embedded in a more complex account of discourse, as including both structural and conscious, third-person and first-person aspects. And meaning, of course, in Lonergan's sense, is not only conscious and life-worldly but essentially linked to linguistic expression as well, and within such expression there is room for third-person, explanatory aspects.

Polymorphism is différance in this more qualified, critical sense, or more precisely, polymorphism is différance in the sense of a variegated, unified ground and context for différance in the linguistic sense, and différance is the linguistic expression of polymorphism. Self-appropriation only fully becomes itself in linking up with polymorphism-différance, and polymorphism-différance must be seen in relation to a self-appropriated consciousness and community. Polymorphism is, again, the middle term between self-appropriation and différance. Postmodernists are right to be critical of a notion of self that minimizes or excludes différance but not of selfhood as such. Selfhood as such is related to différance.

Now, I wish to reflect on some of the implications of my account. First, it opens up to us the possibility of integrating in a positive way other insights of postmodernism. I have done this already in some of my other work. Heidegger's *Denken*, the questioning that is the piety of thinking, does not have to be seen as lying outside the practice of philosophizing or doing metaphysics as he thinks. Rather, if we understand thought in philosophy and science as moving from question to answer, preconceptual to conceptual, evaluation of evidence to judging, then questioning as the piety of thinking before the mystery of being can be seen as part of philosophy and metaphysics. Also, the practice of deconstruction can be seen as a way of applying Lonergan's canon of residues to texts, by being open to the way texts do not hang together and thus deconstruct themselves. Derrida's mistake is not in asserting the value of deconstruction, but in absolutizing it at the expense of other hermeneutical canons. Lonergan shows himself to have a more nuanced, differentiated hermeneutics and thus is a truer friend of différence.[18]

Second, in a similar way, Derrida's "critique of presence," mistaken if it is absolutized, can be fruitfully linked to a critique of the "already out there now" as a critique of the insufficiency and invalidity of immediate presence as a criterion of truth. Derrida's insistence on mediation is, up to a point, similar to Lonergan's, and his critique of philosophy as representational is similar to Lonergan's claim that the history of modern philosophy can be seen as the history of various attempts to conceive knowing as taking a good look. Where Lonergan disagrees with Derrida is that it is not presence as such that is the problem, but one kind of false presence. Once again, Lonergan shows himself to have a more differentiated account of presence and evidence.[19]

Third, if it is not presence as such that is the problem, but rather a certain deficient form of presence, then it is not philosophy as such that is problem, but a certain deficient form of it based on this illegitimate presence. We can as confident philosophers use and learn from this critique, and others very similar as well, such as Rorty's critique of philosophy as an immediate mirror of nature, without conceding one iota to the anti-philosophical thrust of these critiques.[20]

But, fourth, a postmodernist might say that this account of self-appropriation, polymorphism, and différance still stresses unity too much, integrating différance with identity, with self-appropriation, in a way that does violence to its otherness. I answer this objection in two steps. First, one strategy for dealing with this objection is to use "self-appropriation" when I wish to stress unity and to use "polymorphism" when I wish to stress différance. Sometimes, in my practice of philosophizing, I wish to emphasize the task of becoming an authentic, unified self, and sometimes I wish to stress an acceptance and even rejoicing in my polymorphism. "Enjoy your polymorphism." There is no problem of illegitimate privileging as long as I am conscious of what I am doing as a philosopher, as long as I am employing a certain finesse.

A second way of answering the above objection is to distinguish between understanding and judgment. On the level of understanding, I can grasp the otherness of différance as minimizing or denying any relationship to unity or identity, but I do not have to agree with that strong sense of différance. I am legitimately making a judgment that difference with little or no relationship to identity is invalid, and that relationship to identity is essential. Postmodernism in its practice does that all the time, for example, in understanding or misunderstanding the concept of evidential or epistemic presence, and judging that to be invalid.

"Becoming polymorphic," is, then, a "becoming different" – an openness to otherness, a self-transcendence that is the hallmark of authenticity, an objectivity that is the fruit of authentic subjectivity. But this "becoming different" is at the same time the achieving of self-appropriation. There is in such becoming different a self-transcendence that moves from intellectual to moral to religious conversion, falling in love with God, the absolute other. There is at the same time a movement from above that involves a becoming aware of, accepting, and rejoicing in my body, my psyche, my sexual, aesthetic, and political self, that complements intellectual, moral, and religious conversion. Even such apparently outrageous discussions as that of "becoming animal," in Deleuze and Guattari's *A Thousand Plateaus*, the second volume of their *Capitalism and Schizophrenia*, can contribute to this movement from above. "Becoming animal" becomes a complementary aspect, enabling me resist a crypto-idealism, to becoming spirit.[21]

Fifth, As I have already indicated, the relatively negative emphasis on polymorphism needs to be complemented by and lead into the relatively positive account of differentiation in *Method*, something that Walmsley does not do sufficiently; and differentiation implies the achievement of self-appropriation as not only a fully integrated but a fully differentiated consciousness. "Polymorphism" thus relates to "differentiation" as problematic context to a fully worked out account, question to answer, experience to understanding and judgment, metaphysics as troubled or problematic to metaphysics as achieved, consciousness to knowledge. Polymorphism as merely experienced is both problematic and full of possibility; polymorphism as known is differentiated in a full, relatively adequate self-appropriation.[22]

Sixth, for me, certain of these thinkers, especially Foucault, Derrida, Deleuze-Guattari, and Levinas up to point, become partners in my project of social-political critique, adding weight and insight to my claim that intellectual, moral, and religious conversion lead, or should lead, to radical political conversion. Without such conversion, in my opinion, self-appropriation flowing into the other conversions is incomplete, truncated, and self-contradictory. And, of course, the opposite is true as well; radical political conversion without the other conversions is incomplete, truncated, ungrounded, and self-contradictory. To sharpen the point, these thinkers contribute to a legitimate Lonerganian "materialism" or even "historical materialism," the noematic side of critical realism. All of which is not to deny the relevance of postmodernism to liberal or conservative persons. All of us these days, conservatives, liberals, or radicals, need to be concerned with différance and alterity.

For me, of course, the philosophical and socio-political dig into one another. No philosophy is complete without a socio-political component, and the socio-political needs to be grounded in a cognitional theory, epistemology, ethics, and metaphysics. Consequently, these thinkers, in encouraging and forcing us to recognize difference and alterity as these are present in a capitalistic, imperialistic system, educate us. Levinas, for example, forces us to see the way the marginalized other functions or does not function in contemporary society, and Foucault shows us how the disciplinary society in our politics, schools, economies, and prisons expresses and serves capitalism. "Is it surprising that prisons resemble factories, schools, barracks, hospitals, which all resemble prisons?"[23]

I end with a quotation from Derrida's *Specters of Marx* that may be one of the most important philosophical and socio-political statements of the last fifteen to twenty years, and illustrates much of what I have tried to say here about the socio-political implications of taking différance and alterity seriously.

> A "new international" is being sought in these crises of international law; it already denounces the limits of a discourse on human rights that will remain inadequate, sometimes hypocritical, and in any case formalistic and inconsistent with itself as long as the law of the market, the "foreign debt," the inequality of techno-scientific, military, and economic development maintain an effective inequality as monstrous as that which prevails today, to a greater extent than ever in the history of humanity. For it must be cried out, at a time when some have the audacity to neo-evangelize in the name of the ideal of a liberal democracy that has finally realized itself as the ideal of human history; never have violence, inequality, exclusion, famine, and thus economic oppression affected as many human beings in the history of the earth and humanity. Instead of singing the advent of the ideal of liberal democracy and of the capitalist market in the euphoria of the end of history, instead of celebrating the "end of ideologies" and the end of the great emancipatory discourses, let us never neglect this obvious macroscopic fact, made up of innumerable singular sites of suffering: no degree of progress allows one to ignore that never before, in absolute figures, never have so many men, women, and children been subjugated, starved, or exterminated on the earth.[24]

9 Lonergan and Marx on Economics and Social Theory: Some Preliminary Reflections

Our problems stem from our acceptance of this filthy, rotten system.

Dorothy Day[1]

Cardinal Daniélou speaks of the poor. It is a worthy topic, but I feel that the basic step in aiding them in a notable manner is a matter of spending one's nights and days in a deep and prolonged study of economic analysis.

Bernard Lonergan[2]

The quotations are intended by me as indications of a fruitful tension between theory and praxis, reform and revolution, universal analysis of any economy as such and capitalism as a particular economy. The quotation from Day indicates that one can be a radical on non-Marxist grounds; such is also true of the life and thought of Daniel Berrigan. My own radicalism emerges from a decades-long attempt to mediate the influence of Lonergan and various radical sources, some Marxist and some non-Marxist. Indeed, long before I read the above words of Lonergan, I had been engaged in a study not only of economics but of social theory more broadly conceived, including sociology, political science, and history. Thus my formula, summing up the results of my life's work: "Intellectual, moral and religious conversion should lead to radical political conversion." It is thus my sense that Marx, in his life and work, integrates the perspectives of Day and Lonergan. He spent his life, as I have been doing, studying economics because he hated capitalism.

In my pursuing this path of negotiating between the claims of Lonergan and Marx, I have been struck by the largely "positional" aspect of Marx and the many legitimate Marxisms. At the same time, I would say that such positionality is partial and incomplete, requiring qualification, completion, and correction by Lonergan's cognitional theory, epistemology, metaphysics, and theology. But in the political-economic part of his work, which constitutes most of his work, Marx is marvelously positional and insightful.[3]

One strand of the Marxist tradition, of course, Marxism-Leninism or vulgar Marxism, as it is referred to by critical theory, does deserve severe criticism. It is indeed counter-positional, deterministic, reductionistic, scientistic, undemocratic, both bad philosophy and bad Marx. It needs to be said that Marx himself is not a Marxist-Leninist. He has been badly misinterpreted over the years, by thinkers both inside and outside the Marxist tradition, in a way similar to the way naive realists have misinterpreted St Thomas.[4]

Not only is this the case, but there is insufficient awareness of the hermeneutical richness and diversity of the Marxist tradition, including not only Marx himself, but critical theory (for instance, Marcuse and Habermas), Western Marxism (Gramsci and the late Sartre), aesthetic Marxism (Jameson and Eagleton), various thinkers in social theory and history more or less influenced by Marxism (Chomsky, Zinn, and Harvey), and the liberation philosophy and theology of Dussel, Boff, Segundo, and Gutierrez. To return to aesthetic Marxism (my own term), I regard it as the single most important school of aesthetics in the twentieth century. To read Adorno on Beckett or Schoenberg, Benjamin on Baudelaire, Sartre on Flaubert, or Eagleton on the Brontes is to read accounts that are both pleasurable and enlightening.

What can also be missed is the degree to which there has been a process of self-correction and development, starting from the early part of the last century, in the Marxist tradition itself in relation to the bad form of Marxism, Marxism-Leninism. Thus, thinkers as diverse as Karl Korsch, Antonio Gramsci, and the late Sartre have been forceful and cogent in criticizing the defects and limitations of this deficient form of Marxism. We could say, then, that there has been a process of developing positions and overcoming counter-positions, although not in those words, from within this tradition.[5]

An aspect of this self-correcting process includes reflection on markets. Thus, thinkers as diverse as Tony Smith, David Schweikert, and Carol Gould argue for a market socialism: worker-owned and -controlled firms, full economic, political, and social democracy, a minimal welfare state, and a blend of local, regional, and national planning operating to coordinate and complement, not replace, the marketplace. I count myself among such market socialists.[6]

To be fair, of course, it must be said that Lonergan legitimately criticizes Marx and Marxism-Leninism for their rejection of any kind of market and reliance on state planning. What can be missed, however, is the extent to which various thinkers within the Marxist tradition also have criticized Marx and Marxism-Leninism on this issue of markets.

Now, with some of the preliminaries cleared away, it is time to get down to Lonergan's economics proper and its relationship to Marx's. It is possible, I think, to overstate the originality of Lonergan's economics in relationship to Marx. In considering his very illuminating account of the relationship of the two circuits, that producing commodities and that producing means of production, it is easy to forget that seventy-five to one hundred years before Lonergan began to write on economics, there was a book, volume 2 of *Capital,* devoted precisely to this issue. More original in Lonergan is his insistence that these two circuits function or can function in any economy, whereas Marx's focus is on their interaction in a capitalistic context. There is room, therefore, for fruitful interaction, mutual criticism, and complementarity between Lonergan and Marx, between Lonergan's focus on the universal and Marx's on the particular, and between Lonergan's claim that the two circuits can fruitfully interact even in a capitalist economy and Marx's criticisms on that point.[7]

Lonergan's other main discovery is that of the pure cycle, in which a stationary phase is followed by a stage of surplus expansion in producing means of production, after which comes a basic expansion in the sector producing means of consumption for all. As workers must be content with lower wages and accept higher profits for the capitalist in the stage of surplus expansion, so also the capitalist should accept lower profits and higher wages for workers in the phase of basic expansion in order that a beneficial standard of living may arise for all. As "thrift and enterprise" is the motto of the stage of surplus expansion, so "enterprise and benevolence" is the motto for the phase of basic expansion. We see here the way in which a moral, normative criterion operates in the pure cycle.[8]

But here is where questions begin to arise. A Marxist might say, "Certainly Lonergan stipulates in a valid way what should transpire in any economy, including a capitalist economy. But can such a state of affairs be realized or even approximated in a capitalist economy?" And here the main sticking point is the fundamentally undemocratic character of the capitalist firm, its democratic deficit, both in itself and in the way it interacts with the rest of the economy and the state, subordinating them to itself and making them do its bidding. Capitalism as private ownership and control of the means of production is oriented to the private profit of the capitalist and only, with reluctance and pressure from without and resistance from below, to the standard of living and well-being of the workers and the rest of the population.[9]

One could, of course, as a response to this objection, argue that the welfare state as it emerged in the United States and Europe from 1930 to 1980 more closely approximated the pure cycle, and in a sense that is true and is to be applauded; any reform leading to a reduction of human misery is good. But that result was less the result of capitalists suddenly becoming reasonable and more a result of something forced on them from the outside: the welfare state, legislated reforms like social security, Medicare, the Glass-Steagall act, separating investment banking from regular banking, and popular resistance from below. And, of course when it became possible in the late 1970s and 1980s, capitalists and the capitalist state began to "roll back" these reforms. The point is that this approximation to the pure cycle did not come from within, as Lonergan would desire, but was imposed from without.[10]

There are two big obstacles, according to Lonergan, to carrying out surplus and basic expansion and in the transition from one to the other: worker self-interest in higher wages in surplus expansion and capitalist interest in profit during basic expansion. There is a class disagreement or class conflict between capital and labor: the more wages, the less profit, and vice versa. Since class conflict is what blocks the reasonable unfolding of the pure cycle, removing that in principle will facilitate a reasonable process. This is what the democratic socialist form, described earlier, does. The worker would no longer resist surplus expansion and resulting lower wages, because he is the beneficiary of such increased investment, and the capitalist cannot resist a transition to basic expansion because he is nonexistent as distinct from labor. Should Lonergan, for reasons intrinsic to his theory, be a democratic socialist? Should he also be critical of the capitalist firm and capitalist system as in principle incapable of satisfying the requirements of full rationality and justice?

Here is where I would link the pure cycle to Marxist analysis, and my argument here points to an "incipient socialism" in Lonergan that becomes more explicit as he approaches the end of his life. More of that anon. The point I am making here is that the capitalist firm is not and cannot be fully rational or moral. It is as plausible to think so as it is to think the slave owner over the long run will be reasonable in the treatment of his slaves. Just as slavery was an asymmetrical social relationship between slave and master, so capitalism is an asymmetrical social relationship between capital and labor. Because of this asymmetry, full democracy is impossible. Both capitalism and slavery are instances of institutionalized group bias.

This point is important because, even if the capitalist firm were occasionally to become more reasonable and moral in Lonergan's terms, the capitalist social relation to labor would remain even in the period of basic expansion. The worker might receive more wages, but "it is better payment for the slave" in Marx's terms. The asymmetry of the social relation remains, even if the worker momentarily receives more money. Imagine a slave owner inviting his slaves, for a change, up to the plantation house for Christmas dinner. Should a self-respecting slave be satisfied with his situation as a slave, with its exploitation, domination, inequality, and alienation? So also the "wage slave" in capitalism still remains a slave, is still stuck in that same unjust social relationship, even if he or she is better paid.[11]

I am arguing by analogy here, admittedly a weak form of argument, but the argument has an important point, namely, that in capitalism the worker is separated from the means of production and ends up being hired by the capitalist on the capitalist's terms, has little or no say over how production is organized, works part of the day for the capitalist, and that part of the day constitutes the source of capitalist profit. Here is the basis for Marx's famous discussion of alienation in both his early and later work.

This class relationship for Marx implies that labor is alienated. The surplus value appropriated by the capitalist is socially necessary labor time, and that ends up being the core of capitalist profit. Labor under capitalism is essentially alienated, at odds with itself, in a way that contradicts the imperative of self-appropriation. Initially in the *Economic and Philosophical Manuscripts*, Marx lists four different aspects of this alienation: from the object produced and from the means of production, owned by the capitalist in such a way that the workers have to work on the capitalists' terms undemocratically; from the process of work, in which the self-expression and self-fulfillment of the worker in work is subordinated to and sacrificed to efficiency, division of labor, and the machine; from what Marx calls "species life," which is my own self-consciousness as an embodied, intelligent, reasonable, free human being and end in myself being made a means for capitalist profit; and from other human beings, against whom I compete for scarce jobs and resources and whom I am tempted to see as means or obstacles in my upward mobility to Wall Street, Greenwich, or Scarsdale. As capitalism moves more and more into the overall fabric of society, money becomes the real mind and community of all things, and people relate to one another atomistically.[12]

Because labor in capitalism is socially alienated, capitalism essentially and intrinsically violates the imperative of self-appropriation. Interested in the expression and fulfillment and realization of myself, I am continually forced, manipulated, or seduced into loss of self or division of self. As I have argued the point elsewhere, such alienation, already present in the economic sphere, expands into the social and political spheres as capitalism subordinates these spheres to itself, capitalizing them, as it were. Thus, in the United States at the current time we have the best Congress money can buy, and media in their advertising, news, and programming conform to the dictates of capital. Media such as the *New York Times* and *Washington Post* act over and over again as sycophants and sounding boards and stenographers of capital, as they did in pushing the Iraq War of 2003, for which they later apologized.[13]

Finally, the problem of the democratic deficit with the individual firm can be generalized to the interaction between and among firms and especially between and among firms devoted to producing means of consumption and those devoted to means of production. Because capitalism is anarchistic and basically antagonistic to democratic control, coordination of production between and among firms subordinated to the common good and standard of living is not likely or possible. Occasionally, of course, and almost as an accident, such coordination will occur, but the general tendency will be towards overproduction or underproduction, underconsumption or overconsumption. The orientation to democracy and the common good, rightly stressed by both Lonergan and Marx, is basically contradicted by a socio-economic system in which "of, by, and for the people" is subordinated to or sacrificed to "of, by, and for capital." And most recently in the United States, to financial capital both in the initial crisis and in the bailout, Keynesianism for the banks but very little for the bottom 80 per cent of the American people. Again a democratic deficit with very little concern for the common good.[14]

Now here I want to move another stage of this argument and discuss value theory in Marx, which I see as complementary to Lonergan's valid concerns and insights. There is nothing like it, in Lonergan or anybody else, and it has enormous hermeneutical-explanatory power in both depth and breadth. I will go more into detail on this issue in the next chapter. Let us consider depth first. Like Lonergan, Marx gives a primacy to production, but goes much more deeply into that than Lonergan and presents more analytic and empirical detail, devoting the whole first volume of *Capital* to production. In chapter 1 of this volume, Marx asks about the basis of equivalent exchange for commodities. It cannot be anything qualitative because qualities as such are not commensurable and have different functions, different use values as Marx would put it; a coat is not a hat is not a tie. But this possible basis cannot be the physical weight of things or size or density. A very small diamond can be worth much more than a very big vacuum cleaner. The basis of equivalent exchange is, and can only be, abstract labor time, the average socially necessary time it takes to produce a product. Notice here the way the class relationship is built into the definition of value. Abstract labor time implies an exploitative relationship to the capitalist, who appropriates a part of it, surplus labor time, as the basis for his profit.[15]

Abstract labor time as present in the commodity is not something one can touch, taste, hear, or see. It is "immaterial" in this sense; for Lonerganians, this claim would mean that it is something understood and judged. Socially average labor time is the basis of a law, the law of value, the tendency of capital to expand, that like other laws, the theory of relativity and theory of evolution, can illumine a large amount and variety of phenomena. As we move from description to explanation in economics, we come up with abstract labor time as the core of value; this is a point that I develop in my *Critique, Action, and Liberation*.[16]

Now there is another problem, which Marx inherited from Smith and Ricardo, both of whom had versions of the labor theory of value. The problem is this: if it is generally true that equivalents are exchanged in the sphere of circulation, how does the surplus value arise that is the basis and core of capitalist profit. Obviously, it cannot arise in the sphere of circulation because there only equivalents are exchanged. Therefore, the surplus value must arise in the sphere of production. Here there are two possibilities: means of production, which include instruments of production and materials of production, and labor. Means of production, however, only contribute to the product value that they already have from their already having been produced. They cannot create new value. Consequently, the surplus has to come from labor producing surplus value, which is different from necessary labor time, for which the laborer is paid wages necessary to reproduce himself from day to day, week to week, year to year, as he buys the clothing, food, housing, and other items required to survive. This necessary labor time, again, is different from surplus labor time, for which labor is not paid.[17]

Surplus value is, therefore, Marx's greatest discovery and liberates economics from its central dilemma: how can profit emerge from an exchange of equivalents. It is interesting and significant that Marx achieves this end by revolutionizing bourgeois economics in showing that capitalist profit rests on the exploitation of labor. This is a scientific and moral point; Marx takes the account of alienation in the *Manuscripts* and traces it to its economic basis in *Capital*. Capitalism in both basic and surplus expansion is basically exploitative, unjust, irrational. The rate of surplus value as the rate of exploitation, he tells us early in *Capital*, is the ratio between necessary and surplus labor. Although Lonergan, like Marx, gives a priority to production, Marx takes that primacy more seriously and goes deeper. Production is important because surplus value is created in production.[18]

The canon of complete explanation as a hermeneutical-explanatory criterion is also satisfied by the synthetic breadth of Marx's account. *Capital* is a three-volume work, in which volume 1 is devoted to production, volume 2 to circulation, and volume 3 to financial capital. I am a radical philosopher and social theorist, one influenced by Marx and others without being Marxist, not simply because I try to be moral and ethical and see capitalism and its expansion into imperialism and militarism as the dominant, most comprehensive form of social injustice today, but also because I am a philosopher seeking the intelligible. If being is intelligible, then so should social being be intelligible; and radical social theory strikingly illumines our contemporary situation in a way that other theory does not. First of all, the United States has intervened in the Third World hundreds of times in the last two hundred years. Liberal or conservative accounts leave those phenomena relatively opaque. At most or best, the United States comes across as a pitiful, helpless giant, stumbling around the world trying to do good but ending up time after time doing bad. A consistent picture emerges: massive impoverishment of most of the population, enrichment of a sector at the very top of society, growth of unemployment, torture used to keep the population compliant, thus insuring a safe investment climate for US corporations, and a massive transfer of surplus value occurring between the First and Third Worlds. Indeed, such transfer of surplus value is the goal or aim of capitalist imperialism.[19]

Radical social theory, informed by Marx and others, does illumine this situation remarkably, and it ceases to be opaque. If we understand capital as self-expanding value, Marx's initial definition of capital in volume 1, and if he is right to say that the world market is implicit in the notion of capital, then imperialism is built into the notion of capital. In its "vampire-like" or "werewolf-like" thirst for the blood of living labor, expressions that Marx uses in volume 1 of *Capital*, capital must eventually move beyond its national borders and go abroad in search of markets, raw materials, and cheaper labor. Imperialism simply becomes the natural extension of capitalism into other countries and lands. If capitalism is unjust at home, then imperialism is simply the international extension of that. If imperialism is unjust and exploitative abroad, then so also national capitalism must be within our own borders. And if capitalism must extend abroad, then there must be a strong military presence as enforcer of last resort. Native peoples in these regions sooner or later will rise up and resist. Thus, the United States as of this moment has 737 bases in more than 130 countries.[20]

Let's consider another example. On 9/11, my first thought was that the imperial chickens had come home to roost. Thus, what Chalmers Johnson calls "blowback" is an essential aspect of a contradictory imperial logic. Of course, if we have been intervening violently or destructively in the Third World for many decades, then the victims will try to strike back. Of course, if we are regularly transferring value from the Third World to the First World, then the victims are going to resist that. Of course, if we are regularly undermining democracy in the Third World while claiming to support democracy, the people in those countries are going to resent that and begin to resist and fight back (e.g., the recent events in Tunisia and Egypt), but because this point was not understood after 9/11, we plunged into more and more catastrophic depths in Afghanistan, Iraq, and now Pakistan. My point here is that, as bad and horrendous and destructive as US foreign policy has been the last ten years, radical theory informed by Marx and the right kind of Marxism has an enormous light to shed on these events. Why did media like the *New York Times* and *Washington Post* function as cheerleaders for the war in Iraq in ways that even they have apologized for? If they are first and foremost and above all capitalist media devoted to making money and defending money making as a way of life, then, of course, such media are going to support politicians that serve and promote the ends of the capitalist class – for example, to gain more control over the oil in Iraq – and to exclude or marginalize points of view that bring capitalism into question. If being is intelligible, then so also is social being, but this perspective most illumines social being. Therefore ...[21]

I realize that in discussing the history of events since 9/11, I have been somewhat schematic and hypothetical, because of the ground I am trying to cover. But what I am trying to suggest is a brief account of my own journey in coming to understand the relationship between self-appropriation and critical social theory rooted in Marx and certain forms of Marxism. And what I have found is that Marx and positional Marxism have been as fruitful for my version of social theory, ethics, and history as Lonergan has been for my versions of phenomenology, epistemology, and metaphysics.

A possible objection against all of the above is that maybe actually existing capitalism is just a "false fact," inadequate and flawed certainly, but not enough to rule out capitalism in principle or to prove that capitalism is essentially exploitative, irrational, and contradictory. I would argue, however, that Marx's genius lies in showing that capitalism itself is essentially flawed. If we understand what capitalism is, flowing from the exploitation of surplus labor, then talking about a "just capitalism," or "rational capitalism," is as wrong as talking about a "just slavery." It is easier to see that slavery is or was unjust because it is or was mostly in the past. Because capitalism permeates our lived present, it is harder to see it for what it is.

Capitalism as self-expanding value depends on surplus labor derived from the exploitation of labor to make its profits and to expand. Take away that surplus value and you remove the profit and expansion. Capitalism, as self-expanding value, therefore, no matter how benign it is or seems to be, is based on and flows from surplus labor. Just as a more benign or less cruel slavery is still slavery, so as "kinder, gentler" capitalism is still capitalism. To understand truly what capitalism is, therefore, is to understand it as unjust or exploitative.

Conclusion: From the Self-Appropriated Subject to the Revolutionary Subject

In summary, I first note a fruitful interplay among Lonerganian self-appropriation, epistemology, metaphysics, and theology and the Marxist tradition as a whole. That tradition as a whole needs to be complemented and criticized by Lonergan on the issues of authentic selfhood, being, God, and religion.

Second, neither Marx nor Marxism can be reduced to Marxism-Leninism. To do so is to fail egregiously in the functional specialty of hermeneutics. Third, honesty demands that one strand of the Marxist tradition, Marxism-Leninism, needs to be vigorously criticized as counter-positional, reductionist, deterministic, and scientistic. And since all or most regimes from the Soviet Union up to the present are more or less identified with this kind of Marxism, then using the functional specialty of history, one can and should be more critical than one might be in using hermeneutics, where the picture is much brighter and more diverse.

Fourth, we note in a variety of sub-traditions of Marxism an ongoing, developing critique and alternative to Marxism-Leninism. One thinks here of the late Sartre, Gramsci, and Habermas. Fifth, Marx's economics can be fruitfully played off against Lonergan's, and each can complement and correct the other. Lonergan validly criticizes Marx on the issue of the legitimacy of markets, and legitimately articulates the historically invariant notions of basic expansion in relation to surplus expansion and the pure cycle. On the other hand, Marx fruitfully questions Lonergan on how much capitalism can even approximate the requirements of the pure cycle. Should Lonergan be a socialist?

More specifically, one can question Lonergan fruitfully on both historical and structural grounds on this issue. Historically, the greatest approximation to Lonergan's model has come through a welfare state intervening from without into capitalist accumulation. And structurally, if Marx is correct about the basically exploitative relationship of capital to labor as a source of surplus value, then capitalism is or seems to be institutionalization of group bias, just as slavery was. Consequently, for the democratic deficit to be fully and adequately overcome, capitalist firms would have to change basically, become non-capitalist, democratic, non-exploitative.

Fifth, I think Marxian value theory, properly understood, can fruitfully complement Lonergan's account of the two kinds of expansion and the pure cycle. Marx's account of particular capitalist social formations can complement Lonergan's universalistic account, and Marx's value theory has a depth and breadth that satisfies significantly the canon of complete explanation. Sixth, while there is a moral stance in Marx, it falls short of being a moral theory, and thus needs to be complemented by Lonergan. Lonergan's scale of values, moving from economy to state to culture to the person to religious commitment, can fill out and ground Marx's claims in the *Manuscripts* and the *Grundrisse* that capitalism is an era of "universal prostitution" in which money and the rule of money move from being a means to serving higher political, social, personal, and religious goals to being the goal and end of capitalist society, which subordinates and twists all other goals to itself. According to Marx, because of an inversion of values, in which means become ends and ends become means, there is a tendency for everyone and everything to become commodified and a means to make money. Lonergan's scale of values has a much more explicit moral normativity than does Marx's, but Marx's account of the inversion of that scale in capitalist society adds a richness and specificity.[22] In Lonergan's terms, Marx develops a series of inverse insights into the irrationality of capitalism and its absurdity, about the way capitalism, in inverting the scale of values, does not make sense in human terms.

Seventh, it may be that Lonergan is incipiently radical not only because of what I have argued about the socialistic implications of the pure cycle, but also in other ways as well. Lonergan, it turns out, has always been critical of capitalism in different respects. Fred Lawrence, in one of the best articles in the Seton Hall volume on economics that came out in the summer of 2010, points out that, for Lonergan, in capitalism potential contributions to the common good with little or no pecuniary value tend to be brushed aside, the exchange system becomes an exclusive club for businessmen, there is a tendency to make money and the making of money an absolute end in and of itself apart from its impact on the common good, and a tendency for civil society to be subsumed into the market.[23]

In a later essay, "Healing and Creating in History," Lonergan argues that the multinational corporations as an ongoing concern are forever expanding, creating more and more disastrous effects based on a very old principle, that of maximizing profit, that has been operative for centuries. The long-accepted principles are inadequate and suffer from radical oversight. But the new system and principles for our collective well-being do not exist. Lonergan may be articulating here what I have been referring to as an "incipient radicalism" or "non-Marxist radicalism." If I am right in whole or part, do we need to be satisfied with such agnosticism about principles? Is there not room for a blending of Lonerganian and Marxist insights in economic and social theory, and does not such an integration provide a more adequate theory than either Lonergan or Marx alone?[24]

Fifth, what all of this comes to is the movement from the self-appropriated subject to the revolutionary subject. I present this point as an existence possibility in Kierkegaard's sense, argued for in a form of indirect communication. Because of Lonergan, the revolutionary subject is a revolutionary *subject*, more fundamentally grounded and articulated than in Marx, even though Marx is open to such an articulation and even has aspects of it, as in his theory of alienation. Because of Marx, the revolutionary subject is a *revolutionary* subject, giving that project a depth and comprehensiveness and explicitness not present in Lonergan. Indeed, personally, I am a revolutionary for Lonerganian reasons, because I wish my social world to make sense; and I am or try to be a self-appropriated subject for Marxist reasons, because I am outraged by the damage, mutilation, and self-division inflicted on subjects by capitalism.

The revolutionary subject builds on and more fully realizes on a social level the self-appropriated subject; and perceives, feels, understands, judges, and chooses differently from the merely self-appropriated subject. For example, the revolutionary subject perceives and cares for and does not merely pass by or ignore the poor and homeless in our cities, rejoices in the triumph of Chavez over the US-sponsored coup in Venezuela in the early years of this century, comprehensively understands world capitalism in its perversity and destructiveness, judges harshly the use of torture in the Third World to create a "safe investment climate," and chooses the preferential option for the poor and at the same time criticizes the capitalism and imperialism that creates the poor. In support of the poor, the revolutionary subject in her personal and professional life chooses to engage in class struggle against the rich, capital, and empire. Class struggle and self-appropriation go together like hand and glove.

I end with a quotation from Marx that illustrates the movement from circulation to production in his account, his morality, and his concern for subjects.

> When we leave this sphere of simple circulation or the exchange of commodities, which provides the "free trader *vulgaris*" with his views, his concepts, and the standard by which he judges the society of capital and wage-labor, a certain change takes place, or so it appears, in the physiognomy of our *dramatis personae*. He who was previously the money-owner now strides in front as a capitalist; the possessor of labor power as his worker. The one smirks self-importantly and is intent on business; the other is timid and holds back, like someone who has brought his own hide to market and now has nothing else to expect but – a hiding.[25]

10 Intellectual, Moral, and Religious Conversion as Radical Political Conversion

The purpose of this chapter is to establish a connection between conversion as Lonergan understands it and a radical, critical, political stance. What are the socio-political implications of intellectual, ethical, and political conversion? It is the main contention of this chapter that these conversions lead up to, imply, and are completed in radical, political conversion. Short of that, intellectual, moral, and religious conversion remains truncated, incomplete, half-hearted, inconsistent, obscurantist. If the pure desire to know obligates us, as Lonergan argues, always to raise or be open to raising the further question, then one such question is the following: "Is capitalism as a socio-economic system basically and essentially compatible with intellectual, moral, and religious conversion?"

By "radical political conversion" here I refer basically to a line of social critique and action taken up by the tradition of Western Marxism, extending from Marx through Lukács (1971), Gramsci, Korsch (1970), and Bloch (1986), to the Frankfurt School of Adorno, Horkheimer (1972, 1974), Marcuse (1964), and Habermas (1976, 1984), and the phenomenological Marxism of Paci (1972), Kosik (1976), Merleau-Ponty (1973), and Sartre (1976). In contrast to the reprehensible turn taken by Soviet Marxism, this tradition is non-reductionist, democratic, non-positivistic, dialectical, and insistent on the importance of individual subjectivity and freedom. I am in agreement with commentators who see this as the authentic interpretation and development of Marx and for whom the Soviet Union's version of Marxism has about as much to do with genuine Marxism as the Inquisition does with genuine Christianity. Criticisms of Marx and Marxism, even some criticisms made by Lonergan himself, that presume this reductionistic interpretation of Marxism miss the mark.[1]

For many accustomed to an orthodox, positivistic, reductionistic reading of Marx and the Marxist tradition, here are some explanations of what I mean by such a non-reductionistic interpretation that makes Marx more compatible with Lonergan on the issues of knowing, being, and objectivity. First, Rader argues that the base-superstructure model, in which culture and state are seen as passively mirroring structures and values on the economic level, is certainly present, but is not the dominant, all-pervasive model of society in Marx. Rather, what is dominant and all pervasive is an organic model, in which economic, political, and cultural sectors of society reciprocally influence one another. This model of society as an organic totality is present in later Western Marxism as well.[2]

Second, Lukács, Bologh, and Korsch have shown that a notion of thinking as critical, reflective dialectic is the operative method in Marx rather than a naive positivism or copy theory. Critical dialectic commits me to reflecting on the contradiction between subject and object in class-dominated societies in order to transcend that contradiction theoretically and practically. Third, "determine" in Marx means that the economy in all historical epochs is determinant in the sense of providing a basic structure that allows one sector or other of the society to predominate. Only in capitalism is the economy determinant in both senses of basic structure and predominance.[3]

Fourth, even when one sector is predominant as the economy is under capitalism, this still allows other sectors such as the state or culture to be relatively autonomous and to exert a reciprocal influence on the economy, as the feet and legs, for example, do with the heart. Fifth, phrases such as "life is not determined by consciousness but consciousness by life" are unfortunate. However, Avineri points out the way Marx's detractors have missed the point that life, in its economic and political aspects, is already itself a form of consciousness. Also this phrase is used in a polemic against German idealism and is not characteristic of Marx's methods and stance as a whole. In "The Theses on Feuerbach" Marx distinguishes between a passive materialism in which the subject just passively reflects the object and active, transformative materialism in which the subject actively changes its world.[4]

Sixth, to be materialistic in Marx's sense is to insist that human beings are in the world, that their communal praxis influences and transforms that world, and that theory, while not reducible to praxis in that sense, arises on the basis of it. All these claims, as I will show later, are compatible with Lonergan's theory of meaning and historical development. Meaning is not only cognitive, but also efficient, constitutive, and communicative. Meaning, for Lonergan as for Marx, is practical before it is theoretical; theory, however, reflects back on and influences praxis. Following Thomas Aquinas, Lonergan endorses a legitimate "materialism": insight is insight into phantasm, human beings are body-mind, unity-identity-wholes acting in a material world, common sense precedes logically and temporally the theory of science and philosophy, and theory is grounded in and completed by praxis on the fourth level of freedom.[5]

In summary of these points, we can isolate three different hermeneutical stances in relationship to Marxism: that it is all or mostly non-reductionistic, dialectical, reflective in a humane sense; that it is a dialectical, contradictory unity of non-reductionist and reductionistic elements, positions and counter-positions; and that it is all or mostly reductionistic and positivistic. I embrace the first of these alternatives with respect to Western Marxism and the third with respect to the Eastern wing, beginning with Engels and culminating with Lenin and Stalin. Even if my stance proves to be too sanguine, however, with respect to Western Marxism, I would be forced to fall back to the second position, which move still leaves the legitimacy of a rapprochement between Lonergan and Western Marxism intact. Not only are there valid claims and insights to be reclaimed from within the Western Marxist tradition – positions invite development – but, on Lonergan's own principles, counter-positions tend to reverse themselves.[6]

Now, of course, because I am arguing for an interaction or mediation between two traditions, this interaction internally qualifies and affects both traditions. If the effect of Western Marxism on Lonergan's position is to draw out what is mostly implicit in his work and to qualify and criticize certain claims such as the inevitability of class, the impact of Lonergan on Marxism would be the introduction of a theistic, religious, Christian dimension and a criticism of certain claims, such as a tendency in Marxism to reduce all bias to class bias. Here then, the full argument would be one of mutual implication; authentic critique implies full intellectual, moral, and religious conversion; authentic interiority implies radical political conversion. I have argued the former of these claims elsewhere; here I am concentrating on the latter claim.[7]

Now this move of mine is not totally new within religious, Catholic, or even Transcendental Thomist circles. In Europe we have the political theology of Metz and Moltmann, in Latin America the liberation thought of Dussel and Boff, in the United States the breakthroughs of Lamb and Doran. If Metz reacts to an excessively transcendental Rahner by politicizing him, Lamb responds to the riches of Lonergan's thought by relating it to critical theory. I am in basic agreement with Lamb, therefore, that Lonergan's thought, including even the famous manuscripts on economics, is open to and lends itself to such an interpretation. The most adequate interpretation of Lonergan on this question is a left-wing interpretation.[8]

One more introductory note. When I criticize capitalism as structurally unjust, I am not totally condemning it. In its development of the individual as a bearer of dignity of rights, of democracy, and of technology, capitalism has made certain forward moves historically. Even its development of the market is a forward move which I would retain in my conception of democratic socialism, excluding as illegitimate the exchange of wages between capital and labor. My criticism of capitalism is, therefore, a dialectical, nuanced "yes" and "no" avoiding the extremes of simple affirmation or simple negation.

Nor do I wish to give the impression that because capitalism in unjust, all individual capitalists as individuals are evil human beings. In addition to the social, professional dimensions of human life, there is also the private, familial dimension in which it is possible for the capitalist, or anyone else, to treat his spouse, children, relatives, and friends very justly. Even in the social, professional domain there is an indeterminacy that allows for variation in the treatment of workers and employees; that is, even if the wage relationship between capital and labor is structurally unjust, there is variation in the ways that it is realized and carried out. Within the context of that relationship, one capitalist can treat his employees more humanely than another.

Intellectual Conversion

According to Lonergan, conversion in general results from a vertical exercise of freedom whereby I shift from one horizon to another. Such a vertical exercise of freedom contrasts with a horizontal exercise, where my choices all take place within a certain context of assumptions, meanings, and values. Conversion may involve either a progressive deepening or broadening, in which my world gradually expands by building on previous knowledge and commitments; or it may involve a wrenching, in which previous judgments and commitments are overturned. What was real now seems illusory; what was important is unimportant; what was central is now peripheral. The scales have dropped away. Now my life makes sense where before it was absurd, now I see where before I was blind, now I am alive where before I was dead.[9]

Conversion is, then, a function of the whole person, but most fundamentally of the so-called fourth level of freedom, building on, retaining, and going beyond the first three cognitional levels of experience, understanding, and judgment. Conversion in the full sense leads to my choice of a different life and a different world, where I cease to drift and take responsibility for my life. Intellectual conversion, therefore, even though its focus is on cognition, is chosen. I freely choose to live up to and obey the four transcendental precepts corresponding to experience, understanding, judgment, and choice: be attentive, be intelligent, be reasonable, be responsible. Because these precepts themselves are values chosen by freedom, Lonergan rejects the myth of neutral, value-free intelligence.[10]

Lonergan treats intellectual conversion first, then moral conversion, then religious conversion. Really and existentially, however, religious conversion flows over into moral conversion, which then leads to intellectual conversion. The falling in love with God proper to religious conversion attunes me to the values of justice and right essential to moral conversion, which then alerts me to the meaning and reality proper to intellectual conversion. Conversion as self-transcendence gradually expands from the religious through the moral to the intellectual, until the whole person is brought under its sway.[11]

Intellectual conversion is defined by Lonergan as the shift from a very erroneous myth concerning reality, objectivity, and human knowledge. This myth is that "knowing is like looking, that objectivity is seeing what is there to be seen and not seeing what is not there, and that the real is what is out there not to be looked at."[12] This myth overlooks the distinction between the world of immediacy and the world mediated by meaning. The world of immediacy is the sum of what can be sensibly seen, touched, tasted, and so on, and conforms to a degree to the myth's concept of knowing, objectivity, reality. This world of immediacy, however, is but a part, the experiential part, of the world mediated by meaning. The most obvious level of knowing, experience, is not what knowing obviously is. The world mediated by meaning is what is known through individual and social experience, understanding, judgment, and belief.

To know, therefore, is not simply to sensibly experience but to understand and judge and believe. Similarly, the criteria of objectivity lie in inquiring intelligence and reasonableness, and the fully real emerges from a process of experiencing, understanding, and judging. The real force is not simply that which hits me on the head, but the scientific law governing that force and the reality of these laws as affirmed in judgment. The real poem is not simply the words as sensuously heard, but the form and meaning of the poem as understood and affirmed.[13]

Intellectual conversion, then, involves movement from the world of the child to that of the adult, from the world of immediacy to the world mediated by meaning. This is indeed the real world, with which, depending on whether we are empiricists, idealists, or critical realists, we may be more or less in contact. The empiricist restricts objective knowing to sensing; for him understanding and judgment are merely subjective activities. The idealist retains the empiricist's notion of reality but thinks of the world mediated by meaning as only ideal, not real. Only the critical realist does full justice to the facts of human knowing, and only she can pronounce the world mediated by meaning to be fully real. The other positions are those of adult children.[14]

Pure objectivity cut off from subjectivity, is, for the critical realist, a myth. Objectivity is a fruit of authentic subjectivity and authentic subjectivity is a fully appropriated structure of experiencing, understanding, judging, and believing. Lonergan discusses such self-appropriation in terms of transcendental method, which is fully experiencing, understanding, judging, and believing. Lonergan discusses such self-appropriation in terms of transcendental method, which is fully experiencing, understanding, judging, and deciding to live according to my structure of experiencing, understanding, judging, and deciding. The four transcendental precepts corresponding to this structure emerge accordingly: be attentive, be intelligent, be reasonable, be responsible.[15]

A consequence of accepting transcendental method is that variants or offshoots of empiricism, such as objectivism, positivism, and scientism, must be rejected. First of all, such methods ignore the distinction between data of sense and data of consciousness. For empiricists all data are data of sense. Second, empirical methods miss the distinction between empirical method and philosophy as generalized empirical method. Third, these stances miss the reality and importance of philosophy as reflection on interiority, because they have no cognitive access to interiority.[16]

Capitalist Reification as the Cave

The question that faces us is this: what are the implications of transcendental method for my life as a self-appropriated, intellectually converted subject in late capitalist society? The answer is that intellectual conversion and capitalism are flatly contradictory. Capitalism, because it is essentially, structurally objectivistic, fetishistic, reifying, and scientific, is at odds with critical realism. Capitalism, if you like, is in certain essential respects a lived counter-position which a fully reflective, fully appropriated person should reject. I should stress here that because capitalism is essentially contradictory, its counter-positions are in tension with its valid breakthroughs and positions on an intellectual, moral and aesthetic level. "Capitalism" I am here defining as a socio-economic system in which the primary goal governing the whole system is economic profit, in which workers are separated from the means of production privately owned by capitalism, in which workers are free to sell their own labor power to the highest bidder.[17]

To begin at the beginning, in chapter 1 of *Capital*, volume 1, Marx utters a commonplace: that the capitalist social world is characterized by the buying and selling of commodities. Right away, however, he introduces a crucial distinction between use value, the capacity of a commodity to satisfy real human needs, and exchange value, the amount of abstract, socially necessary labor time measured in money that is contained in a product. Labor time is the source of value for Marx here because it alone can serve as a basis for measurement among objects that are diverse in use values: a car, an airplane, and a house have quite distinct use values, but become commensurable because of the labor time contained in each of them.[18]

Because, however, products in a market economy are separated from their producers and because they are measured by a thing, money, and because their value is quantified, commodity fetishism is a necessary result of capitalism. Human beings as subjects produce things as products with value; the human subjectivity, however, that is the source of the value is forgotten. We forget that money is a commodity produced by workers, and money seems to be itself a source of value. "It is nothing but the definite social relations between men themselves which assumes here, for them, the fantastic form of a relation between things."[19]

As capitalism develops, this fetishism extends more and more from production into private consumption. Because of the intrinsic possibility of overproduction, capitalism must develop mechanisms that persuade the populace to consume up to the level required by the system. One mechanism developed for this purpose is advertising, which appeals to us by equating having with being. If I wish to catch the woman or the man, wear Calvin Klein. If I want to get the job, wear expensive Florsheims. If I desire to play good golf, buy this expensive set of

Arnold Palmer golf clubs. I am what I make or wear or own, and the more I have the more I am.[20]

Corresponding to the supremacy of exchange value over use value in the product – profit, after all, is measured in exchange value – is the supremacy of abstract over concrete labor in the activity of laboring itself. Labor, in order to get a job, must sell itself on the open market; labor power becomes a commodity. Contradicting this emphasis on labor as commodity is capital's reliance on labor as use value, as subject, to produce more than the value of its wages. Labor must produce the surplus value that is the source of capitalist profit. Surplus value, then, the amount of labor time over and above necessary labor time, the time necessary to reproduce the value of one's own labor power, arises from labor as subject. Capital simultaneously denies and affirms labor as subject, as use value whose use value for capital is its capacity to produce surplus value. The result, then, of the supremacy of abstract labor over concrete labor is a commodification of labor power. Labor becomes a thing whose distinctiveness from other things, its capacity as subjectivity to produce surplus value, capital must simultaneously affirm and deny.[21]

As capitalism develops, it is an easy step from commodification to reification, that is, the extension from the corporation throughout society of a form of rationality that Horkheimer calls instrumental rationality – scientific, quantitative rationality ordered towards the good of profit. In relationship to this goal, everything becomes a means, everything, as Marx puts it, becomes subject to universal prostitution. Nothing is sacred.[22]

Because it becomes increasingly important for capital, in order to insure its well-being and survival, to extend its sway over everyone and everything, a formal, bureaucratic kind of rationality emerges, a version of instrumental reason that Habermas describes as purposive rational action. Because this rationality is oriented to quantity rather than quality, the abstract rather than the individual, administration rather than participation, any concern for subjectivity or self-appropriation dwindles or dies. The world so aptly described and depicted by Kafka develops – the organization man, the man in the grey flannel suit, the other-directed person. Like Prufrock, my self-confidence drains out of me – "Shall I part my hair behind? Do I dare to each a peach?"[23]

The final flowering of this process of objectification, commodification, and reification is scientism as the form of reason most appropriate to late capitalism. Capitalism, we can say, has moved through four stages historically. First, capital posits the supremacy of exchange value over use value; I must invest money to make money. If the miser is an irrational capitalist, piling up his money in order to make money, the capitalist is a rational miser, investing his money in order to make money, losing his life in order to find it.[24]

Second, there is the supremacy of absolute surplus value in the early stages of capitalism, the acquisition of surplus value by lengthening the working day. Third, there is the supremacy of relative surplus value, in which capital acquires surplus value by decreasing the amount of necessary labor time going to the worker in the form of wages. Capital achieves this end by an increased productivity, based on developing technology and machinery, which allows products necessary to feed, clothe, and house labor to be produced more cheaply and more quickly. Accompanying the reign of relative surplus value is greater investment in technology compared to labor, greater division and cheapening of labor. Already a commodity, labor becomes a degraded commodity, a mere appendage to the machine.[25]

Finally, in the twentieth century, science becomes not only productive force but ideology. Corresponding to a one-dimensional society ruled by a calculus of profit is the reign of one-dimensional thought governed by a logic of quantity. All other forms of rationality, aesthetic, moral, metaphysical, and religious, are shunted to the side as capitalism finds the form of reason most appropriate to itself. If science is essentially descriptive of facts and capitalism is *the* fact, then any kind of critical transcendence of capitalism is by definition impossible. Science becomes a peculiar kind of legitimating ideology, an ideology that denies itself as ideology, an ideology that claims to be value free. If science equals rationality, then such a claim legitimizes the jettisoning of democracy and the rule of experts like Kissinger or Brzezinski.[26]

One commentator on Lonergan has compared his discussion of intellectual conversion to Plato's Parable of the Cave.[27] Movement from knowing as looking to knowing as experience, understanding, and judgment is a movement of the whole person from illusion to truth, analogous to the person staring at images on the wall of the Cave moving out into the sunlight of reality. If my claims here are true, capitalism provides a way of understanding the parable of the Cave in twentieth-century North America and Western Europe. It systematically and structurally produces illusion, mystification, obfuscation, distortion. As late capitalism matures, it moves from "being" to "having" to "appearance" – the society of the spectacle. The spectacle is *capital* to such an extent that it becomes an image. Knowing as looking becomes a way of life.[28] If so, then full liberation from the Cave implies a critique of and liberation from capitalism. Short of such a critique, we have not asked all the relevant questions, come to all the relevant insights, or made all the necessary judgments.

Because capitalism is systematically and structurally productive of illusion and mystification, it covers up the ultimate reality of subjectivity, being and God. The subject becomes a reified object, being becomes a quantified thing, and God becomes a mere projection of feeling. To change Plato's Parable of the Cave a bit, we can imagine a family of four staring at images on their television forty to fifty hours a week, deliberately and systematically produced to convince them that having is being; uncritical patriotism is virtuous; certain persons are inherently evil and certain others inherently good. The loss of being so bemoaned by thinkers such as Heidegger has its roots here. Capitalism is institutionalized group bias reinforcing and legitimizing general, empiricist bias, and thus blocks the unfolding of the desire to know. Capitalism is an institutionalized refusal of insight.[29]

Moral Conversion: Praxis as Constitutive of Ultimate Moral Meaning

Moral conversion occurs when I cease to live a hedonistic, self-indulgent, narcissistic life and begin to commit myself to the genuinely valuable. As Lonergan puts it, I move from satisfaction to value as the controlling norm of my life. Satisfaction is the empirically pleasurable or unpleasurable; value is experienced, understood, affirmed, chosen. When satisfaction and value conflict, the morally unconverted person goes for satisfaction, the morally converted for value.[30]

Moral conversion implies a shift to action or praxis as essential in my life. To know is one thing, to do is another; to know what is right is one thing, to do what is right is another. From the perspective of moral conversion, merely knowing the true and the good is not enough. The question arises about the conformity of my doing to my knowing. If they do not fit, then my life is a lie. If they do fit, then I am integral, authentic, together.[31]

When moral conversion and intellectual conversion take place in the same consciousness, then moral conversion sublates intellectual conversion. What sublates goes beyond what is sublated, introduces something new and at the same time retains and builds upon what is sublated. I go beyond the value truth to values generally as I explicitly become a conscious, practical agent in the world. Such moral transcendence, however, in no way interferes with my devotion to truth. Indeed, I need the truth if I am to know and realize the genuinely good. Now, however, my devotion to truth is on a firmer basis because I am armed against egoistic, group, dramatic, and general bias and because the search for truth is in the far richer context of the pursuit of values.[32]

Moral conversion is lived out and expressed in an adult universe of meaning. There is a cognitive dimension to meaning when I move out of the child's world of immediacy and into the adult's world mediated by science, psychotherapy, philosophy, and theology. In addition to cognitional meaning there is efficient meaning in which human beings work and bring forth products, constitutive meaning in which human beings produce social institutions and cultures, and communicative meaning in which a history of common, shared meanings is built up, transmitted, and enriched within a community. We communicate intersubjectively, artistically, symbolically, incarnately.

Meaning, in other words, is not only discovered cognitively but created practically. For this reason, Lonergan suggests that a conjunction of the constitutive and communicative functions of meaning yields the three key notions of community, existence, and history. A community is not just a number of people living within a certain geographical place, but an achievement of common meaning. Such meaning is potential when there is a common field of experience, formal when there is common understanding, actual when there are common judgments, realized when there are common shared commitments and aversions, values and disvalues, ends and means. Community coheres or divides to the extent that this commonality of meaning holds together or breaks up, survives or perishes, increases or decreases.

The individual develops as an authentic or inauthentic individual in relation to the common meaning of the community. There is minor authenticity or inauthenticity of the subject in relation to the tradition itself. "The chair was still the chair of Moses, but it was occupied by the Scribes and Pharisees. The theology was still scholastic, but the scholasticism was decadent. The religious order still read out the rules, but one wonders whether the home fires were still burning."[33]

History, because it is a human product, differs radically from nature, which unfolds in accordance with law. Logical meaning has invariant structures and elements, but the content of history is the structures subject to cumulative development and decline. Human beings do not simply conform to traditions and institutions the way they would to systematic, scientific law, but are free to shape and transform these traditions and institutions. Meaning in the social-political sphere is not simply discovered but created.[34]

Capitalist Injustice as a Violation of Morality

In spite of the recent crises of the Soviet system, Marx's criticism of capitalism should not be forgotten. For all the thinkers in this tradition, the person is eminently and primarily a practical, creative being, able to create and overturn human institutions. Such an affirmation underlies Marx's critique of capitalism and his projection of different social arrangements beyond it. What had a human beginning can have a human end, what human beings choose to create they can choose to reform or destroy. There is in human practical rationality a necessary going beyond, rooted in the ability to ask the further question, conceive a higher viewpoint, overturn mistaken judgments, reject distorted values.[35]

Because human rationality is essentially utopian in this sense, able to raise the further question, come to the further insight, correct the mistaken judgment, criticize the false value, a rationality unwilling and unable to do this is a mutilated, incomplete, half-hearted rationality. It is the contention of critical theory that bourgeois rationality is such a half-baked rationality, inconsistent, obscurantist, exploitative, absurd. Bourgeois ethical and political rationality is at odds with itself. Counterpositions, however, whether in the intellectual or political realm, invite reversal.

Capitalism, one could say first, is wrong not because it violates moral and political ideals brought in from outside, but because it systematically and structurally violates its own ideals. One example of such a violation is the conflict between such ideals as they are present in the marketplace and in the workplace. In the marketplace, freedom, equality, property, and Bentham's "the greatest happiness of the greatest number" seem to prevail. I am feel to sell what I own, whether it be my car or my own labor power, to someone else and to receive the equivalent in money. In the workplace, however, such values are betrayed and turn into their opposites. Freedom turns into rigid subjection to the capitalist manager or machine, equality turns into domination and appropriation of surplus value, property turns into the appropriation by the capitalist of the product produced by labor, and Bentham turns into the unhappiness of deskilled work within the workplace and poor living conditions – squalor, poverty, and homelessness outside the workplace.[36]

Another example of the same kind of contradictoriness resides in the justification for property. From Locke on, the standard bourgeois justification for private property has been that I put my own labor into what I own: whatever I have worked on, I can legitimately appropriate. What happens, however, in capitalism is that the right to own what I have produced turns into the capitalist's right to own what others have produced.[37]

To take still a third example, we can consider the Kantian commonplace of bourgeois morality that human beings should be treated as ends and not merely as means. Such a claim has the implication that in the production process human beings should be the ends of that process and not mere means to it. This claim is one of the main points made in the US Catholic bishops' pastoral letter on the economy.[38]

Yet what happens is that capitalism necessarily, essentially, structurally violates this imperative in practice. Being treated as an end means doing work that is meaningful and satisfying; capitalism, however, subdivides and mechanizes work in the name of efficiency oriented towards profit and the maintenance of political control so that the worker becomes a mere appendage of the capitalist manager or machine. That which should be the means of her self-expression instead becomes the source of her alienation. Also treating someone as an end means their full participation in the decisions that shape the work process; workers, however, are essentially victims of decisions they have not made and of processes over which they have no control. Finally, being treated as an end means that my work serves and benefits me as a worker; capitalism, however, subordinates the worker's gain to capitalist surplus value and profit. As a result, workers remain at least relatively poor compared to capitalists, and there is enormous poverty, unemployment, and homelessness.[39]

A fourth example of capitalism violating its own moral ideals is the incompatibility between the moral, political imperative of democracy and the domination essential to capitalism. Democracy in the full sense means participation in decisions affecting me, not just a formal exercise every two to four years to choose among candidates chosen by elites. Democracy implies equal claims by all to influence decisions, run for office, voice their opinions, air their grievances. Democracy implies that no arbitrary limit be placed on questions asked, alternatives considered, criticisms offered, proposals made.[40]

Capitalism reveals itself as structurally incompatible with such democracy for several reasons. First, it is difficult or impossible for someone to get elected without money or the support of those with money. This fact means that those with questions, criticisms, or policies offensive to capital will not be supported by capital. Second, just as capitalism economically rests on unequal access to the means of production, so also politically it rests on unequal access to political power. Corporations and the wealthy have much greater access to and influence on decision making through membership in or influence on key government committees and the lobbying of political action committees. Third, because the "business of America is business," government looks after the well-being of the business community more than that of workers and the poor. Because the government depends for its own survival and well-being on the good fortune and support of business, it goes out of its way to please business.

Fourth, because of the preceding point, there is a tendency for Congress and committees in government to favor those alternatives approved by business and not to consider alternatives that displease business. Cutting military spending, for example, is anathema; cutting welfare is not. Fifth, there is a positive correlation between one's wealth and his participation in the political process. One reason for the decreasing participation of workers and the poor is the strong perception that what they do and say makes little or no difference to the outcome, and that their concerns are not being addressed. Sixth, the media, which are primarily financed by business, overwhelmingly express opinions, attitudes, and values that are favorable to business and have the largest audience. Contrast both the opinions and readers of *Time* with those of *The Nation.* Finally, politics, because it functions in a government basically ordered to the good of business, increasingly becomes a politics of public relations and image, insuring that substantive issues are not raised and relevant questions are not asked. In place of honest, full discussion of issues in an election, the emphasis is on selling a presidential candidate.[41]

Capitalist democracies, therefore, rather than being "of, by, and for the people," are "of, by, and for capital and the rich." Democracy, rather than fulfilling Mill's ideal of full, unlimited, equal participation and discussion for all, is reduced to a mere formal exercise. This is not to say that state socialist experiments in Russia and China were any better. Indeed, because of the lack of a democratic tradition, respect for individual rights, and a public sphere of criticism and opinion, they fell behind, at least in some respects, the achievements of bourgeois democracy. Rather than an economic domination peculiar to capitalist societies, state socialist states practiced a bureaucratic, political domination that is equally or more reprehensible. From the point of view of moral conversion, both late capitalism and state socialism are inadequate.[42]

Building on such arguments as these, we can argue that, if we are committed to full political democracy, then we require economic democracy – decentralized worker ownership and control. Not only is economic oligarchy contradictory to political democracy, but, following Walzer, we can see that arguments validating or invalidating the one validate or invalidate the other. If, using *modus ponens*, we are committed to political democracy, then the same reasons oblige us to endorse economic democracy. If A, then B; A, therefore B. If, on the other hand, using *modus tollens*, we wish to endorse capitalist, economic plutocracy, private ownership, and control of the means of production, then the same reasons oblige us to reject political democracy. If A, then B; not B, therefore not A.

Walzer argues this point through using a real historical example: Pullman, Illinois, set up in the nineteenth century by George Pullman as both a town and a business. Pullman thought this investment of money in the town gave him the right to run it like a benevolent dictator. However, Walzer argues, we do not recognize such a claim as valid in the political arena. Essentially, people entering the town would be giving up rights of self-government they already had as American citizens. Nor does the idea that the citizens did not have to live there justify Pullman; that they chose to live in Pullman does not justify denying them rights as citizens.

Now Walzer's point here is that if these arguments are not justified for denying political democracy, then they are not valid for denying economic democracy either. Pullman's entrepreneurial energy and investment went equally into his town and his business; by his standards and his arguments, both were his private property. He had as much right to choose his workers' wives as he did their wages; he could as legitimately control their privacy as their productivity. Since, however, his arguments are clearly not valid for the town, then they are not valid for the plant either. Economic and political democracy are parts of a seamless web; denying or affirming the one implies denying or affirming the other.[43]

Up to this point, we have been performing what critical theory calls immanent critique, measuring capitalism against its own norms and values and finding it wanting. This is an elementary, straightforward form of critique very much in Lonergan's spirit and method. If the doing does not conform to the knowing, then the doing is ethically and politically suspect. Rationality in the cognitive and ethical arena implies performative and logical consistency. If a system is essentially self-contradictory, as capitalism is, then that system is essentially flawed morally and politically.

All of the preceding in this section, then, entitles us to say that capitalism is structurally unjust and, therefore, at odds with moral conversion. Kai Nielsen, basing his conclusions on considerations similar to ours, concludes that a society, in order to be just, must allow individuals maximum freedom to participate in the life of that society and fundamental equality in wealth and income, with some allowances for individual preference, initiative, talent, and need. Capitalism fails on both counts. Freedom is not adequately present because of the conflict between political democracy and capitalist oligarchy and because of the regimentation of the capitalist workplace. Equality is also not present, because of unequal access to means of production and power.[44]

Freedom and equality go together or not at all. Loss of freedom implies inequality because of the domination of one group over another. Fundamental inequality leads to loss of freedom because some have greater resources to realize their aims than others and can impose their preferences on others. In twentieth-century capitalist society, then, there are basically three alternatives: Nozick's minimalist state, Rawls's welfare state, or a decentralized democratic socialism. Nozick's minimalist state is basically inadequate because it intentionally leaves capitalist unfreedom and inequality intact, legitimizes that intactness, and discourages any form of welfare whatsoever. Rawls's welfare state, while it is an improvement over Nozick's, is also deficient, because its difference principle, that inequality in income and wealth is legitimate if the well-being of the worst off in society is increased, legitimates enormous gaps in income and wealth, endorses a contradiction between political democracy and economic oligarchy, and legitimates such economic oligarchy. Since neither the minimalist state nor the welfare state measure up to the standards of justice, only democratic socialism will do.[45]

Full moral conversion, then, implies critique of and transformation of capitalism and movement towards a democratic socialism. The principles of justice are the middle term between moral conversion and democratic socialism. If I am committed to full moral conversion, I must be committed to justice. If I am committed to justice, then I am committed to maximum freedom and equality. If I am committed to maximum freedom and equality, then I must reject capitalism as unjust. If I am fully morally converted, then I must reject capitalism as unjust. Conversely, if I do not reject capitalism as unjust, then I am not fully morally converted. I am either insincere, inconsistent, misguided, misinformed, confused, or all or some of these in combination. A merely bourgeois moral conversion is an incomplete, truncated moral conversion. Justice in the moral sphere is basic reality and meaning; capitalism as injustice contradicts such meaning. As negation of such meaning, capitalism is not only intellectually but morally absurd.

We have been discussing here only the issue of justice in one country. However, I wish at least to note that there is also an international problem of justice arising when capitalism exports its system abroad in various forms of direct or indirect imperialism. Expropriation of surplus value at home expands to become expropriation of surplus value abroad. The limits of this chapter, in which the ground covered is already fairly extensive, do not allow me to go into the issue at length. Here it is only appropriate to note that radical political conversion has international as well as national implications. Condemnation of US capitalism as unjust at home will then, very probably, lead me to condemn it abroad as well. This issue, as US involvement in Central America and the Near East indicate, is not a trivial one.[46]

Religious Conversion: Falling in Love with God

Religious conversion is the peak of self-transcendence. Intellectual conversion promotes self-transcendence by orientation to the totality of being and moral conversion by its commitment to justice in community, but religious conversion is other-worldly falling in love with God without restriction. As such, it occurs primarily on the fourth level of responsibility, choice, commitment. The openness or disposability to the other that has its roots in intellectual and moral conversion flowers in religious conversion and disposability towards God, emptiness for God as absolute mystery.[47]

When religious conversion occurs, my life is put on a new basis. Whereas before the initiative came from me in my own efforts towards intellectual and moral self-transcendence, now the initiative comes from God as I receive God's love. The results are increased peace and joy, attentiveness to God in prayer and to God's loved ones in action, relinquishment of self and love of the other. Religious conversion sublates intellectual and moral conversion in that it retains all that is valid and legitimate in them, but puts them on a new basis. I live now no longer, but Christ lives in me. "It is the first principle. From it flow one's desires and fear, one's joys and sorrows, one's decision and deeds."[48]

It is in the notion of sublation that we find the first connection with radical political conversion. For if the results of our first four sections are true, then we can say that religious conversion sublates radical intellectual and moral conversion. If such sublation occurs, then religious conversion also possesses as part of its meaning and one of its fruits radical political conversion. Otherwise there would be a contradiction between the sublated radical intellectual and moral conversion and the conservative, bourgeois religious conversion. A Christianity that merely legitimates and reproduces the bourgeois, middle-class subject is incomplete and self-denying.

Second, religious conversion also has its own proper content to contribute to radical political conversion. Part of this content is the orientation to community that is at odds with the individualistic, bourgeois subject, regarding others either as obstacles or means on the way to affluent living. If we are, as Christianity says, all members of one Mystical Body, then we are not essentially rugged individuals, would-be entrepreneurs or consumers, "Rambos" or "Ronbos" deriving our meaning from our private property and profit, but social individuals oriented to finding meaning in community. Even when I am most alone, in reflection, writing, or prayer, I am still communal in the language that I use, the traditions that nourish me, the persons about whom and for whom I think, write, or pray.

Third, since love of God is fruitful, it overflows into love of all those whom God loves or might love. Essential to Christianity is the preferential option for the poor, the oppressed, the persecuted, the homeless. Essential to the ultimate reality of God and Christ is that God is on the side of the poor. We side with the oppressed against the oppressors, the elite, the powerful. Here Christianity proclaims an either-or: either we are on the side of the poor or the rich, the oppressed or the oppressors, the powerless or the powerful. There is no middle ground. If I am committed to justice, then I have to be against injustice.[49]

Both a Marxian conceptual reflection on capital logic and the empirical facts give scant comfort to those who wish to defend the possibility of a fully humane, welfare-state capitalism. Indeed, there are significant indications that poverty, unemployment, and gaps between rich and poor are increasing. The general law of capitalist accumulation, then,

Marx states as follows: "The greater the social wealth, the functioning capital, the extent and energy of its growth, and therefore also the greater mass of the proletariat and productivity of its labor, the greater is the industrial reserve army."[50] Capitalism structurally produces unemployment, poverty, homelessness, hunger, and so on. These are the effects of the original relationship of domination in the workplace, in which the worker is hired not for his own self-satisfaction and profit, but for the capitalist's. From this relationship all bad things follow. Capital is a Moloch on whose altar the poor and oppressed are sacrificed.

The religiously converted Christian, then, in her/his preferential option for the poor necessarily is in conflict with the imperatives of capital. Such imperatives require poverty not only as structural effect but as a way of lowering wages and making labor less rebellious. In the context of the twentieth-century welfare state, governments can consciously intend to manipulate such unemployment and poverty in order to reduce the political resistance of the working class and to lower inflation.

Finally, we may note the opposition between religious conversion and capitalist instrumental reason oriented to the useful. If the desire to know is a natural desire to see God, then we can note the natural completion of that in the falling in love with God, in which I become contemplatively, prayerfully attentive to God. From the perspective of instrumental reason, however, nothing could be more impractical and non-functional than such prayerful, contemplative attentiveness. From the perspective of such prayerful openness to God, the dominance of instrumental reason serving only the capital fetish is an offense, and such contemplation constitutes a breach with and form of resistance to the reign of such rationality.

From the perspective of religious conversion, the most valuable things in human life – thought, art, friendship, love, contemplation – are "useless" in this sense. This perversion and absurdity lies in its subordinating the essential to the accidental, the "useless" to the useful, the intrinsically valuable to the instrumentally valuable. That which should be highest becomes lowest and the lowest highest; that which should be the means becomes the end and the end becomes the means.[51]

In summarizing this section, we might say that a radical interpretation is more faithful to the Gospel and Christian tradition than either a conservative or a liberal interpretation. We have supported this claim, first, by insisting that religious conversion sublates radical intellectual and moral conversion. Second, as the US Catholic bishops' economic pastoral letter indicates, a merely individualistic reading of the

Scriptures, experience, and the Christian tradition is less comprehensive than one doing justice both to the individual relationship to God and the social expression of that relationship. A strictly individualistic reading of the Gospels has troubles with such passages as that dealing with the Last Judgment, Matthew 25:31–45, in which personal salvation is linked to the doing of justice.

Third, the preferential option for the poor is necessary if personal conversion is to be authentic. Intellectual, moral, and religious conversion leads to a commitment to justice, which leads to a preferential option for the poor. A radical political conversion is a more consistent expression of the preferential option for the poor. The true God is not a God that protects and legitimizes the bourgeois status quo, but a God that liberates us from such a status quo – Jesus Christ Liberator. The true God is not the God that exploits the poor, but the God, Jesus Christ, who is identified with the poor.[52]

A merely individualistic Christianity produces and reproduces the privatistic bourgeois subject. Such a Christianity does not do justice to the social dimension of the Gospel. The real debate is between those who seriously wish to reform capitalism in the light of the imperative for social justice and those who wish to transcend capitalism altogether.

Conclusion

It might be helpful, at this point, to sum up the usefulness of intellectual, moral, and religious conversion in bringing about social change. Intellectual conversion is useful to the extent that it arms one against positivism, scientism, reductionism, and technocracy. Moral conversion is useful in order to prevent a "cynicism about means," a playing fast and loose with democracy, freedom, equality, and individual rights. Religious conversion is useful in that it prevents a fetishizing or divinizing of the political party or state in a way that short-circuits meaningful reform or revolution.

Now, if intellectual, moral, and religious conversion imply radical conversion, then the opposite is also true. Radical political conversion is incomplete, truncated, and self-contradictory without intellectual, moral, and religious conversion. A positivistic, technocratic, reductionistic politics, a moral cynicism about means, and authoritarian terroristic, totalitarian left movements and government are the results of radical political change severed from the requisite intellectual, moral, and religious conversion. By contrast, religiously inspired liberation movements in Latin America express theoretically and practically a link between Marxism and Christianity.[53]

In arguing for radical political conversion, I do not wish to claim too much for it. Intellectual, moral, and religious conversion are strictly transcendental in a way that radical political conversion is not. While basing itself on these conversions and the preferential option for the poor, radical political conversion is empirical and a posteriori in its response to capitalism as a particular social structure in modernity. Radical political conversion relates to these three conversions and the preferential option for the poor as conclusion to premise, particular to universal, a posteriori to a priori, final ethical, political flowering and completion to what is incomplete.

Heidegger complains that the twentieth century has witnessed a loss of the sense of being. The loss of a sense of being is, to a significant extent, a political problem. Subjectivity, being, and God are covered over by a social system that reduces human beings to objects, equates reality with the technocratic, commodified surface, and turns God into an unverifiable myth. A reasonable conclusion would seem to be that a prolegomenon to any further anthropology, metaphysics, and theology would be a theory of social, economic transformation. Without such a theory, and the corresponding transformation, subjectivity may remain the outmoded remnant of an underconstructed humanism, being an empty word, and God a mere fantasy.

11 Self-Appropriation, Contemplation, and Resistance

The issue of the relationship between contemplation and resistance has been on my mind for a few years. One source for that concern has come from my being involved with certain contemplative-religious groups and finding that the leadership of those groups and many of their members are unwilling to criticize American foreign policy following 9/11 leading to the war on terror, the invasion of Afghanistan, and the invasion of Iraq, even though these merit criticism by even a moderately motivated contemplative-religious group. Another source for my uneasiness is the relative quiescence in the academic community on these same issues, a similar kind of silence to that in the 1960s concerning the Vietnam War. At best, academics began to mount a pragmatic critique of the war as they are doing now, leaving out of consideration any questions about its morality and legality. The argument was that the policy was not working, and, therefore, we should leave Vietnam. But the "doves," the war's pragmatic critics, shared with the hawks the imperial premise of the war, the righteousness of our invasion. It was just too bad that the intervention was not working.[1]

Now, I find this situation problematic, then and now, because I have long had a sense that contemplation and resistance go together or not at all. The more of a contemplative one is, the more one will tend to be critical of and resist unjust structures, policies, and actions that violate the truth leading to justice called for by contemplation. And by contemplation here I mean any form of knowledge-love for its own sake, apart from practical effects and benefits. Contemplation can be natural, directed towards the wondrous material world, interpersonal, scientific, aesthetic, philosophical, or religious.

The link between contemplation and resistance is an instance of a general link between contemplation and action; in Lonergan's terms, doing should conform to knowing.[2] From this premise, one can, depending on the circumstances, conceive a positive action to be done, goods to be supplied, treatment to be meted out. I respond to the beggar with alms or to an act of kindness directed towards me with gratitude. But what if the provoking circumstances for action are all or mostly negative, an unjust social structure, policy, or action? Then the appropriate action is resistance; I say "no" to this violation of what is demanded by the imperative of consistency between knowing and doing. Just social structures, policies, and actions I describe minimally here as those that are consistent with what a community of self-appropriated knowers and choosers would implement in a community. Unjust versions of these are those that are inconsistent with and violate the imperatives and norms of such a community.

The more immediate provocation for my interest in this question is what happened at a major Jesuit, Catholic university, Boston College, in the spring of 2006. At the university's commencement, Condoleezza Rice, George Bush's secretary of state, gave a major address. This invitation, once published, provoked widespread resistance among the Boston College academic community. Petitions were organized against the decision, public and private letters were written to the president of the university, demonstrations were held, people stood up and turned their backs when Ms Rice spoke, and one faculty member even resigned. The event was covered in the secular and religious press, and provoked much comment around the country.

I note the occasion for two reasons. First, there is the very reprehensible or at least problematic decision to invite Ms Rice, in apparent contradiction to the Jesuit imperative to pursue social justice, operative since the early 1970s in the Society of Jesus. Objections were directed against Ms Rice's participation in the lies and misleading propaganda that led up to the Iraq War, and her support for policies designed for the occupation such as torture, preventive detention, and rendition. One cannot plausibly defend the choice of such a speaker for reasons of academic freedom because this is the kind of situation where a university manifests in its choice of a speaker what intellectual, moral, and religious values it takes seriously and what it does not take seriously. That such is the case can be seen by imagining the hue and cry that would legitimately emerge if Hugh Hefner or Bob Guccione had been chosen as a commencement speaker.

I use the Boston College example not just for critical or negative reasons, what went wrong, but for positive reasons. What went right was that a significant number of people were so offended by the decision that they went public with various kinds of objections, protests, questions, challenges, demonstrations, or actions. In other words, they resisted.

That various people, rooted in their academic disciplines and operating out of their own moral and religious sensibilities, said "no," this "no" manifested in different kinds of speech, and action, is what I mean by resistance. And the various academic disciplines can be taken as different forms of contemplation in the intellectual pattern of experience. To the extent that the protest was religiously motivated, it emerged out of a contemplative, religious stance and the demands of justice flowing from that.

Let us look at this religious dimension more closely. According to a fairly standard account of the demands of religious faith, love of God in contemplative prayer should spill over into compassionate love for the neighbor. Since love of neighbor expresses my love of God, there is no essential contradiction between contemplation and action. Because the contemplative loves God, he loves the will of God, and since the will of God is that I love my neighbor, no one who claims to love God cannot love his neighbor.[3]

So far, so good. All of this is pretty straightforward and obvious. But the onset of modernity brings in complicating factors. One is the modern institutional fact of justice and injustice. Not only is there my immediate neighbor whom I may treat justly or unjustly, but mediated institutions can arise that embody justice or injustice; injustice can take the forms of racism, sexism, classism, heterosexism, militarism, and imperialism. Because of this fact, the neighbor whom I am obliged to love is not simply my immediate neighbor, but those who can be affected by just or unjust social institutions giving rise to various kinds of policies, practice, and actions. My neighbor is no longer merely the person next door or the person I encounter on the street, but the peasant in Latin America, the person being tortured in Abu Ghraib or Guantanamo, or workers in Haiti paid starvation wages by US corporations.

I am reminded here in this context of Lonergan's essay "Existenz and Aggiornamento," one of my favorite of his occasional essays, in which he distinguishes between the Christian subject as substance and the Christian as subject. The Christian as substance, while valid and in some cases even holy, is less adequate in today's modern world because of the inability to understand and deal with the complexity of modernity. The Christian as subject, ideally for Lonergan rooted in self-appropriation, is more equal to the task of grasping and responding to modern complexity, and especially for our purposes, the complexity of modern social institutions.[4]

Still another difficulty needs to be faced. The temptation for a certain kind of modern Christian is to emphasize the positive doing of good to the poor, and back off from criticizing the policies and institutions that make the poor poor. As Don Helder Camara, a Latin American cardinal, said a long time ago, "When I feed the poor, they call me a saint. When I ask why they are poor, they call me a communist." What we seem to be less able and less willing to do is prophetically to criticize and resist unjust social structures and policies. And yet it is just such critique and resistance that is called for at times.

Joan Chittister, addressing the issue in *Called to Question*, says the following:

> If there is a major problem in spirituality today it may be that we do not do enough to form Christians for resistance to evil. We form them for patient endurance and for civil conformity. We form them to be "good" but not necessarily to be holy. In the doing of it, we make compliant Christians rather than courageous ones as if bearing evil were more important than confronting it. We go on separating life into parts, one spiritual, one not. This tension between what is profane and what is spiritual makes all the difference between a holy life and a pious life. The pious life seeks consolation, a kind of other worldly disinterest in the secular city. The holy life, if Jesus is any model at all, understands that one without the other is bogus.[5]

But do we not, a person might object, need to emphasize the positive and de-emphasize the negative, to avoid being mere naysayers, to be people of hope? I answer that there is a form of positive thinking that is just a cop-out, and one that is not because it faces up to the negative. It is honest about the evil that afflicts our policies and institutions. It has the courage to confront them in anticipating a more humane and religiously sane future.

There is, then, a form of "positive" thinking that just buries its head in the sand, that is not worth the paper it is written on, what I would call the "impotence of positive unthinking." It is not worthy of the desire to know's demands to be honest, to be open to all questions, to face up to all difficulties. There is, by contrast, a kind of positive thinking that is worthy, that is laudatory, that has fully faced up to the demands of negativity. Let us hear Daniel Berrigan on this issue.

> The changes rung here echo instructions given at the start ([Jeremiah]1:10): "I have appointed you this day over the nations. To pluck up and break down. To destroy and to overthrow. To build and to plant." In the beginning the work is understood as Jeremiah's own; now the same work is declared to be Yahweh's.
>
> Harsh language and unmistakably clear. In each instance the first task – the first word – is a naysaying. No toleration, no minor (or even major) adjustment of an inherently wicked, inhuman system. The "no" precedes the "yes" in the nature of things. What sort of dwelling can be built on rotten foundations?
>
> One notes too that the images of "no" are more detailed than those of "yes": to pluck up, break down, destroy, overthrow. No mistaking the intent – to start over, to grant nothing of legitimacy or place to a discredited system.
>
> More, the "no" is included and presupposed in the "yes." The primary "no" gives the final "yes" ("to build up, to plant") its dignity, seriousness, and insight.
>
> (Let us however avoid extremism. Let us speak of "good" nuclear weapons, good because ours. And of evil ones, brandished by our enemies.
>
> (Let us wage only "just" wars; just because waged by us.
>
> (Let us approve ROTC on Catholic campuses; correctly approved because the students are Catholic, marching under a religious vexilla.
>
> (Let us sanction and honor Christian military chaplains; they after all bring aid and comfort to Christian warriors.)
>
> In other words, let no prophetic "no" be uttered in face of worldly systems of captivation and control, of morbidity and slack morality. Let us "go with what goes." Let us honor the empire with an unmodified, unmitigated, spiritless, spineless "yes."[6]

Berrigan here insists rightfully and righteously on a kind of negativity that must precede any positive setting up of alternative institutions and policies. Otherwise, the results will be affected and discredited by a rotten foundation, corrupt to the core. For me, at least, there are echoes of Marcuse's "Great Refusal" in *One-Dimensional Man*, written in the 1960s. If Berrigan and Marcuse are correct, in certain situations the great refusal is demanded by the desire to know, and one fails to conform to that desire if one does not move in that direction joyfully and passionately, giving into a kind of spiritless conformism and obscurantism, going along in order to get along. And, of course, implied in the great refusal is resistance.[7]

Let us briefly recapitulate. On the religious level, there is a contemplative love of God that manifests itself in love for the immediate and mediated neighbor. Involved and implied in such love is the demand for justice, which in modern, complex societies necessarily takes the form of dealing with big institutions that may or may not have institutionalized different forms of group bias such as racism, sexism, classism, heterosexism, militarism, and imperialism. If these institutions positively embody a commitment to community, justice, and peace, then the practice of justice is significantly and dominantly a positive doing of good. If these institutions are significantly infected with such bias, then the work of justice and love requires resistance of various kinds. And, we say in all honesty, just as there is a one-sided positive that is only worthy of contempt, there is also a one-sided negative that is nihilistic and violent, insufficiently rooted positively in contemplation of various kinds and insufficiently hopeful. The kind of negative that I am calling for, then, is one that is contemplatively rooted and nourished by an appreciative openness to being and God and that is positively hopeful, looking forward to a humane future.

Let us put a little more philosophical underpinning under this religious scaffolding. Going back to basics, we start with self-appropriation as the experiencing, understanding, judging, and choosing of myself as an experiencing, understanding, and choosing subject in relation to being. The method expressing self-appropriation is transcendental method, in which both knowledge and choice operate. Because knowledge operates, there is a contemplative dimension to self-appropriation, knowledge for its own sake. Because I choose myself as a cognitive-existential subject, there is an element of praxis. Self-appropriation expressed in transcendental method is the most fundamental kind of contemplation and the most fundamental kind of praxis.[8]

Lonergan's notion of self-appropriation enables him to relativize while not eliminating the distinction between contemplation and action. This point is underscored in Lonergan's discussion of the way levels of intentionality presuppose and complement one another. Experience is presupposed by and sublated by understanding, understanding is presupposed by and sublated by judgment, and judgment is presupposed by and sublated by choice. One implication of this claim is that even the most sublime kind contemplation is undergirded by decision; I have to choose to marvel at nature, look at works of art, think philosophically, or pray.[9]

Second, the unity of transcendental cognitive-existential structure flows out into the diversity of patterns of experience. Experience, understanding, judgment, and decision operate in all the patterns of experience, but they operate differently and have different criteria of validity and are oriented to different ends, practical ends in common sense and contemplative ends in the aesthetic, intellectual, and religious patterns.[10]

Third, an implication of self-appropriation is its expression in the moral and political arenas. Because knowing is complemented by doing, there is the categorical imperative that doing should conform to knowing. Because there is a hierarchy of levels in transcendental structure, there is a scale of values manifested in social life, moving from the economic to the political to the cultural to the existential to the religious, and lower levels are presupposed and sublated by the higher. On the economic level, for example, justice will be served when there is adequate distribution of goods to everyone and group bias is eliminated in such distribution. Lower levels should serve higher levels rather than twisting them to their own ends. The economic should serve the political and not dominate it to serve narrow class ends; the political should serve the socio-cultural and not twist it to narrow, propagandistic ends in the public sphere; the human person should be the end served by social institutions and not alienated by bureaucratic, corporate structures; and the human person should serve God in a just society, not some economic political structure deified or fetishized into a God substitute. Finally, when such distorted, unequal, alienated societies spill over into the individual arena such that he or she is sacrificed to narrow economic or political ends, then the scale of values is violated on the individual level. Rather than the lower serving the higher, the higher serves the lower all the way up and down the scale of values.[11]

The practical imperatives of morality and justice, then, mediate between the practice of contemplation and resistance. The self-appropriated person moving between and among the patterns of experience and finally into the moral-political is confronted by the greater or lesser inversion of the scale of values in modern societies, whether late capitalist or state socialist; maldistribution of goods occurs across broad reaches of society, propaganda dominates in the public sphere rather than free, rational discussion, and, finally, illegitimate imperial expansion of these already internally unjust societies moves out into other countries. As I see the matter, basing myself on Lonergan but coming to my own conclusions in my own edition of myself, the movement from self-appropriation to different kinds of contemplation and praxis leads to principled anti-capitalism and anti-imperialism and to a principled resistance. Here, briefly displayed and developed, is a Lonerganian basis for resistance. If you like, Lonergan joins Berrigan.[12]

To complete our Lonerganian trajectory, we need to mention religious conversion. Building on intellectual and moral conversion, religious conversion is a total falling in love with God, immersing myself contemplatively in the cloud of unknowing. In the end, such love of God should lead to love of one's neighbor and the work of justice manifested in different kinds of negative and positive praxis. So we rejoin here our earlier religious reflections; the circle is completed.[13]

Conclusion

The main point of my essay is that contemplation and resistance are not contradictories, but are mutually fructifying opposites that lead into one another and imply one another. The more authentic the contemplation, the more it will be open to and lead into resistance if and when that is required. The more authentic the resistance, the more it will be rooted in contemplation of various kinds. There are various social, political, and religious influences that are continually trying to seduce us out of this legitimate unity of contemplation and resistance, inviting us to be "reasonable" and "positive" and "non-ideological."

Second, the most fundamental reality for Lonergan is not contemplation or resistance, but self-appropriation, and that contributes to relativizing the apparent opposition between the two. One reason for that relativizing is that self-appropriation is a work of both intelligence and freedom, thus helping us to avoid the extremes of a bloodless, will-less contemplation and a totally voluntaristic, one-sidedly activistic action.[14]

Third, mediating between contemplation and resistance is moral-political reason operating on the fourth level of freedom. Because doing should conform to knowing, there emerges the imperative of social justice motivated by the scale of values. The categorical imperative and the imperative of justice thus mediate between a contemplation rooted in self-appropriation and resistance. I have pointed out elsewhere how there has been a tendency in Catholic academia to de-emphasize the practical, transformative aspect of reason, making it one-sidedly contemplative and speculative and short-circuiting the connection to resistance. I have also pointed out how such a one-sided emphasis is inadequate even as philosophy. While philosophy has a legitimate contemplative, speculative moment, that needs to be complemented by a practical, transformative moment.[15]

Fourth, I cannot resist reflecting on possible theological implications of what I have said here. Is there a theology that does justice to the imperative for justice, the link between contemplation and resistance, the destructiveness of contemporary systematic injustice, and the plight of the world's poor. In fact there is such a theology really extant, already on the scene for some 40–50 years. It is called "liberation theology." It is, I have argued elsewhere, the most appropriate theology for the twenty-first century.[16]

But is not such theology ideological in a bad sense? In one sense, liberation theology, because it takes on and criticizes various kinds of bias, racist, sexist, and classist, is the least ideological of disciplines. To the extent that it advocates a "preferential option for the poor," this claim is not ideological in the bad sense but an explicit owning up to the demands of a fully self-conscious reason rooted in the desire to know. To the extent that liberation theology is or can be inattentive to the effects of general bias, grafting it onto a Lonerganian philosophy of self-appropriation should help to correct that tendency. To the extent that liberation theology is committed to a certain set of social, political, and religious values, it is ideological in another sense, but so is any other theology, even liberal or conservative theology. The debate among these theologies concerns the question about which one, conservative, liberal, or liberatory, best conforms to the dictates of the desire to know, overcomes the effects of bias, and extends the full range of reason universally to the plight of the world's poor done in by systematic injustice. I have argued elsewhere that liberation theology is superior in these and other respects.[17]

What can happen and does happen is that a liberal-conservative defender of the status quo calls the more radical liberation theology ideological, but there the contrast is not between non-ideological and ideological, but between a defense of the status quo that is implicitly ideological and one that brings that status quo into question in minor or major ways. If Lonergan is correct that the most fundamental sense of "ideological" is lack of conformity to the transcendental precepts, and if a liberation theology is possible that does do that, then where's the rub, where's the objection? I take it that liberation theology, both in itself and as grounded in and corrected by self-appropriation, is not necessarily, fatally subject to the charge that it is "ideological" in the bad sense.[18]

12 On Really Living

Live all you can; it's a mistake not to. It doesn't so much matter what you do in particular, so long as you have your life. If you haven't had that, what have you had?

Henry James[1]

The unlived life is not worth examining.

James L. Marsh[2]

This chapter was stimulated by a film, *A Dangerous Method*, which deals with personal relationships among Freud, Jung, and a (future) female psychiatrist played by Keira Knightly. One of the minor characters in the film is a male psychiatrist sent by Jung to Freud for analysis, whose version of "live all you can" is to seduce and sleep with any and all women whom he encounters. This policy of seduction he recommends to Jung, who responds by entering into a romantic relationship with the Knightly character, at that point (and through most of the film) his patient. One slight, further complication is that Jung was married at that time and continued to be so while continuing to be involved with Knightly, off and on, over many years.

The film, very well done in my opinion, led me to pursue a question that has engaged me off and on over many years: What does it mean to really live? Here I suggest an initial sense of what that means: passionate, intense, committed, all-out involvement in life in its many dimensions, full of risk and joy and love and even, perhaps, suffering. But the suffering in this context is part of the richness of a life well lived.

But, of course, we have to reflect on the different authentic and inauthentic versions of "really living." The first most obvious version is exemplified by the promiscuous psychiatrist, a sensate, empiricist version. A second, equally one-sided version goes in a different direction, that of the "Party of Woollett," Massachusetts, in James's *The Ambassadors*, wishing to rescue the son of Mrs Newsome from the clutches of Mademoiselle de Vionnet, who has taken the young man in hand and has influenced him in a positive way towards becoming more historically and aesthetically aware, more cosmopolitan, assured, and mature, less Woollett-like. Lambert Strether, the "ambassador" sent over from America to reclaim Chad and return him to Woollett, "where the values are unambiguous, and where everyone pays a price – the price of muffled feeling, the conventional, the proscribed,"[3] begins to doubt his mission and actually shifts towards the values of Europe, ceases to live so much by the rule of the clock, which Woollett manufactures, and begins to open up to life in all of its sensate, historical, and aesthetic glory. Chad, by contrast, returns to Woollett.

A third kind of one-sided approach to living is that of the voluntaristic, which picks up on the value of commitment, certainly an aspect of living, but does not do justice to sensate, intellectual, and morally normative aspects. Thinkers whom I have criticized on this score are Sartre and Foucault, but we can easily imagine and recall other examples from our experience: the grim, tight-lipped, political revolutionary or reformer, or the virtuous, upwardly mobile man or woman, who is always saying to herself, "every day in every way, I am getting better and better."[4]

Transcendental method, rooted in and flowing from self-appropriation, gives an initial and basic Lonerganian take on "really living," putting into practice the transcendental precepts in a habitual manner. The more I do that, the more I am really living. It may be, however, that that formula, while being a good beginning, does not go far enough. It does not do full justice to our sense of life as passionate, risk taking, loving, and adventurous, in contrast to a life that is deficient in or lacks these qualities. There is the "Woollett life," if you like, conventional, safe, following the rules, legal, moral, and religious. Such a life can contain real moral or professional achievement, but, in the final analysis, "has not really done much with its life." This is another phrase that I find telling and suggestive as I ask myself whether I have really lived or am really living. But, of course, there also are one-sided sensate, romantic, and voluntaristic answers to this question.

A further clue about our topic might be to note that a life devoid of feeling and emotional expression seems to be one that is deficient. Here I find psychic conversion an important notion that complements the other three, intellectual, moral, and religious conversion.[5] We are aware of people who know and practice the other three conversions, yet are lacking in the emotional dimensions of their lives, inexpressive, non-passionate, and non-vulnerable. We can note also, of course, people who are deficient in another way, that of excess; life is one constant emotional binge, one affair after another, one fad after another, one fashion after another. Here it is useful to consider how the other three conversions, self-appropriation, and transcendental method allow us to distinguish between too little and too much in the domain of feeling.

Another aspect of living is the socio-political. Here I take the preferential option for the poor, whether philosophical or religious, as complementary to the psychic, and as taking conservative, liberal, or radical forms. And here living in the full sense means combating the forms of anti-life, the anti-kingdom as Sobrino puts it, either in the form of passionate service or in the form of prophetic denunciation, feeding the poor or asking why they are poor. I will argue elsewhere in this volume the way psychic conversion and political conversion can be two aspects of a legitimate historical materialism undergirding and grounding the movement upward through economic, political, cultural, existential, and religious levels of the scale of values. Psychic conversion and political conversion, on the other hand, can translate and express the other conversions. And this vertical movement from lowest to highest or highest to lowest among the scale of values can contribute to a comprehensiveness and breadth in our notion of "really living."[6]

Ultimately at the heart of really living, it seems to me, is really loving God and other human beings. We see here that the levels of commitment and love sublate the lower levels of cognition and psychic and social life. Am I really living if I do not have a great love in my life, or merely existing and getting by? If I am not living a fully committed life, am I really living? The activity and content of love and commitment are both important. Hitler, Stalin, and Mussolini were passionately committed in their respective projects of dominating and exploiting human beings, and contrast to other more adequate examples such as Gandhi, King, and Berrigan.

Filling out this notion and complexifying it, I distinguish among a life call, life form, and profession in expressing my love for God and human beings, or, an alternate formulation, among the "who," "how," or "what" of commitment and love.[7] Life call is my fundamental, unique stance before God and human beings, combining in various ways contemplation and action. Life form is the way I live out that call in married or religious or priestly or single living in the world. And profession is what I do in a day-in and day-out manner as I express my life call and life form as professor, thinker, intellectual, housewife, or social activist.

For Lonerganians, it seems to me, that last aspect is important. It is possible and actual that we feel called to live our lives in various forms of the intellectual pattern of experience as historians, economists, sociologists, philosophers, or theologians. We think, write, read, give papers, and go to conferences, and that can be and is, as it was for Lonergan, a steady, concentrated, faithful, dedicated "keeping at it" over the years and decades that can lead to enormous fruitfulness in the influence on students, colleagues, and the larger world, and to enormous scholarly productivity. And here I am reminded of Lonergan's meditation in *Insight* on the difference between being a weekend celebrity and really achieving something as a scholar and intellectual.[8]

Such day-in and day-out persistence and commitment to the scholarly life can be and is for us a legitimate version of "really living." And we can understand why when we see that the opposites of desire and rationality are not only linked but identical. The desire to know is both rationality and desire. And when we link that to the levels of commitment and love and falling in love, as well as to psychic and political conversion, then we have a very complex notion of the intellectual life, much different from the pedantic caricature of it in Casaubon, the dry-as-dust scholar in *Middlemarch*, who married Dorothea and made her life miserable. Because postmoderns and others miss this linking and identity of rationality and desire, they come up with critiques of reason as dominating, oppressive, alienating, and dehumanizing.[9]

Still, I need to qualify these claims a bit. We are more than our professional selves, even our Lonerganian professional selves. We require an ordering of conversions. Just as moral and religious conversion trump intellectual conversion, do also do life form and life call trump professionalism. Ironically, the desire to know leads to the affirmation of realities more important than the intellectual life. Thinking is part of living, but is not the whole or even the most important part of the whole. Loving is more important than thinking, and being a good person is more important than being a philosopher or intellectual. When such ordering occurs, then professional self-aggrandizement, money, and glory can give way to service, justice, and the glory of God. We note here, in contrast, the deep temptation among Americans to sacrifice and subordinate everything to professional success, with the resulting unhappiness and emptiness of life, another false, one-sided version of "really living."

Here I am led to think about patterns of experience, and the importance for us of the intellectual pattern over other patterns. For others, like Joan Mitchell, it is a matter of spending her whole life in the aesthetic pattern and producing a marvelous body of work. And here I am thinking not only of a vertical comprehensiveness in the life of the self, involving a right ordering of the conversions, the transcendental precepts, the levels of experience, understanding, judgment, and decision, and the scale of values; but also a horizontal comprehensiveness among the patterns of experience. And here it seems right to say that, all other things being equal, the more patterns of experience I can live in and experience in a habitual way, the better. I may be a philosopher, but I experience more or less intensely the biological, aesthetic, dramatic, and religious patterns of experience.[10]

But, of course, there are limits to be observed. If I am a full-time artist, I cannot be a full-time political activist. If I am a philosopher or theologian like Lonergan, I may decide that I can serve the poor best by reading and writing about economics. There is a prudential limit to be respected between spreading myself too thin and focusing myself too narrowly, a kind of Aristotelian mean if you like.

One point to make, also, is to note the individual, unique character of "really living." Self-appropriation is not about any Tom, Dick, or Harry, Lonergan tells us in the introduction to *Insight*, but concerns "the personally appropriated structure of one's own experiencing, one's own intelligent inquiry and insights, one's own critical reflecting, judging, and deciding." Self-appropriation as the experiencing, understanding, judging, and choosing of self as an experiencing, understanding, judging, and choosing self in relation to being in the self's unique and universal aspects is the basis of really living for us as philosophers, and falling in love is its flowering. Existential ciphers need not apply. I cannot really live if I am living someone else's life, whether that be another individual or the "crowd."[11]

In a processive world, to live is to change and to change is to grow, and to grow humanly is to develop and to develop is to obey the law of genuineness. To live genuinely is to dwell consciously and deliberately in the tension between limitation and transcendence, and to embrace both of these poles in fruitful complementarity. I neither sink into the level of mere stasis and convention and custom, the way of Woollett, nor plunge indiscriminately into novelty, the way of the seducer in *A Dangerous Method*. I must forever be creatively faithful to what is valid in tradition, and I must at times risk what is new, overcoming "the fear of the cold plunge into becoming other than what one is."[12]

If there is a law of genuineness, then that law is analogous. There is the genuineness of the simple soul, like St Thérèse of Lisieux, and there is the genuineness won in a complex process of self-appropriation. There is the genuineness of the subject as substance, and there is the genuineness of the subject as subject. Living as subject in modernity is living in the twentieth and twenty-first centuries in all their highs and lows, prospects and temptations, achievements and setbacks. The subject as substance keeps her nose to the grindstone, obeys the laws of church and society, and does not rock the boat. The subject as subject reaches out to the world in all of its complexity, anguish, and richness, learns from that world, and in turn brings something to that world, criticizes it, and transforms it. To live, really live in this way, I cannot drift, but must take hold of myself and choose creatively what I will make of myself.[13]

I wish to conclude by reflecting on Dan Berrigan as an example of real, full living, and here I am intending a deliberate contrast with the more limited versions of *A Dangerous Method* and *The Ambassadors*. In Berrigan's autobiography, *To Dwell in Peace*, published in the 1980s, we see the narrative of a rich, fully lived life, full of passion and love, friendship and commitment, creativity and risk, positive commitment to the Kingdom of God and negative resistance to the forces of the anti-Kingdom of capitalism and imperialism and militarism, very much alive and very compassionate towards the victims of the forces of death, the two-thirds to three-quarters of humanity who cannot take for granted the necessities required for getting through the day. As Lonergan also reminds us, Berrigan's life involves the embracing of suffering and the Cross on behalf of the poor in the Third World and, increasingly, in the First World.[14]

Conclusion

As I wrote this essay, I went in some directions I did not intend, especially in bringing in the political, but I found that the socio-political insisted on itself as a part, not the whole, of life. At the end of the essay, we find ourselves with a much richer, more differentiated, and more profound sense of living than was present in the initial examples of the film and James. A Lonerganian account of human living relativizes and contextualizes and criticizes these examples. Sexual erotics, history, morality, and art are certainly aspects of life, but are not the whole story. In developing this point I have tried to negotiate a vertical comprehensiveness moving up and down the levels of feeling, political involvement, knowing and choosing, and the scale of values; and a horizontal comprehensiveness moving between and among the patterns of experience. I also differentiated among life call, life form, and profession, and the proper ordering of these, and also described a movement from the personal to the interpersonal to the socio-historical.

Because this is such a rich, inexhaustible topic, there are issues I have not sufficiently discussed, such as the role of pleasure and enjoyment on sensuous, intellectual, and spiritual levels. "What about just having fun, Marsh?" one might legitimately ask, "the kind of things we do after this conference on Thursday, Friday, and Saturday evenings." And so here too we could chart a movement from relatively superficial kinds of enjoyment and pleasure all the way up to and down into deeper realms of joy and suffering. A full account of living has to do justice to superficial and profound dimensions of pleasure, properly differentiating and ordering them.

I conclude with two quotations, the earlier passage in *Insight* to which I have already referred, and one from Berrigan uttered from the depths of a DC jail.

> Still, even with talent, knowledge makes a slow, if not a bloody, entrance. To learn thoroughly is a vast undertaking that calls for relentless perseverance. To strike out on a new line and become more than a weekend celebrity calls for years in which one's living is more or less constantly absorbed in the effort to understand, in which one's understanding gradually works round and up a spiral of viewpoints with each complementing its predecessor and only the last embracing the whole field to be mastered.[15]
>
> Anyway, here's my translation of that breakthrough. It's the gratitude that wells up in me, unforeseen, almost ecstatic, at being in jail. Now help me figure that one out! It's being here (even here) with Phil. I remember something Sam Melville wrote about Attica. Prison can be ecstasy. It's one's act of faith, in choosing to be here – verified in the eyes, speech, conduct, style of another. Being here with Phil.

This hole. They say even in D.C. jail, you can't go lower than we've gone. We're in deadlock: 24 hour lockup, two in a cell hardly enough for one, sharing space with mice, rats, flies and assorted uninvited fauna. Food shoved in the door, filth, degradation.

And I wouldn't choose to be anywhere else on the planet. I think we've landed where the breakthrough occurs. I think it's occurred already.[16]

13 Self-Appropriation as a Way of Life

As is well known to most of us, self-appropriation is an important notion in Lonergan's thought, maybe the most important. Lonergan in various places, especially in the introduction to *Insight*, has testified as to its importance. *Insight*, he tells us, is an invitation to a decisive, personal act, the intellectual and volitional taking possession of myself. All other disciplines and sub-disciplines in philosophy are, in *Insight*, simply indications or manifestations or examples of self-appropriation.[1] In "Self-Appropriation: Lonergan's Pearl of Great Price," the first essay in this volume, I show how important that notion is in itself and for my own development as a philosopher.

Nonetheless, Lonergan's emphasis in his work and my own orientation in that chapter is on self-appropriation as a basis for the doing of philosophy and theology. What remains in the background and is less emphasized is the relationship between self-appropriation and the rest of one's non-professional, non-philosophical, non-theological life. This is not to say that Lonergan leaves such issues totally unaddressed, but simply that his main attention is directed elsewhere.

Consequently, the question I would like to address is this: what is the relationship of self-appropriation to the rest of human life? Does it make sense to talk about a back-and-forth reciprocal movement between ordinary life and philosophical life? In addition to seeing self-appropriation as a basis of and core of philosophy and theology as professional vocations, do we not also have to see it as a way of life, as a modern version of the examined life? I am reminded here of a claim by one of my first great teachers: 2% of people think, 4% think that they think, and 94% would rather die than think. Self-appropriation is a very contemporary, sophisticated approach enabling us to enter that elite category, the 2% who think.[2]

What I come up with in my preliminary reflection on this issue is that we can discover a general or universal relationship of self-appropriation to daily life as a whole and at least four different sub-levels or aspects: self-appropriation and non-professional intellectual life, aesthetic life or aesthetic conversion, ethical-political praxis, and the religiously converted subject in the world and church. I will treat each of these issues in turn and then in my conclusion reflect on the relationship between and among these levels and aspects.

From Self-Appropriation to Ordinary Human Life

As I conceive self-appropriation, it is the deliberate, conscious experiencing, understanding, judging, and choosing of myself as an experiencing, understanding, judging, and choosing subject in relation to being. One of the best discussions of this theme occurs in *Method in Theology*, in chapter 1 on transcendental method. Transcendental method is the explicit expression and formulation of self-appropriation, and it leads, of course, to epistemology, ethics, and metaphysics as its immediate consequences.[3]

One way to think about extending self-appropriation into daily life is to ask, "Why do that?" And one argument that occurs to me is to see such extension as based on the general imperative that doing in the rest of my life should conform to knowing. This imperative is like the ethical imperative that Lonergan develops in *Insight*,[4] but goes beyond it and includes it as a moment of itself. Let us imagine, then, that we have gone through intellectual conversion, that we have moved from the world of the child to the world of the adult, the world mediated by meaning; that we have moved from the late industrial capitalist or state socialist cave into the sunlight illuminating being. As such people, we are literally and figuratively in love with meaning, being, and the good, and what, therefore, is more natural than to extend that love everywhere and to everything we do? As Lonerganian lovers, we are so in love with our beloved, being, that we seek her everywhere and are on the lookout for her everywhere. "As a hart longs for flowing streams ..."[5]

As I envision this extension, this search is both a desire and an imperative. I link Aristotle and Kant, "is" and "ought," because it is right to do so and because Lonergan does so. Because I am a Lonerganian lover of being animated by the desire to know and grounded in a deeply rooted decision to follow that out, I seek intelligibility everywhere. Because I am intellectually converted, I experience a demand in myself to allow my whole self to fall under this imperative. I sense, in other words, an imperative to be consistent in my professional and private, non-professional life.[6]

Now, we should note that Lonergan has already said some things explicitly about the relationship between self-appropriation and ordinary life. One such place is in *Method in Theology*. Though religious conversion sublates moral conversion and moral conversion sublates intellectual conversion, one is not to infer that intellectual conversion generally comes first chronologically. First is the gift of God's love, then the eye of this love illumines moral values in their splendor and helps bring about their realization, and finally among the values discerned is that of believing the truths taught by the religious tradition, which contains the seed of intellectual conversion. The mature, adult man or woman, then, pursuing and deepening intellectual conversion, is already doing that in a life that is religiously and morally informed and grounded and providing a solidity, security, and habitual willingness in our pursuit of intellectual conversion.[7]

Second, in *Insight* is found Lonergan's discussion of genuineness as that emerges at the climax of his treatment of genetic method. Genuineness as such is a requirement and an aspect of human development, which includes philosophy, of course, but goes beyond that and is more inclusive. Genuineness as law admits the tension between limitation and transcendence into consciousness. As a requirement, the law of genuineness is both conditional and analogous. It is conditional because it arises only insofar as development occurs in human consciousness. It is analogous because the content is different in different cases. There is the development of a simple soul, a St Thérèse of Lisieux, for example; there is also another kind of genuineness "that has to be won back through a self-scrutiny that expels illusion and pretense, and as this enterprise is difficult and its issue doubtful, we do not think of its successful outcome when we cast about for obvious illustrations of genuineness."[8] But in our world of self-appropriated Lonerganian knowers, choosers, and lovers, it is only this latter kind of genuineness that is open to most of us. There is a simplicity that we can attain, but it is a complex, mediated simplicity attained at the end of a long process of differentiation. There is an innocence that can be won, but it is a second innocence, if you like, a second naiveté.

A third place in which the interplay between philosophy and ordinary life occurs is in the discussion of the appropriation of truth in *Insight*. To appropriate the truth is to make it my own authentically, not just repeating the pronouncements of the crowd. I stand on my own intellectually, stand somewhere, step up to the plate. The sensitive appropriation of truth is cognitional. Because reasonableness demands consistency between what we know and what we do, there is a volitional appropriation of truth that consists in our willingness to live up to it, and a sensitive appropriation consisting of an adaptation of our sensibility to the requirements of our knowledge and our decisions. By "sensibility" here I take it that Lonergan means our feelings, psyche, memories, and unconscious. Psychic conversion, therefore, as Bob Doran defines it, my becoming aware of, understanding, affirming, choosing, and integrating my psyche with my intelligence, becomes crucial. Without such psychic conversion, I remain or run the risk of remaining one-sidedly intellectual or volitional, tempted by a false idealism about myself and the world that can block both effective practical living and cognitive, philosophical performance.[9]

There are many fascinating aspects and implications about what we have been discussing. I have, for example, in the essay already noted, drawn attention to the way Lonerganian self-appropriation is not the affair of any generalized Tom, Dick, or Harry, but is an affair of my knowing and my choosing as the individual self that I am. Lonergan picks up here and integrates insights from Kierkegaard and Heidegger on the existential self as individual, but also links such understanding to our universal, cognitive, transcendental structure. We are all unique individuals, but we are also experiencing, understanding, judging, and choosing subjects in community.[10]

When such individuality is translated into daily life, then we can affirm a personal style of the subject, a dramatic artistry and aesthetics of living that approximates some insights of Nietzsche and Foucault, but links these to cognitive and moral normativity more than they did. The subject as cognitive-volitional and as psychic expresses itself in the world in aesthetic self-creation in the way this subject speaks, dresses, eats, laughs, walks, runs, and tells jokes. I am a transcendental subject and have that in common with other transcendental subjects, but as incarnate, self-expressive, and aesthetic in the world, I am a different, individual transcendental subject.[11]

What has also helped me in thinking about this relationship between philosophy and daily life is that Lonergan has already articulated a notion of philosophy performed by the subject as having both subjective and objective poles. The subjective, existential pole is the experience of the philosopher as a lover of wisdom and incarnation of the desire to know oriented to experience, understanding, and judgment. But because philosophy is a search for complete intelligibility, the objective, systematic imperative arises. Even within the objective pole, there is a distinction between subjective and objective. In the former case (subject as object), we have cognitional theory and transcendental method. In the latter case (object as object), we have epistemology, ethics, and metaphysics, along with related domains such as theology and the physical and social sciences. Because the subject as operative subject in the subjective pole already is himself more than a "plaster cast of a man," the subject more easily moves into daily life. Indeed philosophy as philosophy and the engagement in daily life are just two different modes of the subject as subject, in which he moves in and out of different patterns of experience in a more and more accomplished manner. He has become a differentiated subject who has distinguished, related, and verified in himself the distinctions among common sense, theory, interiority, and religious transcendence. More of that anon.[12]

From Professional to Intellectual

Let us imagine a self-appropriated, Lonerganian philosopher, who has been working at her desk for several hours and needs to take a break. Let us imagine the person in mid-afternoon in a city like Toronto or Boston or Los Angeles or New York. The philosopher takes a walk.

Let us imagine further that, because such a person is on her way to self-appropriation and its consequences, she is more and more animated by a sense of second innocence or complex simplicity or second naiveté. More and more she feels her life being taken over not by a primitive wonder, the wonder of a child, but by a subsequent or consequent wonder more and more open to the mystery and gift of being as manifest in daily life. For her wonder can no longer be confined to the study, but insists on spilling over into daily life. At this point the philosopher as professional becomes the philosopher as intellectual, excited by and nourished by the wonder of ordinary life.

I confess in this formulation to being influenced by an older, more traditional book, *The Intellectual Life*, by A.G. Sertillanges, O.P. I was introduced to it many years ago when I was just getting started as a philosopher and intellectual, and return to it regularly for insight and inspiration. And I do this even though Sertillanges is not my kind of Thomist. He is pre-transcendental, conservative, and more one-sidedly contemplative in that he has not linked theory to practice in the way that both Lonergan and I have tried to do. Also, his definition of "intellectual" includes both the thinker as specialist and as engaged in daily life. While I do not reject that definition, the notion of "intellectual" that I am defending here is that of the intellectual as non-specialist, as open to and excited by daily life.[13]

Thus, the philosopher leaving his study and taking his walk sees "his walks as voyages of discovery."[14] He is not leaving his desire to know the truth behind, but broadening it to include everyone and everything and every event he encounters. No person is too insignificant, no place too boring, and no event too banal to evoke wonder. I have had great conversations with salespersons in my neighborhood deli and convenience store; I look forward to meeting again my friends in Mister Donut when I go there to replenish my supply. A waitress working in a restaurant on 57th Street in Manhattan, struggling in her own way to lead an authentic, moral life, has been to me the source of stunning insights about how to do that; a male waiter/manager in the same place has become a model to me of combining strength with restrained gentleness in dealing with unruly customers.

Sertillanges can be remarkably eloquent on this issue:

> So acquire the habit of being present at this activity of the natural and moral universe. Learn to look; compare what is before you with your familiar or secret ideas. Do not see in a town merely houses, but human life and history. Let a gallery or museum show you something more than a collection of objects, let it show you schools of art and of life, conceptions of destiny and of nature, successive or varied tendencies of technique, of inspiration, of feeling. Let a workshop speak to you not only of iron and wood, but of man's estate, of work, of ancient and modern social economy, of class relationships ... If you cannot look thus, you will become, or be, a man of only commonplace mind. A thinker is like a filter, in which truths as they pass through leave their best substance.[15]

Learn to listen, Sertillanges urges us, to everyone. The whole of the human is in everyone, and we can receive a deep-reaching initiation from him. The greatest novelist is found on doorsteps or in the streets, the least in the Sorbonne or the New York Public Library. The thinker is truly a thinker only if he finds in the least external stimulus the occasion of a limitless interior urge. "It is his character to keep all his life the curiosity of childhood, to retain its vivacity of impression, its tendency to see everything under an aspect of mystery, its happy faculty of everywhere finding wonderment full of consequences."[16]

The thinker should be perpetually ready to see, to hear, "to shoot the bird as it flies, like a good sportsman."[17] We should carry our problems about with us. "The hackney horse does his run and goes back to his stall; the free courser always has his nostrils to the wind."[18] We cultivate an attitude of open, wondering, reverent receptivity, because of which we see as enlightening what others find only banal, problematic what others take to be obvious, stimulating what others find to be only boring. "Everyone looks at what I am looking at," says Lamennais, as quoted by Sertillanges, "but nobody sees what I see."[19]

For those who have undergone religious conversion, who have fallen in love with God, there is an additional motivation. For one genuinely in love in God is constantly striving to live in the presence of God, thirsting for God, treading the highways and byways for signs of his presence. Similarly, Sertillanges asks, should not the Christian who is an intellectual live in the presence of truth? For the self-appropriated philosopher, why cannot the presence of God for him take the form of intelligibility or truth? If we are Christians all the time, why cannot we be philosophers or intellectuals all the time? "Truth is, as it were, the special divinity of the thinker."[20] Have we approached here, in this sense of philosopher as contemplative in action, the Ignatian vision of that?

From Intellectual Conversion to Aesthetic Conversion

To some extent, the discussion is rooted here in the distinction of *Insight* between the intellectual and aesthetic patterns of experience. In the intellectual pattern of experience, operative in formal logic, the sciences, philosophy, and theology, we are oriented to knowledge for its own sake and animated by criteria of evidence, rigor, and logicality. In the aesthetic pattern of experience, we are enriched by experience for its own sake, lifted up and liberated from the pragmatic orientation of common sense – only the useful is true – as well as from the serious striving of intellectual inquiry or moral life. Aesthetic experience is "useless," a value in itself and for its own sake, and as such challenges the "seriousness" of philosophy, morality, and religious faith.[21]

Let us imagine somebody who has gone through or is on the way to intellectual, moral, and religious conversion? Why, such a person might be asked, when we consider the state of the world, bother with aesthetic experience? Do not the hungry have to be fed, the naked clothed, and the homeless housed? Do not men and women throughout the world have need of intellectual, moral, and religious truth? Why waste time lingering before a Picasso, a Matisse, or a Kandinsky? What good does that do anybody? Thus, the troubled philosopher may end up in an art museum, perhaps the Museum of Modern Art.

There is a good Lonerganian answer to such a question. It is the very uselessness of art as an end in itself that constitutes its value. Aesthetic experience, Lonergan says, promises a twofold liberation, from rigid biological or common sense purposiveness in which my nose is always focused on the grindstone, and from the seriousness of intellectual inquiry ordered to truth, evidence, and systematicity. The playfulness of art reveals to me my freedom as a subject. Art opens us up to an elemental wonder that is prior to systematic inquiry, and this openness to the non-functional on that elemental level prepares us to accept philosophy in its uselessness and non-functionality. "Philosophy," Heidegger tells us, "is that thinking with which one can start nothing and about which housemaids necessarily laugh."[22]

When we reflect on the historically specific kind of society we are, the role of art is even more salient and important. For is it not the character of capitalistic society to take a capitalized common sense, in which financial profit is the goal of all economic striving, and extend that to the whole of society? And, rather than the useful being subordinated to the useless, to the intrinsically valuable, as would be the case in a truly sane, ethical society, do we not have a systematic ordering of the intrinsically valuable to the useful, the reign of money? And does art not legitimately challenge the absurd tyranny of the useful, in which means become ends and ends means (Beckett and the theatre of the absurd could only arise in a capitalistic society). When I view Matisse's *Red Studio*, I become aware of dimensions in myself and the world that cannot be easily, legitimately subordinated to the reign of money. "Wasting time," tarrying before the work of art, becomes a form of liberation from such tyranny.

Lonergan reminds us that the presence of intelligence is not just formal, the ordering of lines or sounds or color by the artist in a pleasing, challenging aesthetic form, which is also worth contemplating in itself; but also content that can be symbolized. And as Adorno tells us, part of that content is social. Art is both in-itself and for-others, produced by and for others and, as such, in an alienated, totally or mostly administered society, can testify to these aspects. Thus, the dissonance of Bartok or the dark, twelve-tone harmony of Schoenberg, Webern, and Berg can alert us to the dissonant, unhappy, and unjust suffering of millions in capitalist society. Such works give the Lonerganian inquirer other images and possible insights that he might not otherwise have. Maybe he has too easily learned to live with late capitalism and love it. The power of Arthur Miller's *Death of a Salesman* can alert us to the possible nightmare hidden behind the American Dream, the unhappiness lurking underneath the superficial happiness promoted by Madison Avenue, and the ugliness behind the pleasing, commodified images of Hollywood. Great art makes trouble for an unjust, alienated society in different ways, either by calling it into question through images of dissonance or suffering, or by introducing us to the value of the intrinsically valuable, the useless, in such a way that we see the truth of the paradox that the most valuable elements in human life are useless.[23]

Moreover, as good Lonerganians we know that objectivity is the fruit of authentic subjectivity and that objectivity lies in self-transcendence. Good art, really good, challenging art, not the junk on most American television, invites us into its own kind of self-transcendence and objectivity. For to properly respond to a work like Picasso's *Guernica* or Stravinsky's *Rite of Spring*, I have to give myself to it for its own sake and be receptive to it on its own terms in a kind of disposability or hospitality. The question not to ask, according to Adorno, is "What do I get out of it?" but "what do I give to it?" Asking what I can get out of it, like the typical bourgeois consumer of art, is to misuse the work of art, to turn it into another utilitarian object. That which, by its purpose and structure, transcends utility, is turned into a utilitarian object.[24] "Insofar as a function is to be ascribed to artworks," Adorno says, "it is their functionlessness."[25] And again," "Artworks are the plenipotentiaries of things beyond the motivating sway of exchange, profit, and the false needs of a degraded humanity."[26]

From the Ivory Tower to the Streets

Up to this point, in the last two sections, I have been stressing the role of contemplation in daily life and aesthetics. But thought and freedom are also practical, critical, and transformative, and indeed Lonergan himself helps to overcome any false conflict or dichotomy between contemplation and action. In *Method in Theology*, he argues that freedom as a fourth moment sublates cognition, and that the priority of intellect is just the priority of the first three levels of experience, understanding, and judgment. It also follows that speculative intellect or pure reason is just an abstraction. Scientific and philosophical understanding do not occur in a vacuum, but are the operations of an existential subject who has decided to devote himself to the pursuit of understanding and truth. This would be true also of the contemplative lover of beauty in nature and art, as well as of the intellectual pursuing truth in ordinary life. And, then, of course, there is the famous sentence from *Method*. "A life of pure intellect or pure reason without the control of deliberation, evaluation, responsible choice is less than the life of a psychopath."[27]

Consequently, and I take myself to be agreeing with Lonergan here, self-appropriation and transcendental method that follows upon it is contemplation because I am committing myself to philosophical knowledge for its own sake, and a kind of praxis, indeed the most basic praxis, because I choose myself as an experiencing, understanding, judging, and choosing subject. Other kinds of praxis, such as ethical or political action in the world, although they precede self-appropriation psychologically and historically, are derivative from it as founding and giving clarity and direction to these activities. And such activities, although based on knowledge, are dominantly practical and transformative. I aim to change the world and not simply to know it.[28]

Let us imagine, then, the self-appropriated philosopher not simply going for a walk, but going for a walk to an anti-war demonstration. And let us imagine that that demonstration is organized to protest a war in the Middle East carried out by our government for reasons that are manifestly false. There is no demonstrated presence of weapons of mass destruction, there is no link of Saddam Hussein to al Qaeda or bin Laden, and there is no serious commitment to democracy. What kind of sense does it make to spend hundreds of billions of dollars and lay waste a country and lose, so far, over a thousand of our men and women, with thousands more wounded, and hundreds of thousands of murdered Iraqis, to impose a democracy that we directly or indirectly deny to dozens of countries throughout the world and even in the Middle East, nations such as Turkey or Saudi Arabia or the Palestinian people. Something else has to be going on here, functioning as the real reasons for intervention, such as, possibly, gaining more adequate control of oil, securing water resources for Israel, and establishing a stronger, more permanent US military and political presence in the region.

Let us imagine the Lonerganian activist operating on grounds of consistency between knowing and doing. She is offended intellectually by the lies, morally by the sheer injustice of the war, not even coming close to the criteria of just-war theory (violation of the last-resort criterion is the most obvious), religiously by the tendency of the American empire to function as a fetish, a God substitute, and by Bush's fundamentalist use of religion in the service of empire. The Lonerganian activist, in other words, is confronted by the contradiction between her own self-appropriation and its intellectual, moral, and religious implications – and the war. And the reasons for her opposition do not necessarily have to be radical, opposition to capitalism and imperialism in principle, although I think radicalism is the most adequate moral and political response and interpretation. She can oppose the war for conservative reasons, because it violates the UN Charter and US Constitution; and she can oppose it for liberal reasons because it is unjust.

The experience of the Lonerganian activist in this kind of illegal, unjust, and imperial context is one of legitimate offense. She experiences the necessity to speak out, act out, resist, protest, or, be a little more blunt, raise hell. There is or could be a kind of "not being able to look at myself in the mirror" unless she engages in this kind of direct action. The necessarily prophetic nature of philosophy in bad times is striking here, and something I have been acutely aware of as I have been travelling around the country speaking out and acting out against this war and the occupation, as well as the war on terror begun in 2001, equally or more problematic in my opinion. And such speaking and acting out do not have to take the form of direct action, but can be carried out by philosophers and other intellectuals in a forum of public intellectuals, named by Lonergan "cosmopolis" in *Insight*. "Cosmopolis" seems to be nothing more than Lonergan's heuristic projection of the way a self-appropriated community of philosophers, scientists, theologians, and artists could carry out a practical-theoretical discourse about policies and actions that can help or harm our nation and the world.[29]

What I am trying to suggest here is the necessity to combine a professional commitment to philosophy with the role of a public intellectual and activist, *as essential to my vocation as philosopher*. And, unlike Sertillanges, the Lonerganian intellectual in the world is practical and critical as well as wondering and contemplative. Staying in the ivory tower is not enough, in bad and increasingly worse times such as our own, but maybe in all times.

Such a conviction was brought home to me and reinforced in the wake of the events of 9/11, when I was engaged in my usual teaching duties at Fordham. I discussed the event in all three of my classes, inviting students to reflect with me on the following kinds of questions. If we grant that the attack on the World Trade Center was unjustified morally, indefensible in the light of any moral or political theory that would be worth defending, do we not need to think about the imperial context created by our own national and international policies that could make people angry enough to strike out against us. This context includes the first Iraq War in 1990–91, equally as destructive and unjustified in my opinion as the recent war; the sanctions against Iraq leading to the deaths of hundreds of thousands of children, several thousand a month; US bases in Saudi Arabia enraging millions in the Middle East, and US support of Israel in its dispossession and persecution of the Palestinians, denying them rights of nationhood proclaimed by many UN resolutions.

Now, what really surprised me was that after the last class that I taught that week, a graduate class, several students came up to me and thanked me for discussing the event and informed me that no other professor had even mentioned it in class. How could one be silent, I asked myself, about an event that was at least as important in the lives of these students as the Kennedy or King assassinations were in mine. What would it take to motivate my esteemed colleagues to depart from academic business as usual? An earthquake? A nuclear attack that directly hit Fordham? A student riot? In any event, I concluded by noting that probably operative here was a notion of academic professionalism that may have briefly tempted me two or three seconds out of the womb, which I then rejected as inadequate. There had to be something less narrow, more progressive, more radical, a model of professionalism that could motivate me to speak out, demonstrate, resist, and even at times run the risk of arrest. "Why were you arrested?" "I read *Insight*."

Now, I am on record elsewhere in this book as arguing for radical political conversion as flowing from intellectual, moral, and religious conversion. I have not been able to do more than allude to that here and indicate some of its motivation, but I offer it as a possible complement to Doran's psychic conversion and a possible addition to the Lonerganian pantheon of conversions. And, to conclude this section, it does seem to me that there is a fruitful, complementary relationship between the two conversions helping to constitute a legitimate Lonerganian "materialism." Freud and Marx are appropriated by both me and Doran here, but sublated non-reductionistically. One way that such complementarity can operate is that awareness of my own psychic victimization can allow me to be open to and compassionate with and in solidarity with the victims of capitalism, militarism, imperialism, racism, sexism, and heterosexism. Here I have affirmed a preferential option for the poor that can be reached philosophically and that must be affirmed if philosophy is to be fully consistent with itself. And it is also true that, as I become aware of the suffering, marginalized other, I become aware of my own fragile, suffering, vulnerable psyche. There is an internal link, I think, between self-appropriation and alterity, whether that be the poor, oppressed other or the other in myself, my own body and psyche.[30]

From Existenz to Aggiornamento

One of my favorite occasional essays by Lonergan is that published in *Collection*, "Existenz and Aggiornamento." Here Lonergan develops a distinction between substance and subject, between the being proper to a thing and the being proper to the subject, being conscious, intelligent, reasonable, critical, and responsible. One can as a human being and Christian live like or approximate living like a substance. I am obedient, I believe in Christ through an opaque faith, I know true propositions, meditate on them, make resolutions about them, and decide to commit my life to being a lay Christian or Jesuit. Insofar as this being in Jesus Christ is that of a substance, it is a being in love without awareness of being in love. The delicacy, the gentleness, the deftness, the continual operation of God's grace in us misses us.[31]

But insofar as being in Christ Jesus is the being of a subject, the hand of the Lord ceases to be wholly hidden. In ways that many have experienced, the substance in Christ Jesus becomes the subject in Christ Jesus. The love of God, being in love with God, can be as full and as dominant, as overwhelming and as lasting an experience as human love. And being a subject in Christ Jesus rests upon a willingness and ability of the subject to take herself in hand, deliberate, and decide what she is going to make of herself. This making of oneself is open-eyed and deliberate and is opposed to all drifting, going along to get along.[32]

I take it that Lonergan here is reflecting on religious belief and commitment and conversion and their links to self-appropriation. Self-appropriation, we might say, is the first most fundamental form of contemplative praxis, which then paves the way and leads up to the highest form, falling in love with God in the cloud of unknowing. Such contemplation is a faith, the faith that is the knowledge born of religious love. The peak to which self-appropriation leads is a falling in love with God, an appropriation by God as the supreme other. Once again we see the link between self-appropriation and alterity.[33]

Flowing from religious, contemplative love is my involvement in the church and the world, which Lonergan also considers in this essay. There is a way of being Christian and being human that is appropriate to the anguish and achievements of modernity, and there is a way of being Christian that is not appropriate or that is less appropriate, being a subject as substance. The latter is not unacceptable or totally outside the pale or humanity and church, but is less responsive and less comprehensive than the former. "There is the possibility of despoiling the Egyptians," Lonergan says, meaning by "Egyptians" secular modernity, "but that possibility will not be realized unless Catholics, religious, priests exist, and exist not as drifters but creatively and authentically."[34]

In Christian being as substance, we keep our noses to the grindstone, obey the laws of society and church, attend conscientiously to our immediate families and neighborhoods, and do not rock the boat. In Christian being as subject, we reach out to that world in all its complexity, anguish, and richness, learn from that world, and in turn bring something to that world, criticize it, and transform it. To engage in that work most fruitfully, we cannot be content just to remain on the level of immediate, intersubjective encounter, whether it is the kind discussed by Marcel and Buber earlier in the century or by Levinas and Derrida later. Authentic living includes authentic knowing, and far more eagerly do human beings strive for the whole than for the part.

> Nonetheless it remains that the authentic living of anyone reading this paper, though it must start at home, cannot remain confined within the horizons of the home, the workshop, the village. We are citizens of our countries, men of the twentieth century, members of a universal church. If any authenticity we achieve is to radiate out into our troubled world, we need much more objective knowing than men commonly feel ready to absorb.[35]

This quotation, of course, is from another essay in *Collection*, "Cognitional Structure," but links up to "Existenz and Aggiornamento" in interesting ways. The Christian who has fallen in love with God and who has decided to exist as subject, must, to be more effective, use and appropriate objective knowing based on and flowing from self-appropriation. Self-appropriation and the objective knowing to which it leads are not only the basis and starting point that lead to falling in love with God, but also flow from it and are used by it, in a sense, to intervene in a troubled world. Self-appropriation and objective knowing are the basis of and consequence of the knowledge born of religious love.

Not only does Lonergan reflect on the role of the authentic Christian in the world but he also invites us to reflect on the kind of Church that is required. There is a Church, he suggests, that is favorable to the flowering of the subject as subject, the Church of John XXIII and Paul VI and Vatican II; and there is a Church that is not so favorable, that is still more classicist than historical. Inspired by Lonergan, I am also inclined to suggest there is a Church that wishes, if not to repeal Vatican II, at least to put the dampers on it. Inspired by Lonergan, I am inclined to suggest there is a Church that favors the emergence of freedom, and there is a Church that distrusts freedom and hearkens back to outdated notions of authority. There is a Church that plunges headlong prudently and courageously into the adventure of modernity, and there is a Church that tries to retreat from it, burying its head in the sand, moving back into the thirteenth, the greatest of the centuries, and losing its nerve before modernity.

What Lonergan says here inspires me to think creatively and prophetically about our Church as it has existed the last few decades under the reigns of John Paul II and Benedict and promises to exist now under Francis. Does this Church favor the emergence of the Christian as subject or the Christian as substance? In any event, Lonergan leaves us in no doubt as to where he stands. The so-called sin of modernity, he says, is not a sin of frailty, a transient lapse, any lack of advertence or consent. "It is the full deliberate and permanently intended determination to be oneself, to attain the perfection proper to man, and to liberate humanity from the heavy hand of ecclesiastical tradition, ecclesiastical interference, ecclesiastical refusal to allow human beings to grow and be themselves."[36]

Conclusion

As a way of synthesizing and summarizing my reflections here, we might reflect on the various interrelationships uncovered by doing a brief phenomenology of self-appropriation in its relationships to ordinary life and aspects of ordinary life. First of all, we note a reciprocal relationship between self-appropriation and ordinary life in general. Because of self-appropriation and the differentiated consciousness that accompanies it, I am able to negotiate more easily and more competently the various patterns of experience and the transitions between and among them. If there is a practical benefit of philosophy, even when it is pursued disinterestedly, this is certainly it or an aspect on it.

And we are reminded here of Lonergan's claim in the Preface to *Insight* that "insight into insight and oversight is the very key to practicality."[37]

Not only does self-appropriation contribute to clarifying and enhancing practical life, but practical life realizes self-appropriation, makes it effective, makes it fully real. The individual philosophical self, for example, that knows and chooses itself in self-appropriation expresses itself in an aesthetically and practically effective lifestyle.

We can note, second, a relationship between self-appropriation and each of the sub-aspects of human life that I have laid out. When the philosopher goes for a walk, for example, he brings to that walk a desire to know already fully conscious of itself and ready, therefore, to "shoot on the fly" insights that he brings back to the study in a way that enriches and deepens philosophical work. The sublime, revelatory power of a work of art can supply me with images and possible insights that enrich my theoretical work, and that theoretical work allows me to bring to the work of art greater depth, openness, and curiosity. Self-appropriation occurs in such a way that insisting on the conformity of doing to knowing leads me to expect and demand that of social, economic, and political institutions, to praise them when they live up to that demand, and to criticize them when they do not. The experience of protesting an unjust war can reinforce in me a sense of the relevance of critical thinking to concrete political practice. I have always thought that going to a demonstration and seeing signs like "No blood for oil" or "No justice, no peace" or "Why die for Exxon?" enables one to experience on a concrete, lived, pragmatic level truths that are worked up more laboriously and abstractly in the classroom or study. Finally, self-appropriation enables me to see more clearly and rigorously how religious commitment is essential to the full realization of personhood, and how that commitment itself anchors and motivates self-appropriation. I return to my study as a Christian in love with God, animated by the conviction that philosophy is my God-given vocation and that I am doing the work of God in the world.

Finally, we can note the relationship between and among the sub-aspects of ordinary life and between them and practical life in general. The sub-aspects belong to that totality of daily life as parts to a whole. The intellectual relates to the aesthetic as a domain of human life that can stimulate reflection, and the aesthetic as a form of wonder is nourished by the conscious, articulate wonder of the intellectual and clarified by analytic and synthetic understanding and critical judgment. Taste is consciously formed, I think, not just by experiencing works of art, but also by the reciprocal relationship between such experience and reflection. Art can inspire social, political insights that can enable me to be less narrow and ideological, and in turn a powerfully expressed, aesthetically appropriate symbol can inspire ethical, political action and resistance; think of Selma or Cantonsville or the Plowshares actions. Finally, religious experience can be enhanced and deepened by art – consider the sublimity of Notre Dame and Chartres – and religious belief is a source of content for works of art, even modern works of art. The poetry of Gerard Manley Hopkins or T.S. Eliot or Denise Levertov or Daniel Berrigan comes to mind.

I conclude with a fuller quotation from Sertillanges on the intellectual going for a walk.

> Thus the wise man, at all times and on every road, carries a mind ripe for acquisitions that ordinary folk neglect. The humblest occupation is for him a continuation of the loftiest; his formal calls are fortunate chances of investigation; his walks are voyages of discovery, what he hears and his silent answers are a dialogue that truth carries on with herself within him. Wherever he is, his inner universe is comparing itself with the other, his life with Life, his work with the incessant work of all beings; and as he comes from the narrow space in which his concentrated study is done, one gets the impression, not that he is leaving the true behind, but that he is throwing his door wide open so that the world may bring to him all the truth given out in its mighty activities.[38]

Notes

Preface

1 Bernard Lonergan, *Understanding and Being*, vol. 5 of the Collected Works of Bernard Lonergan, ed. Elizabeth Morelli and Mark Morelli (Toronto: University of Toronto Press, 1990), 34–35.
2 James L. Marsh, *Post-Cartesian Meditations* (New York: Fordham University Press, 1988); *Critique, Action, and Liberation* (Albany: SUNY Press, 1995); *Process, Praxis and Transcendence* (Albany: SUNY Press, 1998).
3 Marsh, *Post-Cartesian Meditations*, 45–124.

1. Self-Appropriation: Lonergan's Pearl of Great Price

1 Bernard Lonergan, *Insight: A Study of Human Understanding*, vol. 3 of the Collected Works of Bernard Lonergan, ed. Frederick Crowe and Robert Doran (Toronto: University of Toronto Press, 1992), 12. An earlier version of this chapter was published in *In Deference to the Other*, ed. Jim Kanaris and Mark Doorley (Albany: SUNY Press, 2004), 53–65.
2 Lonergan, *Insight*, 12.
3 Ibid., 12–13.
4 Ibid., 13.
5 Ibid.
6 Martin Heidegger, *Being and Time*, trans. John Macquarrie and Edward Robinson (New York: Harper and Row, 1962).
7 Lonergan, *Method in Theology* (Toronto: University of Toronto Press, 1990), 3–25; *Insight*, 497–504.
8 Lonergan, *Method*, 4.

9 Hans-Georg Gadamer, *Truth and Method*, trans. Garrett Barden and John Cumming (New York: Seabury Press, 1975). See also Lonergan, *Method*, 5–6.

10 See James L. Marsh, *Critique, Action, and Liberation* (Albany: State University of New York Press, 1995), 59–74, 219–34, for a fuller discussion and critique of postmodernism.

11 Lonergan, *Insight*, 25–56, 296–450.

12 For a fuller discussion of Husserl, see James L. Marsh, *Post-Cartesian Meditations*, 13–23, 210–12. See also Marsh, *Critique, Action, and Liberation*, 226–8.

13 Lonergan, *Insight*, 27–56, 296–340.

14 Lonergan, *Insight*, 93–125, 372–80; *Method*, 262–65. For a fuller discussion of Habermas on this issue, see Marsh, *Post-Cartesian Mediations*, 72. By "transcendental precepts," I mean the normative demands to be attentive, be intelligent, be reasonable, and be responsible, corresponding to experience, understanding, judgment, and decision. See *Method*, 20.

The canons of empirical method are the norms for conducting successful scientific inquiry and are rooted in and flow from cognitional structure. They are selection, motivating the scientist to be oriented to theories that have sensible consequences; operations, rules for acting upon objects; relevance, directing inquiry to seeking intelligibility immanent in sensible data; parsimony, excluding from scientific affirmation all statements not verifiable in sensible data; complete explanation, oriented to making sense of as much of the data as possible; and the canon of residues, oriented to making sense of data such as chance events that cannot be explained systematically. See *Insight*, 93–125.

The canons of hermeneutics, analogous to those of science, concern the interpretation of texts. They are the canon of relevance, oriented to making sense of texts; the canon of explanation, committed to making sense of as much of the text as possible; the canon of parsimony, excluding all statements that are not verifiable in the text; the canon of successive approximations, oriented to gradually achieving a more satisfactory understanding of texts; and the canon of residues, prescribing an openness to recognizing what is not systematic or clear or coherent in the text. See *Insight*, 608–17.

15 For a fuller discussion of Nietzsche on this issue, see Marsh, *Post-Cartesian Meditations*, 75–81.

16 Lonergan, *Insight*, 553–72. For a fuller discussion of Heidegger on this issue, see Marsh, *Process, Praxis, and Transcendence*, 10–19, 26.

17 Lonergan, *Method*, 101–107.

18 Lonergan, *Insight*, 412–13.
19 Ibid., 241. See Marsh, *Post-Cartesian Meditations*, 75–91; *Critique, Action, and Liberation*, 3–16, 43–45, 174–76; *Process, Praxis, and Transcendence*, 21–29. See also Lonergan, *The Lonergan Reader*, ed. Mark Morelli and Elizabeth Morelli (Toronto: University of Toronto Press, 1997), 569–71.
20 See Robert Doran, *Theology and the Dialectics of History* (Toronto: University of Toronto Press, 1990), 355–470; Matthew Lamb, *Solidarity with Victims: Toward a Theology of Social Transformation* (New York: Crossroad, 1982); Marsh, *Process, Praxis, and Transcendence*, 192–94, 230–46 and *Post-Cartesian Mediations*, 201–207.
21 See Jacques Derrida, *Specters of Marx*, trans. Peggy Kamuf (New York: Routledge, 1994), 569–71.
22 See Gilles Deleuze and Felix Guattari, *Anti-Oedipus: Capitalism and Schizophrenia*, trans. Robert Hurley, Mark Seem, and Helen R. Lane (Minneapolis: University of Minnesota Press, 1983), xiii.
23 See Doran, *Theology and the Dialectics of History*, 232–53.

2. Thought and Expression in Lonergan

1 Marsh, *Post-Cartesian Meditations*, 1–74.
2 Lonergan, *Insight*, 31–32.
3 Ibid., 32–33.
4 Ibid., 33–34.
5 Ibid., 34–35.
6 Ibid., pp. 306–307.
7 Ibid., 307.
8 Ibid.
9 Ibid., 307–308.
10 Ibid., 576–77.
11 Ibid.
12 Ibid., 577–78.
13 Lonergan is more explicit on the distinction between inner and outer word in his book on Aquinas, *Verbum: Word and Idea in Aquinas*, ed. David B. Burrell (Notre Dame: Notre Dame University Press, 1967), 1–11.
14 Lonergan, *Method*, 253–55.
15 Ibid., 255.
16 Ibid.
17 Ibid., 255–56.
18 Ibid., 256–57.

19 Ibid.
20 Ibid., 86.
21 Marsh, *Post-Cartesian Meditations*, 45–74.
22 Ibid., 45–74, 99–106.

3. Continental Hermeneutics: A Lonerganian Response

1 Ivo Coelho, *Hermeneutics and Method: The "Universal" Viewpoint in Bernard Lonergan* (Toronto: University of Toronto Press, 2001).
2 Lonergan, *Insight*, 587.
3 Ibid., 588–89.
4 Ibid., 589.
5 Ibid., 589–90; Lonergan, *Method*, 81–96.
6 Lonergan, *Insight*, 590.
7 Ibid., 591.
8 Ibid., 600–601.
9 Marsh, *Post-Cartesian Meditations*, 169.
10 Lonergan, *Insight*, 603–608.
11 Hans-Georg Gadamer, *Truth and Method*, trans. Garrett Barden and John Cumming (New York: Seabury Press, 1975), 162–73, quotation from 166–67.
12 Ibid., 235–40, 345–47.
13 Ibid., 91–119, 325–66.
14 Ibid., 235–73, 325–41.
15 Paul Ricoeur, *Interpretation Theory: Discourse and the Surplus of Meaning* (Fort Worth: Texas Christian University Press, 1976), 1–23.
16 Ibid., 8–44, 91–95, quotation from p.12.
17 Ibid., 1–8, 351–52. Gadamer, *Truth and Method*, 351–52.
18 Paul Ricoeur, *Hermeneutics and the Human Services*, ed. and trans. John Thompson (Cambridge: Cambridge University Press, 1981), 87–100, 229–46.
19 Gadamer, *Truth and Method*, 286–87, 327–28.
20 Ibid., 325–28.
21 Ricoeur, *Interpretation Theory*, 75–80.
22 Lonergan, *Insight*, 95–96, 268. *Method*, 3–25.
23 Martin Heidegger, *The Question concerning Technology and Other Essays*, trans. William Lovitt (New York: Harper Torchbooks, 1977), 12–23.
24 Gadamer, *Truth and Method*, 335. Ricoeur, *Interpretation Theory*, 92–93.
25 Lonergan, *Insight*, 28–37. Gadamer, *Truth and Method*, 325–28.
26 Lonergan, *Insight*, 769–70.

27 Bernard Lonergan, *The Lonergan Reader*, ed. Mark D. Morelli and Elizabeth Morelli (Toronto: University of Toronto Press, 1997), 579.
28 Lonergan, *Insight*, 502.

4. Self-Appropriation and Alterity

1 Lonergan, *Insight*, 372–74.
2 Lonergan, *Method*, 104, 205.
3 Lonergan, *Insight*, 410–15, 553–54.
4 Emmanuel Levinas, *Totality and Infinity*, trans. Alphonso Lingis (Pittsburgh: Duquesne University Press, 1969), 39, 46, 49, 52, 53, 87, 89–90, 124–27, 194, 199, 204, 215–16, 290, 291).
5 Lonergan, *Insight*, 12–14.
6 Ibid., 372–76.
7 Ibid., 399–409.
8 Levinas, *Totality and Infinity*, 46, 194; Marsh, *Post-Cartesian Meditations*, 81–85, 125–28.
9 Marsh, *Post-Cartesian Mediations*, 45–53.
10 Ibid., 128.
11 Ibid.
12 Ibid., 128–29.
13 Ibid., 129–30.
14 Ibid., 130–31.
15 Ibid., 143–57.
16 Ibid., 146.
17 Ibid.
18 Ibid., 147–48.
19 Lonergan, *Insight*, 622–24.
20 Marsh, *Critique, Action, and Liberation*, 132–33.
21 Ibid., 172–76, 265–89; Marsh, *Process, Praxis, and Transcendence*, 210–29, 264–97.
22 Marsh, *Critique, Action, and Liberation*, 174–75.
23 Marsh, *Process, Praxis, and Transcendence*, 31.

5. The Unity of the Right and the Good in Lonergan's Ethics

1 See my chapters 7, 8, and 9, *Critique, Action, and Liberation*, 113–76.
2 Lonergan, *Insight*, 618.
3 Ibid., 619–21.
4 Ibid., 621–22.

5 Ibid., 622–23.
6 Ibid., 623.
7 Ibid., 623–24.
8 Ibid., 624.
9 Ibid., 624–25.
10 Ibid., 626. Lonergan's earliest, most simple example of heuristic structure is the unknown "X" present in a mathematical equation. See ibid., 60–62.
11 Ibid., 628–29.
12 Ibid., 629–30. An inverse insight is an insight that something is not intelligible, does not make sense. Classical method is scientific orientation to systematic intelligibilities such as the law of falling bodies or the theory of relativity. Statistical method directs the scientist to ascertaining the probability that events may occur non-systematically. Genetic method concerns itself with development; the theory of evolution is the best example. Dialectical method is reflection on the way contradictory, untrue claims may be understood and reversed. See ibid., 509–10, 766–67.
13 Ibid., 631–32.
14 Ibid., 631–33.
15 Ibid., 633–35, quotation from p. 635. See Paul Ricoeur, *Freedom and Nature: The Voluntary and the Involuntary*, trans. Erazim V. Kohak (Evanston: Northwestern University Press, 1966), 14–76, for an approach that complements Lonergan's. See also my "Ricoeur's Phenomenology of Freedom as an Answer to Sartre," in *Reading Ricoeur*, ed. David Kaplan (Albany: SUNY Press, 2008), 13–29.
16 Lonergan, *Insight*, 635.
17 Ibid., p. 636.
18 Ibid., 636–37.
19 Ibid.
20 Ibid., 641–42.
21 Ibid., 639–42, quotation from p. 642.
22 Bernard Lonergan, *A Third Collection*, ed. Frederick Crowe (New York: Paulist Press, 1985), 172–75.
23 Bernard Lonergan, *Collection*, vol. 4 of the Collected Works of Bernard Lonergan, ed. Frederick Crowe and Robert Doran (Toronto: University of Toronto Press, 1993), pp. 17–51.
24 I am indebted to the work of Professor Pat Brown at Seattle University for insights into the early philosophy of history.
25 See not only Lonergan's use of "liberation" in the subtitle of his third section of this chapter on ethics, which includes reflections on the social sphere, but also my *Process, Praxis, and Transcendence*, 264–97; Doran, *Theology and the Dialectics of History*, 418–70.

6. Rationality and Mystery in Lonergan

1 See my discussion of this issue in *Process, Praxis, and Transcendence*, 26, 76, 97–98.
2 Martin Heidegger, *The Question of Technology and Other Essays*, trans. William Lovitt (New York: Harper & Row, 1977).
3 Lonergan, *Insight*, 372–75.
4 Ibid., 555.
5 Ibid., 556–57, quotation from p. 556.
6 Ibid., 56–57.
7 Ibid., 499–500. See Eric Voegelin, *Order and History*, vol. 1, *Israel and Revelation* (Baton Rouge: Louisiana State University Press, 1956), 1–11; vol. 4, *The Ecumenic Age* (Baton Rouge: Louisiana State University Press, 1974), 1–58. William Desmond, *Being and the Between* (Albany: SUNY Press, 1995), 44–46. This notion of the "between" is somewhat implicit in Lonergan, more explicit in Voegelin, and very explicit in Desmond.
8 William Desmond, *Beyond Hegel and Dialectic: Speculation, Cult and Comedy* (Albany: SUNY Press, 1992), 51.
9 G.W.F. Hegel, *Phenomenology of Spirit*, trans. A.V. Miller (Oxford: Clarendon Press, 1977), 3–4; *Insight*, 446–47.
10 Lonergan, *Insight*, 448–54, quotation from p. 554.
11 Ibid., 263–67.
12 Ibid., 251–63.
13 Lonergan, *Method*, 104–105.
14 Ibid., 106.
15 Ibid., 30–31, 243, 115.
16 Marsh, *Process, Praxis, and Transcendence*, 26.
17 Bernard Lonergan, *A Second Collection*, ed. William Ryan, S.J.; and Bernard Tyrell, S.J. (Toronto: University of Toronto Press, 1974), 229.
18 See William Desmond, *Is There a Sabbath for Thought?* (New York: Fordham University Press, 2005).
19 See Bernard Lonergan, *Philosophical and Theological Papers 1965–1980*, vol. 14 of the Collected Works of Bernard Lonergan, ed. Robert C. Croken and Robert M. Doran (Toronto: University of Toronto Press, 2004), 390.
20 Robert M. Doran, *What Is Systematic Theology* (Toronto: University of Toronto Press, 2005), 182–96.
21 Bernard Lonergan, *The Triune God: Systematics*, trans. Michael G. Shields, vol. 12 of the Collected Works of Bernard Lonergan, ed. Robert Doran and H. Daniel Mansour (Toronto: University of Toronto Press, 2007), 1–20; *Method*, 320–22, 335–40, 344–47.
22 Desmond, *Being and the Between*, 8–13.

7. Postmodernism: A Lonerganian Retrieval and Critique

1 See, for example, Ronald McKinney, "Deconstructing Lonergan," *International Philosophical Quarterly* 31 (March 1991): 81–93, and my "Reply to McKinney on Lonergan: A Deconstruction," *International Philosophical Quarterly* 31 (March 1991): 95–104. An initial version of this chapter appeared in *Postmodernism and Christian Philosophy*, ed. Roman T. Ciapalo (Mishawaka, IN: American Maritain Association, 1997), 149–67.

2 For representative examples of the critique of Western *Ratio*, see Heidegger, *The Question concerning Technology and Other Essays*, 3–35; Michel Foucault, *Discipline and Punish* (New York: Vintage Brooks, 1979); Theodore Adorno and Max Horkheimer, *The Dialectic of Enlightenment*, trans. John Cumming (New York: Seabury Press, 1972); Jacques Derrida, *Of Grammatology*, trans. Gayatri Chakravorty Spivak (Baltimore: Johns Hopkins University Press, 1975–76), 3–93.

3 For examples of the equating of rationality and science and technology, see Heidegger, *The Question concerning Technology*, 3–35; and Adorno and Horkheimer, *The Dialectic of Enlightenment*, 4–14. For Derrida's critique of structuralism see *Of Grammatology*, 27–73. For their critiques of Husserl and Hegel, see Adorno, *Against Epistemology*, trans. Willis Domingo (Cambridge: Massachusetts Institute of Technology Press, 1982); *Negative Dialectics*, trans. E.B. Ashton (New York: Seabury Press, 1973), 300–60; *Drei Studien zu Hegel* (Frankfurt: Suhrkamp verlag, 1971); and Jacques Derrida, *Speech and Phenomena*, trans. D. Allison (Evanston: Northwestern University Press, 1973); and *Glas*, trans. John Leavey and Richard Ran (Lincoln: University of Nebraska Press, 1986).

4 Heidegger, *The Question concerning Technology*, 116–20; Adorno and Horkheimer, *The Dialectic of Enlightenment*, 4–14. For representative quotations, consider Heidegger: "Machine technology remains up to now the most visible outgrowth of the essence of modern technology, which is identical with the essence of modern metaphysics" (4); and Adorno and Horkheimer: "Knowledge, which is power, knows no obstacles: neither in the enslavement of men nor in compliance with the world's rules … Technology is the essence of this knowledge. It does not work by concepts and images, by the fortunate insight, but refers to the method, the exploitation of others' work, and capital" (4).

5 Adorno, *Negative Dialectics*, 3–57; Jacques Derrida, *Margins of Philosophy*, trans. Alan Bass (Chicago: University of Chicago Press, 1982), 329; Martin Heidegger, *What Is Called Thinking*, trans. Fred D. Wieck and J. Glenn Gray (New York: Harper & Row, 1968); Michel Foucault, *The Archeology of*

Knowledge and *The Discourse on Language*, trans. A.M. Sheridan Smith (New York: Harper & Row, 1972), 3–17.

6 Adorno and Horkheimer, *The Dialectic of Enlightenment*, 3–42; Derrida, *Of Grammatology*, 6–26; Martin Heidegger, *Discourse on Thinking*, trans. John Anderson and E. Hans Freund (New York: Harper & Row, 1966), 43–57.

7 Herbert Marcuse, *One-Dimensional Man* (Boston: Beacon Press, 1964), 1–120; Foucault, *Discipline and Punish*; Adorno and Horkheimer, *The Dialectic of Enlightenment*, 120–67; B.F. Skinner, *Beyond Freedom and Dignity* (New York: Vintage, 1971); Niklaus Luhmann, *The Differentiation of Society* (New York: Columbia Press, 1982)

8 See Jürgen Habermas, *The Philosophical Discourse of Modernity*, trans. Frederick Lawrence (Cambridge: Massachusetts Institute of Technology Press, 1987), 119, 136, 185–86, 277–86, 336–37, 294–95.

9 Lonergan, *Insight*, 343–46, 349–52, 352–57.

10 Ibid., 346–48.

11 Ibid.

12 Ibid.

13 Jürgen Habermas, *The Theory of Communicative Action II: Reason and the Rationalization of Society*, trans. Thomas McCarthy (Boston: Beacon Press, 1984), 387, 389–90.

14 Michel Foucault, *The Order of Things: An Archeology of the Human Sciences* (New York: Vintage Books, 1973), 386–87.

15 Lonergan, *Method*, 3–25.

16 Lonergan, *Insight*, 296–303.

17 Ibid., 204–12.

18 Ibid., 27–37, 242–63.

19 Lonergan, *Method*, 20, 104, 265, 291.

20 Heidegger, *The Question concerning Technology*, 35; Derrida, *Of Grammatology*, 27–73, 230–54.

21 Lonergan, *Insight*, 348–50, 530–49; *Method*, 104–107, 120–21.

22 Lonergan, *Method*, 85–99; *Insight*, 410–55.

23 Lonergan, *Insight*, 458–87, 484–511.

24 Ibid., 586–94; Derrida, *Of Grammatology*, xliii–1.

25 Lonergan, *Insight*, 386–88.

26 Martin Heidegger, *Introduction to Metaphysics*, trans. Ralph Manheim (Garden City, NY: Anchor Books, 1961), 79–172.

27 Lonergan, *Insight*, 408–11.

28 Ibid., 226–38.

29 See Doran, *Theology and the Dialectics of History*, esp. 355–470, for an insightful unfolding of the social-political implications of Lonergan's thought.

30 See my chapter 10 in this volume. For a further development of radical political conversion and its links to Lonergan's thought, see Lamb, *Solidarity with Victims.*
31 Lonergan, *Method*, 27–55, 165.
32 Michel Foucault, *Power/Knowledge*, ed. Colin Gordon, trans. C. Gordon, L. Marshall, J. Mepham, and K. Soper (New York: Pantheon Books, 1980), 78–133.
33 See Habermas's critique of Foucault's "crypto-normativism" in *The Philosophical Discourse of Modernity*, 279–86.
34 Lonergan, *Insight*, 204–12. Jürgen Habermas, *Knowledge and Human Interests*, trans. Jeremy Shapiro (Boston: Beacon Press, 1971), 301–17.
35 Habermas, *The Philosophical Discourse of Modernity*, 284.
36 Foucault, *Power/Knowledge*, 81–82; Lonergan, *Insight*, 232–69; Doran, *Theology and the Dialectics of History*, 387–417.
37 See the whole of *Discipline and Punish*, esp. 135–94, and my chapter 10.
38 Lonergan, *Insight*, 412–14; Michel Foucault, *A Foucault Reader*, ed. Paul Rabinow (New York: Pantheon Books, 1984), 76–97, 292–389. Lonergan correlates empiricism, idealism, and critical realism with the three regions of experience, understanding, and judgment respectively. Critical realism embraces all three levels in proper proportion and relation; see *Insight*, 426–55. Idealism and empiricism represent a one-sided emphasizing of either understanding or experience, and a tendency to reduce knowing to one of those levels.

When one considers transcendental method as a conscious experiencing, understanding, judging, and choosing of myself as an experiencing, understanding, judging, and choosing subject in relation to being, then a fourth possibility arises, a reduction of the levels of knowing to that of freedom, which is Foucault's tendency. Such a tendency is to be contrasted to an authentic sublating of cognition by the fourth level of freedom while maintaining cognition's distinctiveness and validity, which is Lonergan's option (see *Method*, 120–22). The difference may seem slight, but it is enormous.

For a critique of Derrida's idealism using Ricoeur's notion of discourse, see my "Ambiguity, Language, and Communicative Praxis," in *Modernity and Its Discontents*, eds. and co-authors, James L. Marsh, John Caputo, and Merold Westphal (New York: Fordham University Press, 1992), 105–106.

8. Self-Appropriation, Polymorphism, and Différance

1 James L. Marsh, *Unjust Legality: A Critique of Habermas's Philosophy of Law* (New York: Rowman & Littlefield, 2001). An initial version of this

chapter appeared in *Method: Journal of Lonergan Studies* 2, no. 1 (Spring 2011): 1–12.

2 As I wrote my trilogy, I realized that there is a somewhat close parallel between my three volumes and Lonergan's claim in *Insight* that in any philosophy we should distinguish between its cognitional theory and its pronouncements on metaphysical, ethical, and theological issues. Consequently, *Post-Cartesian Meditations* functions as my basis, and the last two volumes as the expansion of my philosophy. See *Insight*, 412–13.

3 I dealt with these issues twenty years ago in a book co-authored with John Caputo and Merold Westphal, *Modernity and Its Discontents.*

4 William Shakespeare, *Julius Caesar*, act 3, scene 2: "I come to bury Caesar, not to praise him."

5 Gerard Walmsley, *Lonergan and Philosophical Pluralism: The Polymorphism of Consciousness as the Key to Philosophy* (Toronto: University of Toronto Press, 2008), 47–52. Mentioned the most by Walmsley among the many commentators on Lonergan is Mark Morelli, who is thus the hero of this discussion. See, among other citations, pp. 6, 9, 11, and 252–53.

6 Lonergan, *Insight*, 452.

7 Ibid., 410.

8 Ibid., 410–11.

9 *Hamlet*, act 1, scene 5.

10 Walmsley, *Lonergan and Philosophical Pluralism*, 51.

11 Ibid.,138–69; *Insight*, 293, 410–11. Walmsley mentions Elizabeth Murray as one who develops the notion of a moral pattern of experience; see pp. 160–68.

12 Bernard Lonergan, *Understanding and Being*, ed. Elizabeth Morelli and Mark Morelli, vol. 5 of the Collected Works of Bernard Lonergan, revised and augmented by Frederick Crowe with the collaboration of Elizabeth Morelli, Mark Morelli, Robert Doran, and Thomas Daly (Toronto: University of Toronto Press, 1997), 309.

13 Lonergan, *Insight*, 412.

14 Jacques Derrida, *Margins of Philosophy*, trans. Alan Bass (Chicago: University of Chicago Press, 1982), 7–8. I am indebted to my friend and colleague Marty De Nys for some of the content and form of the following discussion.

15 Lonergan, *Insight*, 274–79.

16 Rodolphe Gasché, *The Tain of the Mirror: Derrida and the Philosophy of Reflection* (Cambridge: Harvard University Press, 1986), 6–7; John Caputo, *The Prayers and Tears of Jacques Derrida: Religion without Religion* (Bloomington: University of Indiana Press, 1997), 12–13.

17 Jacques Derrida, *Positions*, trans. Alan Bass (Chicago: University of Chicago Press, 1981), 27–29; *Specters of Marx*, trans. Peggy Kamuf (New York: Routledge & Kegan Paul, 1994), 59.
18 Marsh, *Post-Cartesian Mediations*, 118; Ricoeur, *Interpretation Theory*; Lonergan, *Insight*, 316–24; Lonergan, *Method*, 86.
19 Marsh, *Process, Praxis, and Transcendence*, 16–17; *Post-Cartesian Mediations*, 169. Lonergan, *Insight*, 437–41.
20 Richard Rorty, *Philosophy as the Mirror of Nature* (Princeton: Princeton University Press, 1979), 12–13.
21 Gilles Deleuze and Felix Guattari, *A Thousand Plateaus*, trans. Brian Massumi (Minneapolis: University of Minnesota Press, 1987), 232–309.
22 Lonergan, *Method*, 302–305.
23 Foucault, *Discipline and Punish*, 228.
24 Derrida, *Specters of Marx*, 85.

9. Lonergan and Marx on Economics and Social Theory: Some Preliminary Reflections

1 From a poster of Dorothy Day at a United Farm Workers picket line.
2 Bernard Lonergan, "Sacralizing and Secularization," in *Philosophical and Theological Papers, 1965–1980*, vol. 17 of the Collected Works of Lonergan, ed. Robert Doran and Robert Croken (Toronto: University of Toronto Press, 2004), 280.
3 See my *Post-Cartesian Meditations, Critique, Action, and Liberation*, and *Process, Praxis, and Transcendence*.
4 For example, one of the best refutations of Marx as Marxist-Leninist is Melvin Rader's *Marx's Interpretation of History* (New York: Oxford University Press, 1979). Rader argues that there are three models of history in Marx, base-superstructure, dialectical, and organic, in which there is reciprocal interaction among the parts of the social totality, economic, political, and socio-cultural. Even the base-superstructure model, for which a reductionistic reading is not implausible, does not have to be read that way, and is more plausibly read in a non-reductionistic way. "Bedingt" is sometimes taken to mean "determines'" but is most plausibly read as "conditions." The economy, therefore, conditions or motivates human beings to behave in a certain way. Freedom for Marx is not unlimited but situated. Human beings are free, but inherit a situation that they must struggle against. On freedom, Rader quotes Marx as saying, "Freedom is so much the essence of man that even its opponents implement it while combatting its reality; they want to appropriate for themselves as a most precious ornament

what they have rejected as an ornament of human nature. No one combats freedom; at most he combats the freedom of others" (223). Moreover, theory is not simply a passive result of economic forces, but itself can react back on those forces and influence them. Again, Marx as quoted by Rader: "Material force can only be overthrown by material force; but theory itself becomes a material force when it is seized by the masses. Theory is capable of seizing the masses … as soon as it becomes radical" (212). Marx wrote *Capital* to educate the working man as to his state and its causes. In a very real sense, *Capital* is a liberatory work aiming at the radical political conversion of the workers and other persuadable people.

5 See Antonio Gramsci, *Prison Notebooks*, ed. and trans. Quentin Hoare and Geoffrey Nowell Smith (New York: International Books, 1971); Karl Korsch, *Marxism and Philosophy*, trans. Fred Halliday (New York: Monthly Review Press); Jean-Paul Sartre, *Search for a Method*, trans. Hazel Barnes (New York: Vintage, 1963).

6 On the issue of democratic socialism and markets, see the last two chapters of my *Critique, Action, and Liberation*, 313–55. For other versions of market socialism within the Marxist tradition, see David Schweikert, *After Capitalism* (New York: Roman & Littlefield, 2002); Carol Gould, *Rethinking Democracy* (Cambridge: Cambridge University Press, 1988); and Tony Smith, *Globalisation: A Systematic Marxian Account* (Boston: Brill Academic Publishers, 2006), 296–344.

7 Karl Marx, *Capital*, vol. 2, trans. David Fernbach (New York: Penguin Books, 1978).

8 Bernard Lonergan, *For a New Political Economy*, vol. 21 of the Collected Works of Lonergan, ed. Phillip McShane (Toronto: University of Toronto Press, 1998), 231–44; Michael Shute, *Lonergan's Discovery of the Science of Economics* (Toronto: University of Toronto Press, 2010), 126–53.

9 Marsh, "Is Late Capitalism Rational?" in *Critique, Action, and Liberation*, 265–89.

10 David Harvey, *The Enigma of Capital and the Crises of Capitalism* (New York: Oxford University Press, 2010), 1–39.

11 Karl Marx, *The Economic and Philosophic Manuscripts of 1844 and the Communist Manifesto* (with Frederick Engels) (Amherst, NY: Prometheus Books, 1988), 81–82.

12 Ibid., 74–79.

13 James L. Marsh, "Justice, Difference, and the Possibility of Metaphysics," in *Philosophy at the Boundary of Reason: Proceedings of the American Catholic Philosophical Association*, vol. 76, ed. Michael Baur (Charlottesville, VA: Philosophy Documentation Center, 2003), 57–76. Marx also discusses the

extension and expansion of capital into other non-economic spheres. See *Manuscripts*, 115–40.

14 Harvey, *The Enigma of Capital*, 1–39.

15 Karl Marx, *Capital*, vol. 1, trans. Ben Fowkes (New York: Vintage Books, 1977), 125–30.

16 Marsh, *Critique, Action, and Liberation*, 27–45, 265–89.

17 Marx, *Capital*, 1: 258–80.

18 Ibid., 320–39.

19 Marsh, "Beyond the New World Order: A Critique of Neoimperialism," in *Process, Praxis and Transcendence*, 264–97.

20 Marx, *Capital*, 1: 240–44, 342, 353, 367; Chalmers Johnson, *Nemesis: The Last Days of the American Republic* (New York: Metropolitan Books, 2006), 5.

21 Johnson, *Nemesis*, 1–11.

22 Marx, *Manuscripts*, 115–40; Karl Marx, *Grundrisse*, trans. Martin Nicolaus (New York: Penguin Books, 1973), 163; Lonergan, *Method*, 31–32; Robert M. Doran, *What Is Systematic Theology?* (Toronto: University of Toronto Press, 2005), 170–79.

23 Fred Lawrence, "Money, Institutions, and the Human Good," *The Lonergan Review* 2, no. 1 (South Orange, NJ: Seton Hall University, 2010): 187–96.

24 Lonergan, *The Lonergan Reader*, 569–70.

25 Marx, *Capital*, 1: 280

10. Intellectual, Moral, and Religious Conversion as Radical Political Conversion

1 Marsh, *Process, Praxis, and Transcendence*, 192–94; Lonergan, *Insight*, 242–43, 258–59, 262–63, 648. An initial version of this chapter appeared in *Ultimate Reality and Meaning* 13, no. 3 (September 1990): 222–40.

2 Rader, *Marx's Interpretation of History*; Martin Jay, *Marxism and Totality: The Adventures of a Concept from Lukács to Habermas* (Berkeley: University of California Press: 1984).

3 George Lukács, *History and Class Consciousness*, trans. Rodney Livingstone (Cambridge, MA: MIT Press, 1971); Roslyn Wallach Bologh, *Dialectical Phenomenology: Marx's Method* (Boston: Routledge & Kegan Paul, 1979); Korsch, *Marxism and Philosophy*.

4 Shlomo Avineri, *The Social and Political Thought of Karl Marx* (London: Cambridge University Press), 75–76; Karl Marx, *Selected Writings*, ed. David McClellan (New York: Oxford University Press), 156–58, 164.

5 Lonergan, *Insight*, 27–31, 196–204, 232–44, 538–44; *Method*, 76–81, 120–22, 141–43.

6 Lonergan, *Insight*, 412.
7 Ibid., 262–63, 266; James L. Marsh, "Interiority and Revolution," *Philosophy Today* 29 (1985): 191–202.
8 Lamb, *Solidarity with Victims*; Johann Baptist Metz, *Faith in History and Society: Towards a Practical Fundamental Theology*, trans. David Smith (New York: Seabury Press, 1980); Doran, *What Is Systematic Theology*, 40–41, 199–201.
9 Lonergan, *Method*, 237–44.
10 Ibid., 20, 267–69.
11 Ibid., 243.
12 Ibid., 238.
13 Ibid.
14 Ibid., 238–39.
15 Ibid., 3–25, 83–85.
16 Ibid., 83–85; *Insight*, 298–300, 448–55.
17 Marx, *Grundrisse*, 459–524.
18 Marx, *Capital*, 1: 125–31.
19 Ibid., 165.
20 Stuart Ewen, *Captains of Consciousness* (New York: McGraw Hill, 1976); John Kenneth Galbraith, *The Affluent Society* (New York: Mentor Books, 1958), 114–23.
21 Marx, *Grundrisse*, 266–75, 281–89.
22 Ibid., 163; Lukács, *History of Class Consciousness*, 83–222; Marx Horkheimer, *Critique of Instrumental Reason*, trans. Matthew O'Connell et al. (New York: Seabury Press), vii–x.
23 T.S. Eliot, *The Waste Land and Other Poems* (New York: Harvest Books, 1962), 8; Jürgen Habermas, *Towards a Rational Society*, trans. Jeremy Shapiro (Boston: Beacon Press, 1970), 90–122.
24 Marx, *Grundrisse*, 228–37, 239–64; *Capital*, 1: 254.
25 Marx, *Capital*, 1: 429–38, 492–639.
26 Marcuse, *One-Dimensional Man*, 1–18. Habermas, *Towards a Rational Society*, 120–22.
27 Bernard Tyrrell, *Bernard Lonergan's Philosophy of God* (South Bend: University of Notre Dame Press, 1974), 39.
28 Guy Debord, *Society of the Spectacle* (Detroit: Black and Red, 1983), para. 12, 34.
29 Lonergan, *Insight*, 250–59; Heidegger, *Introduction to Metaphysics*, 40–41.
30 Lonergan, *Method*, 34–41, 241–42.
31 Lonergan, *Insight*, 618–28.
32 Ibid., 214–31, 244–57; *Method*, 240–42.
33 Lonergan, *Method*, 76–80.
34 Ibid., 79–81.

35 Horkheimer, *Critique of Instrumental Reason*, 188–243; Ernst Bloch, *Principle of Hope*, vol. 1, trans. Neville Plaice, Stephen Plaice, and Paul Knight (Cambridge: MIT Press, 1986), 1–18.

36 Marx, *Capital*, 280.

37 Marx, *Grundrisse*, 459–71.

38 United States Conference of Catholic Bishops, *Economic Justice for All: Pastoral Letter on Catholic School Teaching and the U.S. Economy* (Washington: U.S. Conference of Catholic Bishops, 1986), 15.

39 Ibid., 65–165; Marx, *The Economic and Philosophical Manuscripts*, 106–19; Harry Braverman, *Labor and Monopoly Capital: The Degradation of Work in the Twentieth Century* (New York: Monthly Review Press, 1974).

40 Jürgen Habermas, *Legitimation Crisis*, trans. Thomas McCarthy (Boston: Beacon Press, 1976), 111–14; U.S. Conference of Catholic Bishops, *Economic Justice for All*, 145–62.

41 William Domhoff, *Who Rules America* (Englewood Cliffs, NJ: Prentice Hall, 1967); Charles Lindblom, *Politics and Markets* (New York: Basic Books, 1977), 161–233; E.E. Schattschneider, *The Semisovereign People* (New York: Holt, Rinehart, and Winston, 1960). Habermas, *Towards a Rational Society*, 90–122.

42 Lindblom, *Politics and Markets*, 237–309; Andrew Arato, "Critical Sociology and Authoritarian State Socialism," in *Habermas: Critical Debates*, ed. John Thompson and David Held (Cambridge, MA: MIT Press), 196–218; John Stuart Mill, *Utilitarianism and Other Debates*, ed. Mary Warnock (New York: Meridian Books, 1970), 126–83.

43 Michael Walzer, *Spheres of Justice* (New York: Basic Books, 1983), 295–303.

44 Kai Nielsen, *Equality and Liberty: A Defense of Radical Egalitarianism* (Totowa, NJ: Roman & Allanheld, 1985), 46–61, 78–99.

45 Ibid., 76–99, 191–277.

46 Walter Lafeber, *Inevitable Revolutions: The United States in Central America* (New York: W.W. Norton, 1983); William Appleman Williams, *Empire as a Way of Life* (New York: Oxford University Press, 1980).

47 Lonergan, *Method*, 104–107, 240–42.

48 Ibid., 104–18, quotation from p. 105.

49 U.S. Conference of Catholic Bishops, *Economic Justice for All*, 28; Gustavo Gutierrez, *The Power of the Poor in History*, trans. Robert R. Barr (Maryknoll, NY: Orbis Books, 1984).

50 Marx, *Capital*, 1: 798.

51 Lonergan, *Method*, 101–109.

52 U.S. Conference of Catholic Bishops, *Economic Justice for All.*

53 Marsh, "Interiority and Revolution"; Lafeber, *Inevitable Revolutions*, 219–26.

11. Self-Appropriation, Contemplation, and Resistance

1 Noam Chomsky, *The Essential Chomsky*, ed. Anthony Arnove (New York: New Press, 2008), 39–62, 160–86).
2 Lonergan, *Insight*, 637–38.
3 Thomas Merton, *New Seeds of Contemplation* (New Directions: New York, 1961), 76–77.
4 Lonergan, *Collection*, 222–31.
5 Joan Chittister, *Called to Question: A Spiritual Memoir* (New York: Sheed & Ward, 2004), 129–30.
6 Daniel Berrigan, *Jeremiah: The World, The Wound of God* (Minneapolis: Fortress Press, 1999), 81–82.
7 Marcuse, *One-Dimensional Man*, 63.
8 Lonergan, *Method*, 3–25.
9 Ibid., 316–40.
10 Lonergan, *Insight*, 204–14; *Method*, 266.
11 Lonergan, *Method*, 31–33; Doran, *Theology and the Dialectics of History*, 1–11, 26–27, 29–30.
12 Marsh, *Critique, Action, and Liberation*, 149–76, 265–89; *Process, Praxis, and Transcendence*, 264–320.
13 Lonergan, *Method*, 105–109.
14 Ibid., 316–17, 340.
15 James L. Marsh, "Self Appropriation and Liberation: Philosophizing in the Light of Cantonsville," in *Social Justice, Its Theory and Practice: Proceedings of the American Catholic Philosophical Association*, vol. 79 (Charlottesville, VA: Philosophy Documentation Center, 2006): 1–18.
16 Marsh, *Process, Praxis and Transcendence*, 191–209.
17 Ibid.
18 Lonergan, *Method*, 55.

12. On Really Living

1 Henry James, *The Ambassadors* (New York: Signet Books, 1960), 134.
2 James L. Marsh, *Radical Fragments* (New York: Peter Lang, 1992), 96.
3 Leon Edel, *Henry James: A Life* (London: HarperCollins, 1996), 536.
4 Marsh, *Critique, Action, and Liberation*, 43–45.
5 Doran, *What Is Systematic Theology*, 109–43.
6 See the last essay in this volume. Jon Sobrino, *Jesus the Liberator: A Historical-Theological View* (Maryknoll, NY: Orbis Books, 2001), 25–35. On the scale of values, see Lonergan, *Method*, 31–32; and Doran, *What Is Systematic Theology*, 180–97.

7 Adrian van Kaam, *In Search of Spiritual Identity* (Denville, NJ: Dimension Books, 1975), 138–71; Frances Kelly Nemeck and Marie Theresa Coombs, *Called by God: A Theology of Vocation and Lifelong Commitment* (Collegeville, MN: The Liturgical Press, 1992).
8 Lonergan, *Insight*, 186.
9 George Eliot, *Middlemarch* (New York: Oxford University Press, 1996).
10 Patricia Albers, *Joan Mitchell, Lady Painter* (New York: Alfred A. Knopf, 2011). On patterns of experience, see Lonergan, *Insight*, 181–90.
11 Lonergan, *Insight*, xviii–xix.
12 Ibid., 477.
13 Lonergan, "Existenz and Aggiornamento," 222–31.
14 Daniel Berrigan, *To Dwell in Peace* (San Francisco: Harper & Row, 1987).
15 Lonergan, *Insight*, 186.
16 Daniel Berrigan, *The Nightmare of God* (Baltimore: Fortkamp, 1989), 3–4. Phil, in this quotation, refers to Phil Berrigan, Daniel's brother.

13. Self-Appropriation as a Way of Life

1 Lonergan, *Insight*, 12–14. An initial version of this chapter appeared in *Meaning and History in Systematic Theology: Essays in Honor of Robert M. Doran, SJ*, ed. John Dadosky (Milwaukee: Marquette University Press, 2009), 311–29.
2 The teacher was William Weller, a Jesuit in the philosophy department at Seattle University.
3 Lonergan, *Method*, 3–25.
4 Lonergan, *Insight*, 621–22.
5 "Psalm 42," in *Psalms for Praying*, ed. Nan Merrill (New York: Continuum, 1996), 81.
6 For this union of desire and demand in Lonergan, see the whole of his chapter on ethics in *Insight*, 618–56.
7 Lonergan, *Method*, 241–43.
8 Lonergan, *Insight*, 500.
9 *Insight*, 581–85; Doran, *Theology and the Dialectics of History*, 8–9.
10 See chapter 1.
11 On self-creation as aesthetic self-creation, see Michel Foucault, *The Use of Pleasure: The History of Sexuality*, vol. 2, trans. Robert Hurley (New York: Vintage Books, 1986). For a more nuanced discussion of this issue, see Doran, *Theology and the Dialectics of History*, 85–86.
12 Thomas McPartland, *Lonergan and the Philosophy of Historical Existence* (Columbia: University of Missouri Press, 2001), 147–54.

13 A.G. Sertillanges, *The Intellectual Life: Its Sprit, Conditions, Methods,* trans. Mary Ryan (Washington, DC: Catholic University of American Press, 1987).
14 Ibid., 81.
15 Ibid., 74.
16 Ibid., 74–75, quotation from p. 75.
17 Ibid., 77.
18 Ibid.
19 Ibid., 73.
20 Ibid., p. 78.
21 *Insight*, 207–10.
22 Martin Heidegger, *What Is a Thing?* trans. W. Barton and V. Deutsch (Chicago: Henry Regnery, 1967), 3.
23 Theodore Adorno, *Aesthetic Theory*, trans. Robert Hullot-Kentor (Minneapolis: University of Minnesota Press, 1997), pp. 3–8.
24 Ibid., 13, 17.
25 Ibid., 227.
26 Ibid.
27 *Method*, 122.
28 Marsh, *Post-Cartesian Mediations*, 110–12.
29 Lonergan, *Insight*, 263–67.
30 Marsh, *Post-Cartesian Mediations*, 183–238; Marsh, *Critique, Action, and Liberation*, 174–75, 376–79, n. 52; Doran, *Theology and the Dialectics of History*, 42–63, 232–53, 523–24.
31 Bernard Lonergan, "Existenz and Aggiornamento," 222–31.
32 Ibid., 232–24, 230–31.
33 Lonergan, *Method*, 115–16.
34 Lonergan, "Existenz and Aggiornamento," 229.
35 Lonergan, "Cognitional Structure," *Collection*, 221.
36 "Existenz and Aggiornamento," 228.
37 *Insight*, 8.
38 Sertillanges, *The Intellectual Life*, 81.

Index

www.ingramcontent.com/pod-product-compliance
Lightning Source LLC
LaVergne TN
LVHW090200080826
844660LV00013B/880/J

* 9 7 8 1 4 4 2 6 4 8 9 7 5 *